CONTENTS

HOW TO USE YOUR
MOON SIGN BOOK

We get a number of letters and phone calls every year from readers asking the same types of questions. Most of these have to do with how to find certain information in the *Moon Sign Book* and how to use this information.

The best advice we can give is to read the entire introduction, in particular the section on how to use the tables. We provide examples, using the current Moon and Aspect Tables, so that you can follow along and easily figure out the best dates for all of your important activities.

The information in the remaining part of the book is divided into categories. If you want to find out when to cut your hair, look in the Health & Beauty section. Sections are listed in the Table of Contents for your convenience.

The Moon Tables do *not* take into account the Moon void of course. Just before the Moon enters a new sign it will have one last aspect to a planet. From that point until it enters the next sign, it is void. It is said that decisions made while the Moon is void never come to fruition. Sometimes purchases made during a Moon void turn out to be poorly made or a bad investment. If you want to avoid making your decisions during a void of course Moon, please refer to the "Moon Void of Course" section in this book. Many people do not pay attention to the voids, as it is virtually impossible to bypass all of them when making decisions.

Although we have included a list of retrograde planets in this year's *Moon Sign Book*, the Astro-Almanac does *not* take into account planetary retrogrades. For more information on these see Llewellyn's *Astrological Calendar*.

Note: All times given in the *Moon Sign Book* are set in Eastern Standard Time. You must adjust for your time zone and for daylight-saving time.

THE MOON'S PHASES

Everyone has seen the Moon wax and wane, growing progressively larger and smaller through a period of approximately 29 1/2 days. This circuit from New Moon, when the surface of the Moon is completely dark, to Full Moon, when it is totally lit, and back again, is called the *lunation cycle*. It is the result of a relationship between the Sun, Moon and Earth; it reflects the light of the Sun in varying degrees, depending on the angle between the Sun and Moon as viewed from Earth. During the year, the Moon will make 13 such trips (lunations).

This cycle is divided into parts called *phases*. There are several methods by which this can be done, and the system used in the *Moon Sign Book* will not necessarily correspond to those used in other almanacs and calendars. It is important, when using the Moon as a guide, to use Llewellyn's *Astrological Calendar* or *Daily Planetary Guide*, as these have been designed for astrological use.

The method used by Llewellyn divides the lunation cycle into **four phases or quarters**. These are measured as follows.

The **first quarter** begins when the Sun and Moon are in the same place, or *conjunct* (the New Moon). The Moon is not visible at first, since it rises at the same time as the Sun. But toward the end of this phase, a silver thread can be seen just after sunset as the Moon follows the Sun over the western horizon.

The **second quarter** begins halfway between the New Moon and Full Moon, when the Sun and Moon are at right angles, or a 90-degree *square* to each other. This half-moon rises around noon, and sets around midnight, so it can be seen in the western sky during the first half of the night.

The **third quarter** begins with the Full Moon, when the Sun and Moon are opposite one another and the full light of the Sun can shine on the full sphere of the Moon. The round Moon can be seen rising in the east at sunset, and then rising progressively a little later each evening.

The **fourth quarter** begins about halfway between the Full Moon and New Moon, when the Sun and Moon are again at 90 degrees, or *square*. This decreasing Moon rises at midnight, and can be seen in the east during the last half of the night, reaching the overhead position just about as the Sun rises.

THE PHASES AND SIGNS
OF THE MOON

New Moon
Finalization, rest, hidden reorganizations, incipient beginnings, or chaos, disorganization, confusion, regret, stagnation, covert revenge.

Full Moon
Fulfillment, culmination, completion, activity, social awareness, or unfulfilled longing, unrest, fretfulness, sentimentality, overt revenge.

First Quarter
Germination, emergence, beginnings, outwardly directed activity.

Second Quarter
Growth, development, articulation of things which already exist.

Third Quarter
Maturity, fruition, assumption of full form of expression.

Fourth Quarter
Disintegration, drawing back for reorganization, rest, reflection.

Moon in Aries
Good for starting things, but lacking in staying power. Things occur rapidly, but also quickly pass.

Moon in Taurus
Things begun now last the longest and tend to increase in value. Things begun now become habitual and hard to alter.

Moon in Gemini
An inconsistent and fickle position for the Moon. Things begun now are easily moved by outside influences.

Moon in Cancer
Stimulates emotional rapport between people. Pinpoints need, supports growth and nurturance.

Moon in Leo
Draws emphasis to the self, to central ideas or institutions, away from connections with others and emotional needs.

Moon in Virgo
Favors accomplishment of details and commands from higher up while discouraging spontaneous initiative.

Moon in Scorpio
Increases awareness of psychic power. Precipitates psychic crises and ends connections thoroughly.

Moon in Sagittarius
Encourages expansionary flights of the imagination and confidence in the flow of life.

Moon in Capricorn
Artificial, disciplined, controlled and institutional activities are favored. Develops strong structure.

Moon in Aquarius
Idealized conditions lead to potential emotional disappointment and disruption in the natural flow of life.

Moon in Pisces
Energy withdraws from the surface of life, hibernates within, secretly reorganizing and realigning for a new day.

Note: All times given in the *Moon Sign Book* are set in Eastern Standard Time. You must adjust for your time zone and for daylight-saving time.

NOT ALL COMMON ALAMANACS
ARE THE SAME

For **astronomical** calculations the Moon's place in almanacs is given as being in the **constellation**. For **astrological** purposes the Moon's place is figured in the **zodiacal sign**, which is its true place in the zodiac, and nearly one sign (30 degrees) different from the astronomical constellation.

To illustrate: If the common almanac gives the Moon's place in Taurus (constellation) on a certain date, its true place in the zodiac is in Gemini (zodiacal sign). Thus, it is readily seen that those who use the common almanac may be planting seeds, or engaging in other endeavors, when they think the Moon is in a **fruitful sign**, while in reality it would be in one of the most **barren signs** in the zodiac.

Common almanacs are worthless to follow for planting. Some almanacs even make a bad matter worse by inserting at the head of their columns "Moon's Sign" when they mean "Moon's Constellation," and this has brought much unmerited discredit to the value of planting by the Moon. The constellations form a belt outside the zodiac, but do not conform with the signs in position or time.

The constellations are correct in astronomical but not in astrological calculations. This fact not being generally known has incurred a great deal of criticism and skepticism regarding the Moon's influence in planting. To obtain desired results, planting must be done according to the Moon's place in the signs of the zodiac.

Therefore, using Llewellyn's *Moon Sign Book* for all of your planting and planning purposes is the best thing to do!

HOW TO USE THE MOON SIGN BOOK TABLES AND ACTIVITY INFORMATION

Timing your activities is one of the most important things you can do to ensure success. In many Eastern countries, timing by the planets is so important that practically no event takes place without first setting up a chart for it. Weddings have taken place in the middle of the night because that was when the influences were the best. You may not want to take it that far, and you don't really need to set up a chart for each activity, but you may as well make use of the influences of the Moon whenever possible. It's easy and it works!

In the *Moon Sign Book* you will find all of the information you need to plan just about any activity: weddings, fishing, buying a car or house, cutting your hair, traveling and more. Not all of the things you need to do will fall on particularly favorable days, but we provide the guidelines you need to pick the best day out of the several from which you have to choose.

Let's run through some examples. Say you need to make an appointment to have your hair cut. You have thin hair and would like it to look thicker. Look in the Health & Beauty section under Hair Care. You see that you should cut hair during a Full Moon (marked FM in the Moon Tables or O under the Sun in the Lunar Aspectarian). You should, however, avoid the Moon in Virgo. We'll say that it is the month of March. Look up March in the Moon Tables. The Full Moon falls on March 27th at 6:10 AM. It is in the sign of Libra, which is good for beauty treatments. Because the Full Moon occurs relatively early in the morning, the entire day is good for cutting hair. If the Full Moon happened late in the evening, the next day would be just as good. The times are fairly flexible; you do not have to use the exact time of the Moon change.

That was easy. Let's move on to a more difficult example that uses the phase and sign of the Moon. You want to buy a house for a permanent home. Look in the Home & Family section under House. It says that you should buy a home when the Moon is in Taurus, Leo, Scorpio or Aquarius (fixed signs). You need to get a loan, so you should look in the Business, Finance & Legal section under Loans. Here it says that the third and fourth quarters favor the borrower (you). You are going to buy the house in December. Look up December in the Moon Tables. The Moon is in the fourth quarter on

December 1st, in the third quarter December 18th through the 24th, and in the fourth quarter again December 25th through the 31st. These dates are good for getting a loan. Now look at the signs. The Moon is in Scorpio (good) on the 1st, 28th and 29th. It is in Leo the 21st, 22nd and 23rd. It is in Taurus and Aquarius (the other good signs) during the first and second quarters—not good for getting a loan. So, the best dates are the 1st, 21st, 22nd, 23rd, 28th and 29th. You just match the best signs and phases (quarters) to come up with the best dates.

With all activities, be sure to check the Favorable and Unfavorable Days for your Sun sign in the table adjoining the Lunar Aspectarian. If there is a choice between several dates, pick the one most favorable for you (marked F).

Now let's look at an example that uses signs, phases and aspects. You will find the aspects listed in the Lunar Aspectarian on the pages facing the Moon Tables. The letters listed under the planets stand for specific aspects: C=conjunction, X=sextile, Q=square, T=trine and O=opposition. You will be using the squares and oppositions more than the other aspects as these are considered negative.

Our example this time is fixing your car. We will use June as the sample month. Look in the Home & Family section under Automobile Repair. It says that the Moon should be in a fixed sign (Taurus, Leo, Scorpio, Aquarius) in the first or second quarter and well-aspected to the Sun. (Good aspects are sextiles and trines, marked X and T.) It also tells you to avoid negative aspects to Mars,

Saturn, Uranus, Neptune and Pluto. (Negative aspects are squares and oppositions, marked Q and O.) Look in the Moon Tables under June. You will see that the Moon is in the first and second quarters from June 10th through the 22nd. The dates that the Moon is in a fixed sign are the 13th and 14th (Leo) and the 20th and 21st (Scorpio). You can eliminate all of the other dates.

Now look at the Lunar Aspectarian for June to find the aspects. All June 13th has is a square to Mars, which discounts it immediately. The 14th has a sextile to the Sun (good) and a square to Pluto (not good). Although there is an adverse aspect present, the positive aspect to the Sun indicates that it may be okay to have your car repaired on this day. The 20th has an opposition to Mars, a sextile to Uranus, a sextile to Neptune and a conjunction to Pluto. This day is not extremely favorable. The 21st has a trine to Venus (good) and a square to Saturn (not good). As the good aspect on this date does not involve the Sun, it is less than ideal for car repair. Use the Favorable and Unfavorable Table for your Sun sign to determine the best date.

You have just gone through the entire process of choosing the best dates for a special event. With practice, you will be able to scan the information in the tables and do it very quickly. You will also begin to get a feel for what works best for you. Everyone has his or her own high and low cycles.

Gardening activities depend on many outside factors, weather being the most influential. Obviously, you can't go out and plant when there is still a foot of snow on the ground or when it is raining cats and dogs. You have to adjust to the conditions at hand. If the weather was bad or you were on vacation during the first quarter when it was best to plant, do it during the second quarter while the Moon is in a fruitful sign instead. If the Moon is not in a fruitful sign during the first or second quarter, choose a day when it is in a semi-fruitful sign. The best advice is to choose either the sign or phase that is *most* favorable when the two don't coincide.

To summarize, in order to make the most of your plans and activities, check with the *Moon Sign Book*. First, look up the activity in the corresponding section under the proper heading. Then, look for the information given in the tables (the Moon Tables, Lunar Aspectarian or Favorable and Unfavorable Days, or all three). Choose the best date according to the number of positive factors in effect. If most of the dates are favorable, then there is no problem choosing the one that will best fit your schedule. However, if there just don't seem to be any really good dates, pick the ones with the least number of negative influences. We guarantee that you will be very pleased with the results if you use nature's influences to your advantage.

For quick reference, use the Astro-Almanac. This is a general guide for planning certain events and activities.

HOW TO USE THE TABLES

First, read the preceding section on how to use your *Moon Sign Book*. You will be using the tables on the following pages in conjunction with the information given in the individual sections: Home & Family, Leisure & Recreation, Health & Beauty, Business, Finance & Legal and Farm & Garden.

The Moon Tables include the date, sign the Moon is in, the element of that sign, the nature of the sign, the Moon's phase and the times that it changes sign or phase. The abbreviation FM signifies Full Moon and NM signifies New Moon. The times listed directly after the date are the times when the Moon changes sign. The times listed after the phase indicate the times when the Moon changes phase. All times are listed in Eastern Standard Time. You need to adjust them according to your own time zone. (Conversion tables have been provided for your convenience.)

On the pages opposite the Moon Tables you will find the Lunar Aspectarian and the Favorable and Unfavorable Days. To use the Lunar Aspectarian, find the planet that the activity lists and run down the column to the date desired. If you want to find a favorable aspect (sextile or trine) to Mercury, run you finger down the column under Mercury until you find an X or T; positive or good aspects are signified by these letters. Negative or adverse aspects (square or opposition) are signified by a Q or O. A conjunction, C, is sometimes good, sometimes bad, depending on the activity or planets involved. The Lunar Aspectarian gives the *aspects of the Moon to the other planets.*

The Favorable and Unfavorable Days table lists all of the Sun signs. To find out if a day is positive for you, find your sign and then look down the column. If it is marked F, it is very favorable. If it is marked f, it is slightly favorable. U means very unfavorable and u means slightly unfavorable.

KEY OF ABBREVIATIONS

X: sextile/positive
T: trine/positive
Q: square/negative
O: opposition/negative
C: conjunction/positive/negative/neutral

F: very favorable
f: slightly favorable
U: very unfavorable
u: slightly unfavorable

FM: Full Moon
NM: New Moon

To find out the exact times of the daily aspects, see Llewellyn's *1994 Daily Planetary Guide.* This will help you refine your timing even more.

LUNAR ACTIVITY GUIDE

ACTIVITY	SIGN	PHASE
Buy animals		New Moon, 1st
Baking	Aries, Cancer, Libra, Capricorn	1st or 2nd
Hair care: permanents, straightening, coloring	Aquarius	1st
Cut hair to stimulate growth	Cancer, Scorpio, Pisces	1st or 2nd
Cut hair for thickness	Any except Virgo	Full Moon
Cut hair to decrease growth	Gemini, Leo, Virgo	3rd or 4th

ACTIVITY	SIGN	PHASE
Start a diet to lose weight	Aries, Leo, Virgo, Sagittarius, Aquarius	3rd or 4th
Start a diet to gain weight	Cancer, Scorpio, Pisces	1st or 2nd
Buy clothes	Taurus, Libra	1st or 2nd
Buy antiques	Cancer, Scorpio, Capricorn	
Borrow money	Leo, Sagittarius, Aquarius, Pisces	3rd or 4th
Start a savings account	Taurus, Scorpio, Capricorn	1st or 2nd
Join a club	Gemini, Libra, Aquarius	
Give a party	Gemini, Leo, Libra, Aquarius	
Travel for pleasure	Gemini, Leo, Sagittarius, Aquarius	1st or 2nd
Begin a course of study	Gemini, Virgo, Sagittarius	1st or 2nd
Begin a new job	Taurus, Virgo, Capricorn	1st or 2nd
Canning	Cancer, Scorpio, Pisces	3rd or 4th

ACTIVITY	SIGN	PHASE
Make preserves and jellies	Taurus, Scorpio, Aquarius	3rd or 4th
Dry fruits and vegetables	Aries, Leo, Sagittarius	3rd
Remove teeth	Gemini, Virgo, Sagittarius, Capricorn, Pisces	1st or 2nd
Fill teeth	Taurus, Leo, Scorpio, Aquarius	3rd or 4th
Dressmaking, mending		1st or 2nd
Buy health foods	Virgo	
Buy medicine	Scorpio	
Buy permanent home	Taurus, Leo, Scorpio, Aquarius	
Buy property for speculation	Aries, Cancer, Libra, Capricorn	
Send mail	Gemini, Virgo, Sagittarius, Pisces	
Cut wood	Any except Cancer, Scorpio	3rd or 4th

ACTIVITY	SIGN	PHASE
Beauty treatments	Taurus, Cancer, Leo, Libra, Scorpio, Aquarius	1st or 2nd
Brewing	Cancer, Scorpio, Pisces	3rd or 4th
Start building	Taurus, Leo, Aquarius	3rd or 4th
Bulbs for seed	Cancer, Scorpio, Pisces	2nd or 3rd
Pour cement	Taurus, Leo, Aquarius	Full Moon
Plant cereals	Cancer, Scorpio, Pisces	1st or 2nd
Cultivate	Aries, Gemini, Leo, Virgo, Sagittarius, Aquarius	4th
Break habits	Gemini, Leo, Virgo	3rd or 4th
Fix your car	Taurus, Virgo	1st or 2nd
Weddings	Taurus, Cancer, Leo, Libra, Pisces	2nd
Move	Taurus, Leo, Scorpio, Aquarius	

Paint	Taurus, Leo, Scorpio, Aquarius	3rd or 4th
Train a pet	Taurus	3rd or 4th
Buy a car	Taurus, Leo, Scorpio, Aquarius	3rd or 4th
Collect debts	Aries, Cancer, Libra, Capricorn	3rd or 4th

MOONRISE

The New Moon always rises with the Sun in the east to start a new lunar month. The Sun blots out the visibility of the New Moon as it comes up, but it can be seen as a thin crescent setting in the west at sunset a day or two after its rise.

The waxing or increasing Moon is known and easily remembered as the "right-hand Moon." The curve of the right-hand index finger and thumb follows the curve of the increasing crescent. Similarly, the waning or decreasing Moon can be remembered as the "left-hand Moon."

To establish the time of moonrise for each day of the month, add fifty minutes for each day after the beginning of a phase or subtract that amount for each day from the beginning of a new phase.

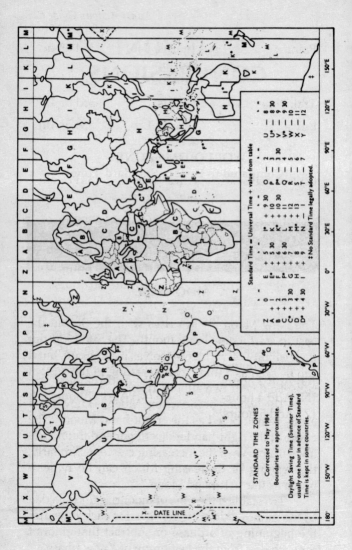

STANDARD TIME ZONES

Corrected to May 1984

Boundaries are approximate.

Daylight Saving Time (Summer Time), usually one hour in advance of Standard Time is kept in some countries.

Standard Time = Universal Time + value from table

N	0	A	+ 1	N	− 1
Z	0	B	+ 2	O	− 2
		C	+ 3	P	− 3
		C*	+ 3 30	Q	− 4
		D	+ 4	R	− 5
		D*	+ 4 30	S	− 6
		E	+ 5	T	− 7
		E*	+ 5 30	U	− 8
		F	+ 6	U*	− 8 30
		F*	+ 6 30	V	− 9
		G	+ 7	V*	− 9 30
		H	+ 8	W	− 10
		H*	+ 8 30	X	− 11
		I	+ 9	Y	− 12
		I*	+ 9 30		
		K	+ 10		
		K*	+ 10 30		
		L	+ 11		
		L*	+ 11 30		
		M	+ 12		
		M*	+ 13		

‡ No Standard Time legally adopted.

X · · · DATE LINE

TIME ZONE CONVERSIONS

WORLD TIME ZONES
(Compared to Eastern Standard Time)

(R) EST—Used
(S) CST—Subtract 1 hour
(T) MST—Subtract 2 hours
(U) PST—Subtract 3 hours
(V) Subtract 4 hours
(W) Subtract 5 hours
(X) Subtract 6 hours
(Y) Subtract 7 hours
(Q) Add 1 hour
(P) Add 2 hours
(O) Add 3 hours
(N) Add 4 hours
(Z) Add 5 hours

(A) Add 6 hours
(B) Add 7 hours
(C) Add 8 hours
(D) Add 9 hours
(E) Add 10 hours
(F) Add 11 hours
(G) Add 12 hours
(H) Add 13 hours
(I) Add 14 hours
(K) Add 15 hours
(L) Add 16 hours
(M) Add 17 hours

JANUARY MOON TABLE

DATE	MOON'S SIGN	ELEMENT	NATURE	MOON'S PHASE
1 Sat. 3:15 PM	Virgo	Earth	Barren	3rd
2 Sun.	Virgo	Earth	Barren	3rd
3 Mon. 6:31 PM	Libra	Air	Semi-fruit	3rd
4 Tue.	Libra	Air	Semi-fruit	4th 7:01 PM
5 Wed. 9:29 PM	Scorpio	Water	Fruitful	4th
6 Thu.	Scorpio	Water	Fruitful	4th
7 Fri.	Scorpio	Water	Fruitful	4th
8 Sat. 12:34 AM	Sagit.	Fire	Barren	4th
9 Sun.	Sagit.	Fire	Barren	4th
10 Mon. 4:16 AM	Capri.	Earth	Semi-fruit	NM 6:10 PM
11 Tue.	Capri.	Earth	Semi-fruit	1st
12 Wed. 9:25 AM	Aquar.	Air	Barren	1st
13 Thu.	Aquar	Air	Barren	1st
14 Fri. 5:03 PM	Pisces	Water	Fruitful	1st
15 Sat.	Pisces	Water	Fruitful	1st
16 Sun.	Pisces	Water	Fruitful	1st
17 Mon.3:42 AM	Aries	Fire	Barren	1st
18 Tue.	Aries	Fire	Barren	1st
19 Wed. 4:22 PM	Taurus	Earth	Semi-fruit	2nd 3:27 PM
20 Thu.	Taurus	Earth	Semi-fruit	2nd
The SUN enters Aquarius at 2:08 AM				
21 Fri.	Taurus	Earth	Semi-fruit	2nd
22 Sat. 4:35 AM	Gemini	Air	Barren	2nd
23 Sun.	Gemini	Air	Barren	2nd
24 Mon. 1:56 PM	Cancer	Water	Fruitful	2nd
25 Tue.	Cancer	Water	Fruitful	2nd
26 Wed. 7:39 PM	Leo	Fire	Barren	2nd
27 Thu.	Leo	Fire	Barren	FM 8:23 AM
28 Fri. 10:39 PM	Virgo	Earth	Barren	3rd
29 Sat.	Virgo	Earth	Barren	3rd
30 Sun.	Virgo	Earth	Barren	3rd
31 Mon. 12:34 AM	Libra	Air	Semi-fruit	3rd

Set in Eastern Standard Time

JANUARY 1994

Lunar Aspectarian   Favorable & Unfavorable Days

	SUN	MERCURY	VENUS	MARS	JUPITER	SATURN	URANUS	NEPTUNE	PLUTO	ARIES	TAURUS	GEMINI	CANCER	LEO	VIRGO	LIBRA	SCORPIO	SAGITTARIUS	CAPRICORN	AQUARIUS	PISCES
1						O			Q	f	u	f		F		f	u	f		U	
2	T	T	T	T	X						f	u	f		F		f	u	f		U
3							T	T	X		f	u	f		F		f	u	f		U
4	Q	Q	Q	Q						U		f	u	f		F		f	u	f	
5						T	Q	Q		U		f	u	f		F		f	u	f	
6			X	X	C					U		f	u	f		F		f	u	f	
7	X	X				Q	X	X	C		U		f	u	f		F		f	u	f
8											U		f	u	f		F		f	u	f
9										f		U		f	u	f		F		f	u
10					X	X				f		U		f	u	f		F		f	u
11	C		C	C			C	C		u	f		U		f	u	f		F		f
12		C							X	u	f		U		f	u	f		F		f
13					Q					f	u	f		U		f	u	f		F	
14						C			Q	f	u	f		U		f	u	f		F	
15						T					f	u	f		U		f	u	f		F
16	X		X	X			X	X	T		f	u	f		U		f	u	f		F
17		X									f	u	f		U		f	u	f		F
18									Q	F		f	u	f		U		f	u	f	
19	Q		Q	Q		X	Q			F		f	u	f		U		f	u	f	
20		Q		O							F		f	u	f		U		f	u	f
21				T			T	T	O		F		f	u	f		U		f	u	f
22	T		T			Q					F		f	u	f		U		f	u	f
23		T								f		F		f	u	f		U		f	u
24						T				f		F		f	u	f		U		f	u
25						T				u	f		F		f	u	f		U		f
26				O		O	O	O	T	u	f		F		f	u	f		U		f
27	O		O	Q						u	f		F		f	u	f		U		f
28		O				O			Q	f	u	f		F		f	u	f		U	
29				X						f	u	f		F		f	u	f		U	
30							T	T	X		f	u	f		F		f	u	f		U
31	T			T							f	u	f		F		f	u	f		U

FEBRUARY MOON TABLE

DATE	MOON'S SIGN	ELEMENT	NATURE	MOON'S PHASE
1 Tue.	Libra	Air	Semi-fruit	3rd
2 Wed. 2:49 AM	Scorpio	Water	Fruitful	3rd
3 Thu.	Scorpio	Water	Fruitful	4th 3:06 AM
4 Fri. 6:14 AM	Sagit.	Fire	Barren	4th
5 Sat.	Sagit.	Fire	Barren	4th
6 Sun. 11:02 AM	Capri.	Earth	Semi-fruit	4th
7 Mon.	Capri.	Earth	Semi-fruit	4th
8 Tue. 5:17 PM	Aquar.	Air	Barren	4th
9 Wed.	Aquar.	Air	Barren	4th
10 Thu.	Aquar.	Air	Barren	NM 9:30 AM
11 Fri. 1:23 AM	Pisces	Water	Fruitful	1st
12 Sat.	Pisces	Water	Fruitful	1st
13 Sun. 11:50 AM	Aries	Fire	Barren	1st
14 Mon.	Aries	Fire	Barren	1st
15 Tue.	Aries	Fire	Barren	1st
16 Wed. 12:20 AM	Taurus	Earth	Semi-fruit	1st
17 Thu.	Taurus	Earth	Semi-fruit	1st
18 Fri. 1:06 PM	Gemini	Air	Barren	2nd 12:48 PM
The SUN enters Pisces at 4:23 PM				
19 Sat.	Gemini	Air	Barren	2nd
20 Sun. 11:28 PM	Cancer	Water	Fruitful	2nd
21 Mon.	Cancer	Water	Fruitful	2nd
22 Tue.	Cancer	Water	Fruitful	2nd
23 Wed. 5:48 AM	Leo	Fire	Barren	2nd
24 Thu.	Leo	Fire	Barren	2nd
25 Fri. 8:27 AM	Virgo	Earth	Barren	FM 8:15 PM
26 Sat.	Virgo	Earth	Barren	3rd
27 Sun. 9:06 AM	Libra	Air	Semi-fruit	3rd
28 Mon.	Libra	Air	Semi-fruit	3rd

Set in Eastern Standard Time

FEBRUARY 1994

Lunar Aspectarian Favorable & Unfavorable Days

	SUN	MERCURY	VENUS	MARS	JUPITER	SATURN	URANUS	NEPTUNE	PLUTO	ARIES	TAURUS	GEMINI	CANCER	LEO	VIRGO	LIBRA	SCORPIO	SAGITTARIUS	CAPRICORN	AQUARIUS	PISCES
1			T				Q	Q		U		f	u	f		F		f	u	f	
2		T		Q		T				U		f	u	f		F		f	u	f	
3	Q		Q		C		X	X			U		f	u	f		F		f	u	f
4		Q		X		Q			C		U		f	u	f		F		f	u	f
5	X		X							f		U		f	u	f		F		f	u
6		X				X				f		U		f	u	f		F		f	u
7				X						u	f		U		f	u	f		F		f
8							C	C	X	u	f		U		f	u	f		F		f
9				C	Q					f	u	f		U		f	u	f		F	
10	C		C						Q	f	u	f		U		f	u	f		F	
11		C				C				f	u	f		U		f	u	f		F	
12				T				X			f	u	f		U		f	u	f		F
13							X		T		f	u	f		U		f	u	f		F
14				X						F		f	u	f		U		f	u	f	
15	X						Q	Q		F		f	u	f		U		f	u	f	
16		X	X			X				F		f	u	f		U		f	u	f	
17				Q	O			T			F		f	u	f		U		f	u	f
18	Q	Q				Q	T		O		F		f	u	f		U		f	u	f
19			Q							f		F		f	u	f		U		f	u
20				T						f		F		f	u	f		U		f	u
21	T	T	T			T				f		F		f	u	f		U		f	u
22					T		O	O		u	f		F		f	u	f		U		f
23								T		u	f		F		f	u	f		U		f
24				O	Q					f	u	f		F		f	u	f		U	
25	O	O				O			Q	f	u	f		F		f	u	f		U	
26			O	X				T			f	u	f		F		f	u	f		U
27						T		X			f	u	f		F		f	u	f		U
28		T						Q		U		f	u	f		F		f	u	f	

MARCH MOON TABLE

DATE	MOON'S SIGN	ELEMENT	NATURE	MOON'S PHASE
1 Tue. 9:43 AM	Scorpio	Water	Fruitful	3rd
2 Wed.	Scorpio	Water	Fruitful	3rd
3 Thu. 11:54 AM	Sagit.	Fire	Barren	3rd
4 Fri.	Sagit.	Fire	Barren	4th 11:54 AM
5 Sat. 4:25 PM	Capri.	Earth	Semi-fruit	4th
6 Sun.	Capri.	Earth	Semi-fruit	4th
7 Mon. 11:15 PM	Aquar.	Air	Barren	4th
8 Tue.	Aquar.	Air	Barren	4th
9 Wed.	Aquar.	Air	Barren	4th
10 Thu. 8:10 AM	Pisces	Water	Fruitful	4th
11 Fri.	Pisces	Water	Fruitful	4th
12 Sat. 6:59 PM	Aries	Fire	Barren	NM 2:05 AM
13 Sun.	Aries	Fire	Barren	1st
14 Mon.	Aries	Fire	Barren	1st
15 Tue. 7:28 AM	Taurus	Earth	Semi-fruit	1st
16 Wed.	Taurus	Earth	Semi-fruit	1st
17 Thu. 8:29 PM	Gemini	Air	Barren	1st
18 Fri.	Gemini	Air	Barren	1st
19 Sat.	Gemini	Air	Barren	1st
20 Sun. 7:54 AM	Cancer	Water	Fruitful	2nd 7:14 AM

The SUN enters Aries at 3:28 PM

DATE	MOON'S SIGN	ELEMENT	NATURE	MOON'S PHASE
21 Mon.	Cancer	Water	Fruitful	2nd
22 Tue. 3:39 PM	Leo	Fire	Barren	2nd
23 Wed.	Leo	Fire	Barren	2nd
24 Thu. 7:14 PM	Virgo	Earth	Barren	2nd
25 Fri.	Virgo	Earth	Barren	2nd
26 Sat. 7:47 PM	Libra	Air	Semi-fruit	2nd
27 Sun.	Libra	Air	Semi-fruit	FM 6:10 AM
28 Mon. 7:15 PM	Scorpio	Water	Fruitful	3rd
29 Tue.	Scorpio	Water	Fruitful	3rd
30 Wed. 7:42 PM	Sagit.	Fire	Barren	3rd
31 Thu.	Sagit.	Fire	Barren	3rd

Set in Eastern Standard Time

MARCH 1994

Lunar Aspectarian — Favorable & Unfavorable Days

Day	SUN	MERCURY	VENUS	MARS	JUPITER	SATURN	URANUS	NEPTUNE	PLUTO	ARIES	TAURUS	GEMINI	CANCER	LEO	VIRGO	LIBRA	SCORPIO	SAGITTARIUS	CAPRICORN	AQUARIUS	PISCES
1				T		T	Q			U		f	u	f		F		f	u	f	
2	T	Q			C			X			U		f	u	f		F		f	u	f
3			T	Q		Q	X		C		U		f	u	f		F		f	u	f
4	Q									f		U		f	u	f		F		f	u
5		X	Q	X						f		U		f	u	f		F		f	u
6	X				X	X				u	f		U		f	u	f		F		f
7			X				C	C	X	u	f		U		f	u	f		F		f
8										u	f		U		f	u	f		F		f
9		C			Q					f	u	f		U		f	u	f		F	
10			C			C			Q	f	u	f		U		f	u	f		F	
11				T							f	u	f		U		f	u	f		F
12	C						X	X	T		f	u	f		U		f	u	f		F
13			C							F		f	u	f		U		f	u	f	
14							Q	Q		F		f	u	f		U		f	u	f	
15		X		X		X				F		f	u	f		U		f	u	f	
16					O						F		f	u	f		U		f	u	f
17	X	Q					T	T	O		F		f	u	f		U		f	u	f
18			X	Q		Q				f		F		f	u	f		U		f	u
19										f		F		f	u	f		U		f	u
20	Q	T				T				u	f		F		f	u	f		U		f
21			Q	T	T					u	f		F		f	u	f		U		f
22	T						O	O	T	u	f		F		f	u	f		U		f
23				Q						f	u	f		F		f	u	f		U	
24			T						Q	f	u	f		F		f	u	f		U	
25		O		O	X	O				f	u	f		F		f	u	f		U	
26							T	T	X		f	u	f		F		f	u	f		U
27	O										f	u	f		F		f	u	f		U
28			O				Q	Q		U		f	u	f		F		f	u	f	
29		T		T	C	T				U		f	u	f		F		f	u	f	
30							X	X	C	U		f	u	f		F		f	u	f	
31	T	Q				Q				U		f	u	f		F		f	u	f	

APRIL MOON TABLE

DATE	MOON'S SIGN	ELEMENT	NATURE	MOON'S PHASE
1 Fri. 10:38 PM	Capri.	Earth	Semi-fruit	3rd
2 Sat.	Capri.	Earth	Semi-fruit	4th 9:56 PM
3 Sun.	Capri.	Earth	Semi-fruit	4th
4 Mon. 4:46 AM	Aquar.	Air	Barren	4th
5 Tue.	Aquar.	Air	Barren	4th
6 Wed. 1:51 PM	Pisces	Water	Fruitful	4th
7 Thu.	Pisces	Water	Fruitful	4th
8 Fri.	Pisces	Water	Fruitful	4th
9 Sat. 1:09 AM	Aries	Fire	Barren	4th
10 Sun.	Aries	Fire	Barren	NM 7:17 PM
11 Mon. 1:47 PM	Taurus	Earth	Semi-fruit	1st
12 Tue.	Taurus	Earth	Semi-fruit	1st
13 Wed.	Taurus	Earth	Semi-fruit	1st
14 Thu. 2:48 AM	Gemini	Air	Barren	1st
15 Fri.	Gemini	Air	Barren	1st
16 Sat. 2:41 PM	Cancer	Water	Fruitful	1st
17 Sun.	Cancer	Water	Fruitful	1st
18 Mon. 11:45 PM	Leo	Fire	Barren	2nd 9:35 PM
19 Tue.	Leo	Fire	Barren	2nd
20 Wed.	Leo	Fire	Barren	2nd

The SUN enters Taurus at 2:37 AM

DATE	MOON'S SIGN	ELEMENT	NATURE	MOON'S PHASE
21 Thu. 4:59 AM	Virgo	Earth	Barren	2nd
22 Fri.	Virgo	Earth	Barren	2nd
23 Sat. 6:41 AM	Libra	Air	Semi-fruit	2nd
24 Sun.	Libra	Air	Semi-fruit	2nd
25 Mon. 6:19 AM	Scorpio	Water	Fruitful	FM 2:46 PM
26 Tue.	Scorpio	Water	Fruitful	3rd
27 Wed. 5:49 AM	Sagit.	Fire	Barren	3rd
28 Thu.	Sagit.	Fire	Barren	3rd
29 Fri. 7:05 AM	Capri.	Earth	Semi-fruit	3rd
30 Sat.	Capri.	Earth	Semi-fruit	3rd

Set in Eastern Standard Time

Lunar Aspectarian — Favorable & Unfavorable Days

	SUN	MERCURY	VENUS	MARS	JUPITER	SATURN	URANUS	NEPTUNE	PLUTO	ARIES	TAURUS	GEMINI	CANCER	LEO	VIRGO	LIBRA	SCORPIO	SAGITTARIUS	CAPRICORN	AQUARIUS	PISCES
1			T	Q						f		U		f	u	f		F		f	u
2	Q				X	X				f		U		f	u	f		F		f	u
3		X		X			C	C		u	f		U		f	u	f		F		f
4			Q						X	u	f		U		f	u	f		F		f
5	X				Q					f	u	f		U		f	u	f		F	
6									Q	f	u	f		U		f	u	f		F	
7			X		T	C					f	u	f		U		f	u	f		F
8		C		C			X	X	T		f	u	f		U		f	u	f		F
9											f	u	f		U		f	u	f		F
10	C									F		f	u	f		U		f	u	f	
11							Q	Q		F		f	u	f		U		f	u	f	
12			C		O	X					F		f	u	f		U		f	u	f
13							T	T	O		F		f	u	f		U		f	u	f
14		X		X		Q					F		f	u	f		U		f	u	f
15										f		F		f	u	f		U		f	u
16	X			Q						f		F		f	u	f		U		f	u
17		Q			T	T				u	f		F		f	u	f		U		f
18	Q		X				O	O	T	u	f		F		f	u	f		U		f
19				T	Q					u	f		F		f	u	f		U		f
20		T	Q							f	u	f		F		f	u	f		U	
21	T				X	O				f	u	f		F		f	u	f		U	
22								T		f	u	f		F		f	u	f		U	
23			T	O			T		X	f	u	f		F		f	u	f		U	
24								Q		U		f	u	f		F		f	u	f	
25	O	O			C	T	Q			U		f	u	f		F		f	u	f	
26							X	X			U		f	u	f		F		f	u	f
27			O	T		Q			C		U		f	u	f		F		f	u	f
28										f		U		f	u	f		F		f	u
29	T	T			X					f		U		f	u	f		F		f	u
30				Q		X		C		u	f		U		f	u	f		F		f

MAY MOON TABLE

DATE	MOON'S SIGN	ELEMENT	NATURE	MOON'S PHASE
1 Sun. 11:35 AM	Aquar.	Air	Barren	3rd
2 Mon.	Aquar.	Air	Barren	4th 9:32 AM
3 Tue. 7:47 PM	Pisces	Water	Fruitful	4th
4 Wed.	Pisces	Water	Fruitful	4th
5 Thu.	Pisces	Water	Fruitful	4th
6 Fri. 7:01 AM	Aries	Fire	Barren	4th
7 Sat.	Aries	Fire	Barren	4th
8 Sun. 7:50 PM	Taurus	Earth	Semi-fruit	4th
9 Mon.	Taurus	Earth	Semi-fruit	4th
10 Tue.	Taurus	Earth	Semi-fruit	NM 12:07 PM
11 Wed. 8:44 AM	Gemini	Air	Barren	1st
12 Thu.	Gemini	Air	Barren	1st
13 Fri. 8:28 PM	Cancer	Water	Fruitful	1st
14 Sat.	Cancer	Water	Fruitful	1st
15 Sun.	Cancer	Water	Fruitful	1st
16 Mon. 5:59 AM	Leo	Fire	Barren	1st
17 Tue.	Leo	Fire	Barren	1st
18 Wed. 12:32 PM	Virgo	Earth	Barren	2nd 7:51 AM
19 Thu.	Virgo	Earth	Barren	2nd
20 Fri. 3:55 PM	Libra	Air	Semi-fruit	2nd
21 Sat.	Libra	Air	Semi-fruit	2nd

The SUN enters Gemini at 1:49 AM

DATE	MOON'S SIGN	ELEMENT	NATURE	MOON'S PHASE
22 Sun. 4:51 PM	Scorpio	Water	Fruitful	2nd
23 Mon.	Scorpio	Water	Fruitful	2nd
24 Tue. 4:43 PM	Sagit.	Fire	Barren	FM 10:39 PM
25 Wed.	Sagit.	Fire	Barren	3rd
26 Thu. 5:17 PM	Capri.	Earth	Semi-fruit	3rd
27 Fri.	Capri.	Earth	Semi-fruit	3rd
28 Sat. 8:19 PM	Aquar.	Air	Barren	3rd
29 Sun.	Aquar.	Air	Barren	3rd
30 Mon.	Aquar.	Air	Barren	3rd
31 Tue. 3:03 AM	Pisces	Water	Fruitful	4th 11:02 PM

Set in Eastern Standard Time

MAY 1994

Lunar Aspectarian   Favorable & Unfavorable Days

	SUN	MERCURY	VENUS	MARS	JUPITER	SATURN	URANUS	NEPTUNE	PLUTO	ARIES	TAURUS	GEMINI	CANCER	LEO	VIRGO	LIBRA	SCORPIO	SAGITTARIUS	CAPRICORN	AQUARIUS	PISCES
1							C		X	u	f		U		f	u	f		F		f
2	Q	Q	T	X	Q					f	u	f		U		f	u	f		F	
3									Q	f	u	f		U		f	u	f		F	
4			Q		T	C				f	u	f		U		f	u	f		F	
5	X	X					X	X		f	u	f		U		f	u	f			F
6									T	f	u	f		U		f	u	f			F
7			X	C						F		f	u	f		U		f	u	f	
8							Q	Q		F		f	u	f		U		f	u	f	
9				O	X					F		f	u	f		U		f	u	f	
10	C							T			F		f	u	f		U		f	u	f
11		C					T		O		F		f	u	f		U		f	u	f
12					Q						f	F		f	u	f		U		f	u
13			C	X							f	F		f	u	f		U		f	u
14				T	T						f	F		f	u	f		U		f	u
15	X			Q			O	O	T	u	f	F		f	u	f		U			f
16				Q						u	f	F		f	u	f		U			f
17		X								f	u	f			F	f	u	f		U	
18	Q		X	T					Q	f	u	f			F	f	u	f		U	
19		Q		X	O						f	u	f		F	f	u	f			U
20	T		Q				T	T	X		f	u	f		F	f	u	f			U
21										U		f	u	f		F	f	u	f		
22		T	T	O			Q	Q		U		f	u	f		F	f	u	f		
23				C	T						U		f	u	f		F	f	u	f	
24	O						X	X	C		U		f	u	f		F	f	u	f	
25						Q					f	U		f	u	f		F	f		u
26		O		T							f	U		f	u	f		F	f		u
27			O		X	X				u	f		U		f	u	f		F		f
28							C	C	X	u	f		U		f	u	f		F		f
29	T			Q	Q					u	f		U		f	u	f		F		f
30									Q	f	u	f		U		f	u	f		F	
31	Q	T			X	T				f	u	f		U		f	u	f		F	

JUNE MOON TABLE

DATE	MOON'S SIGN	ELEMENT	NATURE	MOON'S PHASE
1 Wed.	Pisces	Water	Fruitful	4th
2 Thu. 1:31 PM	Aries	Fire	Barren	4th
3 Fri.	Aries	Fire	Barren	4th
4 Sat.	Aries	Fire	Barren	4th
5 Sun. 2:14 AM	Taurus	Earth	Semi-fruit	4th
6 Mon.	Taurus	Earth	Semi-fruit	4th
7 Tue. 3:04 PM	Gemini	Air	Barren	4th
8 Wed.	Gemini	Air	Barren	4th
9 Thu.	Gemini	Air	Barren	NM 3:27 AM
10 Fri. 2:23 AM	Cancer	Water	Fruitful	1st
11 Sat.	Cancer	Water	Fruitful	1st
12 Sun. 11:29 AM	Leo	Fire	Barren	1st
13 Mon.	Leo	Fire	Barren	1st
14 Tue. 6:17 PM	Virgo	Earth	Barren	1st
15 Wed.	Virgo	Earth	Barren	1st
16 Thu. 10:48 PM	Libra	Air	Semi-fruit	2nd 2:57 PM
17 Fri.	Libra	Air	Semi-fruit	2nd
18 Sat.	Libra	Air	Semi-fruit	2nd
19 Sun. 1:20 AM	Scorpio	Water	Fruitful	2nd
20 Mon.	Scorpio	Water	Fruitful	2nd
21 Tue. 2:32 AM	Sagit.	Fire	Barren	2nd

The SUN enters Cancer at 9:48 AM

DATE	MOON'S SIGN	ELEMENT	NATURE	MOON'S PHASE
22 Wed.	Sagit.	Fire	Barren	2nd
23 Thu. 3:37 AM	Capri.	Earth	Semi-fruit	FM 6:33 AM
24 Fri.	Capri.	Earth	Semi-fruit	3rd
25 Sat. 6:10 AM	Aquar.	Air	Barren	3rd
26 Sun.	Aquar.	Air	Barren	3rd
27 Mon. 11:45 AM	Pisces	Water	Fruitful	3rd
28 Tue.	Pisces	Water	Fruitful	3rd
29 Wed. 9:07 PM	Aries	Fire	Barren	3rd
30 Thu.	Aries	Fire	Barren	4th 2:31 PM

Set in Eastern Standard Time

JUNE 1994

Lunar Aspectarian   Favorable & Unfavorable Days

	SUN	MERCURY	VENUS	MARS	JUPITER	SATURN	URANUS	NEPTUNE	PLUTO	ARIES	TAURUS	GEMINI	CANCER	LEO	VIRGO	LIBRA	SCORPIO	SAGITTARIUS	CAPRICORN	AQUARIUS	PISCES
1			T			C		X			f	u	f		U		f	u	f		F
2		Q					X		T		f	u	f		U		f	u	f		F
3	X		Q							F		f	u	f		U		f	u	f	
4						Q	Q			F		f	u	f		U		f	u	f	
5		X		C	O					F		f	u	f		U		f	u	f	
6			X			X					F		f	u	f		U		f	u	f
7							T	T	O		F		f	u	f		U		f	u	f
8						Q				f		F		f	u	f		U		f	u
9	C									f		F		f	u	f		U		f	u
10		C			T					f		F		f	u	f		U		f	u
11				X		T		O		u	f		F		f	u	f		U		f
12			C	Q	O				T	u	f		F		f	u	f		U		f
13			Q							f	u	f		F		f	u	f		U	
14	X								Q	f	u	f		F		f	u	f		U	
15		X			X	O					f	u	f		F		f	u	f		U
16	Q			T			T	T	X		f	u	f		F		f	u	f		U
17		Q	X								f	u	f		F		f	u	f		U
18	T						Q	Q		U		f	u	f		F		f	u	f	
19		T	Q		C	T				U		f	u	f		F		f	u	f	
20				O			X	X	C		U		f	u	f		F		f	u	f
21			T			Q					U		f	u	f		F		f	u	f
22										f		U		f	u	f		F		f	u
23	O	O		X						f		U		f	u	f		F		f	u
24				T		X	C	C	X	u	f		U		f	u	f		F		f
25						Q				u	f		U		f	u	f		F		f
26			O							f	u	f		U		f	u	f		F	
27	T	T		Q	T				Q	f	u	f		U		f	u	f		F	
28						C					f	u	f		U		f	u	f		F
29		Q		X			X	X	T		f	u	f		U		f	u	f		F
30	Q										f	u	f		U		f	u	f		F

JULY MOON TABLE

DATE	MOON'S SIGN	ELEMENT	NATURE	MOON'S PHASE
1 Fri.	Aries	Fire	Barren	4th
2 Sat. 9:24 AM	Taurus	Earth	Semi-fruit	4th
3 Sun.	Taurus	Earth	Semi-fruit	4th
4 Mon. 10:13 PM	Gemini	Air	Barren	4th
5 Tue.	Gemini	Air	Barren	4th
6 Wed.	Gemini	Air	Barren	4th
7 Thu. 9:18 AM	Cancer	Water	Fruitful	4th
8 Fri.	Cancer	Water	Fruitful	NM 4:38 PM
9 Sat. 5:43 PM	Leo	Fire	Barren	1st
10 Sun.	Leo	Fire	Barren	1st
11 Mon. 11:48 PM	Virgo	Earth	Barren	1st
12 Tue.	Virgo	Earth	Barren	1st
13 Wed.	Virgo	Earth	Barren	1st
14 Thu. 4:15 AM	Libra	Air	Semi-fruit	1st
15 Fri.	Libra	Air	Semi-fruit	2nd 8:12 PM
16 Sat. 7:35 AM	Scorpio	Water	Fruitful	2nd
17 Sun.	Scorpio	Water	Fruitful	2nd
18 Mon. 10:09 AM	Sagit.	Fire	Barren	2nd
19 Tue.	Sagit.	Fire	Barren	2nd
20 Wed. 12:31 PM	Capri.	Earth	Semi-fruit	2nd
21 Thu.	Capri.	Earth	Semi-fruit	2nd
22 Fri. 3:39 PM	Capri.	Earth	Semi-fruit	FM 3:16 PM

The SUN enters Leo at 8:41 PM

DATE	MOON'S SIGN	ELEMENT	NATURE	MOON'S PHASE
23 Sat.	Aquar.	Air	Barren	3rd
24 Sun. 8:57 PM	Pisces	Water	Fruitful	3rd
25 Mon.	Pisces	Water	Fruitful	3rd
26 Tue.	Pisces	Water	Fruitful	3rd
27 Wed. 5:31 AM	Aries	Fire	Barren	3rd
28 Thu.	Aries	Fire	Barren	3rd
29 Fri. 5:13 PM	Taurus	Earth	Semi-fruit	3rd
30 Sat.	Taurus	Earth	Semi-fruit	4th 7:40 AM
31 Sun.	Taurus	Earth	Semi-fruit	4th

Set in Eastern Standard Time

JULY 1994

Lunar Aspectarian   Favorable & Unfavorable Days

	SUN	MERCURY	VENUS	MARS	JUPITER	SATURN	URANUS	NEPTUNE	PLUTO	ARIES	TAURUS	GEMINI	CANCER	LEO	VIRGO	LIBRA	SCORPIO	SAGITTARIUS	CAPRICORN	AQUARIUS	PISCES
1			T				Q	Q		F		f	u	f		U		f	u	f	
2		X				O				F		f	u	f		U		f	u	f	
3	X						X				F		f	u	f		U		f	u	f
4			Q				T	T	O		F		f	u	f		U		f	u	f
5				C		Q					F		f	u	f		U		f	u	f
6										f		F		f	u	f		U		f	u
7		C	X		T					f		F		f	u	f		U		f	u
8	C					T				u	f		F		f	u	f		U		f
9							O	O	T	u	f		F		f	u	f		U		f
10				X	Q					f	u	f		F		f	u	f		U	
11									Q	f	u	f		F		f	u	f		U	
12		X	C	Q	X	O				f	u	f		F		f	u	f		U	
13	X						T	T	X		f	u	f		F		f	u	f		U
14		Q		T							f	u	f		F		f	u	f		U
15	Q						Q	Q		U		f	u	f		F		f	u	f	
16		T	X		C					U		f	u	f		F		f	u	f	
17						T		X			U		f	u	f		F		f	u	f
18	T						X		C		U		f	u	f		F		f	u	f
19			Q	O	Q					f		U		f	u	f		F		f	u
20				X						f		U		f	u	f		F		f	u
21		O	T				X			u	f		U		f	u	f		F		f
22	O						C	C	X	u	f		U		f	u	f		F		f
23				T	Q					f	u	f		U		f	u	f		F	
24									Q	f	u	f		U		f	u	f		F	
25					T	C				f	u	f		U		f	u	f		F	
26		T	O	Q			X	X	T		f	u	f		U		f	u	f		F
27	T										f	u	f		U		f	u	f		F
28		Q		X						F		f	u	f		U		f	u	f	
29							Q	Q		F		f	u	f		U		f	u	f	
30	Q				O	X					F		f	u	f		U		f	u	f
31		X	T				T	T	O		F		f	u	f		U		f	u	f

AUGUST MOON TABLE

DATE	MOON'S SIGN	ELEMENT	NATURE	MOON'S PHASE
1 Mon. 6:05 AM	Gemini	Air	Barren	4th
2 Tue.	Gemini	Air	Barren	4th
3 Wed. 5:22 PM	Cancer	Water	Fruitful	4th
4 Thu.	Cancer	Water	Fruitful	4th
5 Fri.	Cancer	Water	Fruitful	4th
6 Sat. 1:31 AM	Leo	Fire	Barren	4th
7 Sun.	Leo	Fire	Barren	NM 3:45 AM
8 Mon. 6:42 AM	Virgo	Earth	Barren	1st
9 Tue.	Virgo	Earth	Barren	1st
10 Wed. 10:07 AM	Libra	Air	Semi-fruit	1st
11 Thu.	Libra	Air	Semi-fruit	1st
12 Fri. 12:56 PM	Scorpio	Water	Fruitful	1st
13 Sat.	Scorpio	Water	Fruitful	1st
14 Sun. 3:54 PM	Sagit.	Fire	Barren	2nd 12:58 AM
15 Mon.	Sagit.	Fire	Barren	2nd
16 Tue. 7:18 PM	Capri.	Earth	Semi-fruit	2nd
17 Wed.	Capri.	Earth	Semi-fruit	2nd
18 Thu. 11:34 PM	Aquar.	Air	Barren	2nd
19 Fri.	Aquar.	Air	Barren	2nd
20 Sat.	Aquar.	Air	Barren	2nd
21 Sun. 5:28 AM	Aquar.	Air	Barren	FM 1:47 AM
22 Mon.	Pisces	Water	Fruitful	3rd
23 Tue. 1:55 PM	Aries	Fire	Barren	3rd

The SUN enters Virgo at 3:44 AM

DATE	MOON'S SIGN	ELEMENT	NATURE	MOON'S PHASE
24 Wed.	Aries	Fire	Barren	3rd
25 Thu.	Aries	Fire	Barren	3rd
26 Fri. 1:13 AM	Taurus	Earth	Semi-fruit	3rd
27 Sat.	Taurus	Earth	Semi-fruit	3rd
28 Sun. 2:07 PM	Gemini	Air	Barren	3rd
29 Mon.	Gemini	Air	Barren	4th 1:40 AM
30 Tue.	Gemini	Air	Barren	4th
31 Wed. 1:59 AM	Cancer	Water	Fruitful	4th

Set in Eastern Standard Time

AUGUST 1994

Lunar Aspectarian Favorable & Unfavorable Days

Day	SUN	MERCURY	VENUS	MARS	JUPITER	SATURN	URANUS	NEPTUNE	PLUTO	ARIES	TAURUS	GEMINI	CANCER	LEO	VIRGO	LIBRA	SCORPIO	SAGITTARIUS	CAPRICORN	AQUARIUS	PISCES
1							T	T			F		f	u	f			U	f	u	f
2	X			C		Q				f		F	f	u	f			U	f	u	
3			Q							f		F	f	u	f			U	f	u	
4					T	T				u	f		F		f	u	f		U		f
5			X				O	O	T	u	f		F		f	u	f		U		f
6		C				Q				u	f		F		f	u	f		U		f
7	C			X					Q	f	u	f		F		f	u	f	U		
8				X						f	u	f		F		f	u	f	U		
9							O	T	T		f	u	f		F		f	u	f		U
10			C	Q					X		f	u	f		F		f	u	f		U
11	X	X						Q		U		f	u	f		F		f	u	f	
12				T		Q				U		f	u	f		F		f	u	f	
13					C	T				U		f	u	f			F		f	u	f
14	Q	Q					X	X	C	U		f	u	f			F		f	u	f
15			X			Q				f		U	f	u	f			F	f	u	
16	T	T		O						f		U	f	u	f			F	f	u	
17			Q		X	X				f		U	f	u	f			F	f	u	
18							C	C	X	u	f		U		f	u	f		F		f
19			T		Q					u	f		U		f	u	f		F		f
20									Q	f	u	f		U		f	u	f		F	
21	O	O		T	T	C				f	u	f		U		f	u	f		F	
22								X		f	u	f		U		f	u	f			F
23			Q			X		T		f	u	f		U		f	u	f			F
24										F		f	u	f		U		f	u	f	
25			O				Q	Q		F		f	u	f		U		f	u	f	
26	T			X	O	X				F		f	u	f		U		f	u	f	
27		T					T	T			F		f	u	f		U		f	u	f
28									O		F		f	u	f		U		f	u	f
29	Q					Q				f		F	f	u	f			U	f	u	
30		Q	T							f		F	f	u	f			U	f	u	
31	X			C	T	T				f		F	f	u	f			U	f	u	

SEPTEMBER MOON TABLE

DATE	MOON'S SIGN	ELEMENT	NATURE	MOON'S PHASE
1 Thu.	Cancer	Water	Fruitful	4th
2 Fri. 10:37 AM	Leo	Fire	Barren	4th
3 Sat.	Leo	Fire	Barren	4th
4 Sun. 3:34 PM	Virgo	Earth	Barren	4th
5 Mon.	Virgo	Earth	Barren	NM 1:33 PM
6 Tue. 5:57 PM	Libra	Air	Semi-fruit	1st
7 Wed.	Libra	Air	Semi-fruit	1st
8 Thu. 7:26 PM	Scorpio	Water	Fruitful	1st
9 Fri.	Scorpio	Water	Fruitful	1st
10 Sat. 9:26 PM	Sagit.	Fire	Barren	1st
11 Sun.	Sagit.	Fire	Barren	1st
12 Mon.	Sagit.	Fire	Barren	2nd 6:34 AM
13 Tue. 12:45 AM	Capri.	Earth	Semi-fruit	2nd
14 Wed.	Capri.	Earth	Semi-fruit	2nd
15 Thu. 5:42 AM	Aquar.	Air	Barren	2nd
16 Fri.	Aquar.	Air	Barren	2nd
17 Sat. 12:31 PM	Pisces	Water	Fruitful	2nd
18 Sun.	Pisces	Water	Fruitful	2nd
19 Mon. 9:29 PM	Pisces	Water	Fruitful	FM 3:00 PM
20 Tue.	Aries	Fire	Barren	3rd
21 Wed.	Aries	Fire	Barren	3rd
22 Thu. 8:47 AM	Taurus	Earth	Semi-fruit	3rd
23 Fri.	Taurus	Earth	Semi-fruit	3rd
The SUN enters Libra at 1:19 AM				
24 Sat. 9:41 PM	Gemini	Air	Barren	3rd
25 Sun.	Gemini	Air	Barren	3rd
26 Mon.	Gemini	Air	Barren	3rd
27 Tue. 10:12 AM	Cancer	Water	Fruitful	4th 7:24 PM
28 Wed.	Cancer	Water	Fruitful	4th
29 Thu. 7:56 PM	Leo	Fire	Barren	4th
30 Fri.	Leo	Fire	Barren	4th

Set in Eastern Standard Time

SEPTEMBER 1994

Lunar Aspectarian   Favorable & Unfavorable Days

	SUN	MERCURY	VENUS	MARS	JUPITER	SATURN	URANUS	NEPTUNE	PLUTO	ARIES	TAURUS	GEMINI	CANCER	LEO	VIRGO	LIBRA	SCORPIO	SAGITTARIUS	CAPRICORN	AQUARIUS	PISCES
1							O	O		u	f		F		f	u	f		U		f
2		X							T	u	f		F		f	u	f		U		f
3					Q					f	u	f		F		f	u	f		U	
4			X						Q	f	u	f		F		f	u	f		U	
5	C			X	X	O					f	u	f		F		f	u	f		U
6							T	T	X		f	u	f		F		f	u	f		U
7		C		Q						U		f	u	f		F		f	u	f	
8			C				Q	Q		U		f	u	f		F		f	u	f	
9				T	C	T				U		f	u	f		F		f	u	f	
10	X						X	X	C		U		f	u	f		F		f	u	f
11		X				Q					U		f	u	f		F		f	u	f
12	Q									f		U		f	u	f		F		f	u
13			X		X	X				f		U		f	u	f		F		f	u
14	T	Q		O			C	C	X	u	f		U		f	u	f		F		f
15			Q							u	f		U		f	u	f		F		f
16		T			Q					f	u	f		U		f	u	f		F	
17									Q	f	u	f		U		f	u	f		F	
18			T		T	C					f	u	f		U		f	u	f		F
19	O			T			X	X	T		f	u	f		U		f	u	f		F
20											f	u	f		U		f	u	f		F
21		O		Q			Q	Q		F		f	u	f		U		f	u	f	
22						X				F		f	u	f		U		f	u	f	
23			O		O						F		f	u	f		U		f	u	f
24				X			T	T	O		F		f	u	f		U		f	u	f
25	T					Q					F		f	u	f		U		f	u	f
26										f		F		f	u	f		U		f	u
27	Q	T								f		F		f	u	f		U		f	u
28			T		T	T				u	f		F		f	u	f		U		f
29				C			O	O	T	u	f		F		f	u	f		U		f
30	X	Q		Q						u	f		F		f	u	f		U		f

OCTOBER MOON TABLE

DATE	MOON'S SIGN	ELEMENT	NATURE	MOON'S PHASE
1 Sat.	Leo	Fire	Barren	4th
2 Sun. 1:40 AM	Virgo	Earth	Barren	4th
3 Mon.	Virgo	Earth	Barren	4th
4 Tue. 3:57 AM	Libra	Air	Semi-fruit	NM 10:56 PM
5 Wed.	Libra	Air	Semi-fruit	1st
6 Thu. 4:22 AM	Scorpio	Water	Fruitful	1st
7 Fri.	Scorpio	Water	Fruitful	1st
8 Sat. 4:47 AM	Sagit.	Fire	Barren	1st
9 Sun.	Sagit.	Fire	Barren	1st
10 Mon. 6:44 AM	Capri.	Earth	Semi-fruit	1st
11 Tue.	Capri.	Earth	Semi-fruit	2nd 2:17 PM
12 Wed. 11:09 AM	Aquar.	Air	Barren	2nd
13 Thu.	Aquar.	Air	Barren	2nd
14 Fri. 6:18 PM	Pisces	Water	Fruitful	2nd
15 Sat.	Pisces	Water	Fruitful	2nd
16 Sun.	Pisces	Water	Fruitful	2nd
17 Mon. 3:56 AM	Aries	Fire	Barren	2nd
18 Tue.	Aries	Fire	Barren	2nd
19 Wed. 3:35 PM	Aries	Fire	Barren	FM 7:18 AM
20 Thu.	Taurus	Earth	Semi-fruit	3rd
21 Fri.	Taurus	Earth	Semi-fruit	3rd
22 Sat. 4:28 AM	Gemini	Air	Barren	3rd
23 Sun.	Gemini	Air	Barren	3rd
The SUN enters Scorpio at 10:36 AM				
24 Mon. 5:16 PM	Cancer	Water	Fruitful	3rd
25 Tue.	Cancer	Water	Fruitful	3rd
26 Wed.	Cancer	Water	Fruitful	3rd
27 Thu. 4:05 AM	Leo	Fire	Barren	4th 11:45 AM
28 Fri.	Leo	Fire	Barren	4th
29 Sat. 11:22 AM	Virgo	Earth	Barren	4th
30 Sun.	Virgo	Earth	Barren	4th
31 Mon. 2:46 PM	Libra	Air	Semi-fruit	4th

Set in Eastern Standard Time

OCTOBER 1994

Lunar Aspectarian — Favorable & Unfavorable Days

	SUN	MERCURY	VENUS	MARS	JUPITER	SATURN	URANUS	NEPTUNE	PLUTO	ARIES	TAURUS	GEMINI	CANCER	LEO	VIRGO	LIBRA	SCORPIO	SAGITTARIUS	CAPRICORN	AQUARIUS	PISCES
1			Q						Q	f	u	f		F		f	u	f		U	
2		X				O				f	u	f		F		f	u	f		U	
3			X		X		T	T	X		f	u	f		F		f	u	f		U
4	C			X							f	u	f		F		f	u	f		U
5						Q	Q			U		f	u	f		F		f	u	f	
6		C		Q		T				U		f	u	f		F		f	u	f	
7			C		C		X	X	C		U		f	u	f		F		f	u	f
8			T		Q						U		f	u	f		F		f	u	f
9	X									f		U		f	u	f		F		f	u
10		X			X					f		U		f	u	f		F		f	u
11	Q		X		X		C	C		u	f		U		f	u	f		F		f
12		Q		O					X	u	f		U		f	u	f		F		f
13			Q		Q					f	u	f		U		f	u	f		F	
14	T								Q	f	u	f		U		f	u	f		F	
15		T				C					f	u	f		U		f	u	f		F
16			T		T		X	X	T		f	u	f		U		f	u	f		F
17			T								f	u	f		U		f	u	f		F
18								Q		F		f	u	f		U		f	u	f	
19	O	O						Q		F		f	u	f		U		f	u	f	
20				Q	X						F		f	u	f		U		f	u	f
21			O		O		T	T	O		F		f	u	f		U		f	u	f
22					Q						F		f	u	f		U		f	u	f
23				X						f		F		f	u	f		U		f	u
24	T	T								f		F		f	u	f		U		f	u
25			T			T				u	f		F		f	u	f		U		f
26		Q			T		O	O	T	u	f		F		f	u	f		U		f
27	Q									u	f		F		f	u	f		U		f
28		X	Q	C	Q					f	u	f		F		f	u	f		U	
29	X					O			Q	f	u	f		F		f	u	f		U	
30			X					T			f	u	f		F		f	u	f		U
31				X			T		X		f	u	f		F		f	u	f		U

NOVEMBER MOON TABLE

DATE	MOON'S SIGN	ELEMENT	NATURE	MOON'S PHASE
1 Tue.	Libra	Air	Semi-fruit	4th
2 Wed. 3:19 PM	Scorpio	Water	Fruitful	4th
3 Thu.	Scorpio	Water	Fruitful	NM 8:35 AM
4 Fri. 2:46 PM	Sagit.	Fire	Barren	1st
5 Sat.	Sagit.	Fire	Barren	1st
6 Sun. 3:01 PM	Capri.	Earth	Semi-fruit	1st
7 Mon.	Capri.	Earth	Semi-fruit	1st
8 Tue. 5:48 PM	Aquar.	Air	Barren	1st
9 Wed.	Aquar.	Air	Barren	1st
10 Thu.	Aquar.	Air	Barren	2nd 1:14 AM
11 Fri. 12:04 AM	Pisces	Water	Fruitful	2nd
12 Sat.	Pisces	Water	Fruitful	2nd
13 Sun. 9:44 AM	Aries	Fire	Barren	2nd
14 Mon.	Aries	Fire	Barren	2nd
15 Tue. 9:45 PM	Taurus	Earth	Semi-fruit	2nd
16 Wed.	Taurus	Earth	Semi-fruit	2nd
17 Thu.	Taurus	Earth	Semi-fruit	2nd
18 Fri. 10:42 AM	Taurus	Earth	Semi-fruit	FM 1:58 AM
19 Sat.	Gemini	Air	Barren	3rd
20 Sun. 11:21 PM	Cancer	Water	Fruitful	3rd
21 Mon.	Cancer	Water	Fruitful	3rd
22 Tue.	Cancer	Water	Fruitful	3rd

The SUN enters Sagittarius at 8:06 AM

DATE	MOON'S SIGN	ELEMENT	NATURE	MOON'S PHASE
23 Wed. 10:33 AM	Leo	Fire	Barren	3rd
24 Thu.	Leo	Fire	Barren	3rd
25 Fri. 7:09 PM	Virgo	Earth	Barren	3rd
26 Sat.	Virgo	Earth	Barren	4th 2:04 AM
27 Sun.	Virgo	Earth	Barren	4th
28 Mon. 12:22 AM	Libra	Air	Semi-fruit	4th
29 Tue.	Libra	Air	Semi-fruit	4th
30 Wed. 2:22 AM	Scorpio	Water	Fruitful	4th

Set in Eastern Standard Time

NOVEMBER 1994

Lunar Aspectarian   Favorable & Unfavorable Days

Day	SUN	MERCURY	VENUS	MARS	JUPITER	SATURN	URANUS	NEPTUNE	PLUTO	ARIES	TAURUS	GEMINI	CANCER	LEO	VIRGO	LIBRA	SCORPIO	SAGITTARIUS	CAPRICORN	AQUARIUS	PISCES
1				X						U		f	u	f		F		f	u	f	
2		C					Q	Q		U		f	u	f		F		f	u	f	
3	C		C	Q		T					U		f	u	f		F		f	u	f
4					C	Q	X	X	C		U		f	u	f		F		f	u	f
5				T						f		U		f	u	f		F		f	u
6		X								f		U		f	u	f		F		f	u
7	X		X			X				u	f		U		f	u	f		F		f
8		Q			X		C	C	X	u	f		U		f	u	f		F		f
9			Q							f	u	f		U		f	u	f		F	
10	Q			O	Q				Q	f	u	f		U		f	u	f		F	
11		T	T			C				f	u	f		U		f	u	f		F	
12	T				T		X	X			f	u	f		U		f	u	f		F
13									T		f	u	f		U		f	u	f		F
14										F		f	u	f		U		f	u	f	
15				T			Q	Q		F		f	u	f		U		f	u	f	
16		O	O			X				F		f	u	f		U		f	u	f	
17				Q			T	T			F		f	u	f		U		f	u	f
18	O				O	Q			O		F		f	u	f		U		f	u	f
19										f		F		f	u	f		U		f	u
20				X						f		F		f	u	f		U		f	u
21			T			T				f		F		f	u	f		U		f	u
22							O	O		u	f		F		f	u	f		U		f
23	T		Q		T				T	u	f		F		f	u	f		U		f
24										f	u	f		F		f	u	f		U	
25		Q	X	C	Q				Q	f	u	f		F		f	u	f		U	
26	Q					O				f	u	f		F		f	u	f		U	
27		X			X		T	T	X		f	u	f		F		f	u	f		U
28	X										f	u	f		F		f	u	f		U
29				X			Q	Q		U		f	u	f		F		f	u	f	
30			C			T				U		f	u	f		F		f	u	f	

DECEMBER MOON TABLE

DATE	MOON'S SIGN	ELEMENT	NATURE	MOON'S PHASE
1 Thu.	Scorpio	Water	Fruitful	4th
2 Fri. 2:13 AM	Sagit.	Fire	Barren	NM 6:54 PM
3 Sat.	Sagit.	Fire	Barren	1st
4 Sun. 1:43 AM	Capri.	Earth	Semi-fruit	1st
5 Mon.	Capri.	Earth	Semi-fruit	1st
6 Tue. 2:52 AM	Aquar.	Air	Barren	1st
7 Wed.	Aquar.	Air	Barren	1st
8 Thu. 7:25 AM	Pisces	Water	Fruitful	1st
9 Fri.	Pisces	Water	Fruitful	2nd 4:07 PM
10 Sat. 4:04 PM	Aries	Fire	Barren	2nd
11 Sun.	Aries	Fire	Barren	2nd
12 Mon.	Aries	Fire	Barren	2nd
13 Tue. 3:56 AM	Taurus	Earth	Semi-fruit	2nd
14 Wed.	Taurus	Earth	Semi-fruit	2nd
15 Thu. 4:59 PM	Gemini	Air	Barren	2nd
16 Fri.	Gemini	Air	Barren	2nd
17 Sat.	Gemini	Air	Barren	FM 9:17 PM
18 Sun. 5:25 AM	Cancer	Water	Fruitful	3rd
19 Mon.	Cancer	Water	Fruitful	3rd
20 Tue. 4:13 PM	Leo	Fire	Barren	3rd
21 Wed.	Leo	Fire	Barren	3rd

The SUN enters Capricorn at 9:23 PM

DATE	MOON'S SIGN	ELEMENT	NATURE	MOON'S PHASE
22 Thu.	Leo	Fire	Barren	3rd
23 Fri. 1:01 AM	Virgo	Earth	Barren	3rd
24 Sat.	Virgo	Earth	Barren	3rd
25 Sun. 7:28 AM	Libra	Air	Semi-fruit	4th 2:07 PM
26 Mon.	Libra	Air	Semi-fruit	4th
27 Tue. 11:18 AM	Scorpio	Water	Fruitful	4th
28 Wed.	Scorpio	Water	Fruitful	4th
29 Thu. 12:46 PM	Sagit.	Fire	Barren	4th
30 Fri.	Sagit.	Fire	Barren	4th
31 Sat. 12:58 PM	Capri.	Earth	Semi-fruit	4th

Set in Eastern Standard Time

DECEMBER 1994

Lunar Aspectarian Favorable & Unfavorable Days

Day	SUN	MERCURY	VENUS	MARS	JUPITER	SATURN	URANUS	NEPTUNE	PLUTO	ARIES	TAURUS	GEMINI	CANCER	LEO	VIRGO	LIBRA	SCORPIO	SAGITTARIUS	CAPRICORN	AQUARIUS	PISCES
1				Q	C		X	X	C		U		f	u	f		F		f	u	f
2	C	C				Q					U		f	u	f		F		f	u	f
3				T						f		U		f	u	f		F		f	u
4			X			X				f		U		f	u	f		F		f	u
5							C	C		u	f		U		f	u	f		F		f
6		X	Q		X				X	u	f		U		f	u	f		F		f
7	X									f	u	f		U		f	u	f		F	
8			T	O	Q	C			Q	f	u	f		U		f	u	f		F	
9	Q	Q									f	u	f		U		f	u	f		F
10				T			X	X	T		f	u	f		U		f	u	f		F
11										F		f	u	f		U		f	u	f	
12	T	T					Q	Q		F		f	u	f		U		f	u	f	
13			O	T		X				F		f	u	f		U		f	u	f	
14											F		f	u	f		U		f	u	f
15				Q	O		T	T	O		F		f	u	f		U		f	u	f
16						Q				f		F		f	u	f		U		f	u
17	O									f		F		f	u	f		U		f	u
18		O		X		T				f		F		f	u	f		U		f	u
19			T							u	f		F		f	u	f		U		f
20				T			O	O	T	u	f		F		f	u	f		U		f
21			Q							f	u	f		F		f	u	f		U	
22									Q	f	u	f		F		f	u	f		U	
23	T	T		C	Q	O				f	u	f		F		f	u	f		U	
24			X				T	T			f	u	f		F		f	u	f		U
25	Q		X		X				X		f	u	f		F		f	u	f		U
26		Q						Q		U		f	u	f		F		f	u	f	
27	X			X		Q				U		f	u	f		F		f	u	f	
28		X	C			T					U		f	u	f		F		f	u	f
29				Q	C		X	X	C		U		f	u	f		F		f	u	f
30					Q					f		U		f	u	f		F		f	u
31				T						f		U		f	u	f		F		f	u

ASTRO-ALMANAC

Llewellyn's unique Astro-Almanac is provided for quick reference. Because the dates indicated may not be the best for you personally, be sure to read the instructions starting with "How to Use the Moon Sign Book Tables and Activity Information," then go to the proper section of the book and read the detailed description provided for each activity.

For the most part, the dates given in the Astro-Almanac will correspond to the ones you can determine for yourself from the detailed instructions. But just as often, the dates given may not be favorable for your Sun sign or for your particular interests. *That's why it's important for you to learn how to use the entire process to come up with the most beneficial dates for you.*

The following pages are provided for easy reference for those of you who do not want detailed descriptions. The dates provided are determined from the sign and phase of the Moon and the aspects to the Moon. These are approximate dates only and do not take into account retrogrades or Moon voids. For more information, please see "Retrogrades" and "Moon Void of Course."

Please read the instructions on how to come up with the dates yourself. This is very important in some instances (such as planning surgery or making big purchases). You will find other lists of dates in the proper sections of the *Moon Sign Book*. We have special lists for Fishing and Hunting Dates, Gardening Dates, Dates for Destroying Plant and Animal Pests, and other types of activities. See the Table of Contents for a complete listing.

•JANUARY•

Entertain: 3-5, 12-14, 22-24, 26-28, 31
Sports activities: 27
Marriage for happiness: 15, 22, 25
End a romance or file for divorce: 5-8
Cut hair to increase growth: 14-17, 24-26
Cut hair to retard growth: 27-28
Cut hair for added thickness: 26
Permanents and hair coloring: 13-14
Start a weight loss program: 1-3, 8-9, 27-31
Stop a bad habit: 1-3, 27-31
See dentist for fillings: 6
See dentist for extractions: 12, 15-17, 23-24
Consult physician: 3-5, 9-12, 17-19, 24-26, 31
Purchase major appliances: None
Buy a car or have repairs done: 7, 22
Purchase electronic equipment: 23
Buy antiques or jewelry: 22
Buy real estate for speculation: 35, 9-12, 17-19, 24-26, 31
Buy permanent home: 5-8, 12-14, 19-22, 26-28
Sell home, property or possessions: 2, 6, 10-12, 15-17, 21, 23, 25, 29, 31
Sign important papers: 7
Building: None
Ask for credit or loan: 8-9
Start new ventures or advertise: 13, 20-21, 25
Apply for job: 21
Ask for raise or promotion: 7, 12, 17, 23
Collect money: 10, 25
Move into new home: 6
Painting or roofing: 5-8, 27-28
Cut timber: 4-5, 8-11
Travel for business: 2, 10, 15, 17, 23, 25, 29
Travel for pleasure: 2, 6, 10, 15-16, 25, 29, 31
Air travel: 23
Buy animals: 13-15, 18
Neuter or spay an animal: 8-10, 12-14
Dock or dehorn animals: 4-14
Brewing: 5-8, 26
Canning: 5-8
Mow lawn to retard growth: 1-11, 27-31

•FEBRUARY•

Entertain: 1-2, 8-11, 18-20, 23-25, 27-28
Sports activities: 21-22
Marriage for happiness: 12, 16, 21-22
End a romance or file for divorce: 2-3
Cut hair to increase growth: 11-13, 20-23
Cut hair to retard growth: None
Cut hair for added thickness: None
Permanents and hair coloring: None
Start a weight loss program: 3-6, 8-10, 25-27
Stop a bad habit: 25-27
See dentist for fillings: 3, 10
See dentist for extractions: 11-13, 19-20
Consult physician: 1-2, 6-8, 13-16, 20-23, 27-28
Purchase major appliances: 9
Buy a car or have repairs done: None
Purchase electronic equipment: 28
Buy antiques or jewelry: None
Buy real estate for speculation: 1-2, 6-8, 13-16, 20-23, 27-28
Buy permanent home: 2-3, 8-11, 16-18, 23-25
Sell home, property or possessions: 3, 6-7, 9, 11-12, 14, 16, 20-22, 26, 28
Sign important papers: 2
Building: 2, 16
Ask for credit or loan: 5
Start new ventures or advertise: 16, 21-23
Apply for job: 16
Ask for raise or promotion: 11, 28
Collect money: 1, 7, 21-22
Move into new home: 16
Painting or roofing: 2-3, 8-10
Cut timber: 3-10
Travel for business: 6-7, 12, 16, 21-22, 26, 28
Travel for pleasure: 1, 5, 7, 12, 15-16, 21-22, 26
Air travel: 28
Buy animals: 12-14, 17-18
Neuter or spay an animal: 7-9, 11-13
Dock or dehorn animals: 3-11
Brewing: 2-3, 25
Canning: 2-3
Mow lawn to retard growth: 1-10, 25-28

•MARCH•

Entertain: 1, 7-10, 17-20, 22-24, 26-28
Sports activities: 24
Marriage for happiness: 24
End a romance or file for divorce: 1-3, 28-30
Cut hair to increase growth: 12, 20-22
Cut hair to retard growth: None
Cut hair for added thickness: 27
Permanents and hair coloring: None
Start a weight loss program: 3-5, 7-10, 30-31
Stop a bad habit: None
See dentist for fillings: 2, 8, 10, 29-30
See dentist for extractions: 12, 19-20, 26
Consult physician: 1, 5-7, 12-15, 20-22, 26-28
Purchase major appliances: 10
Buy a car or have repairs done: 2, 17
Purchase electronic equipment: 20
Buy antiques or jewelry: 17, 22
Buy real estate for speculation: 1, 5-7, 12-15, 20-22, 26-28
Buy permanent home: 1-3, 7-10, 15-17, 22-24, 28-30
Sell home, property or possessions: 1-2, 5-6, 9-11, 15, 20-21, 29
Sign important papers: 9, 29
Building: None
Ask for credit or loan: 10-11
Start new ventures or advertise: 16-17, 21-22
Apply for job: None
Ask for raise or promotion: 9
Collect money: 6-7, 21
Move into new home: 24
Painting or roofing: 1-3, 7-10, 28-30
Cut timber: 4-10
Travel for business: 5-6, 11, 15, 20-21, 29
Travel for pleasure: 2, 6-7, 11, 17, 21-22, 24
Air travel: 20
Buy animals: 14, 16, 19
Neuter or spay an animal: 8-10, 12-14
Dock or dehorn animals: 4-10
Brewing: 10-12, 27
Canning: 1-3, 10-12, 28-30
Mow lawn to retard growth: 1-12, 27-31

•APRIL•

Entertain: 3-6, 14-16, 18-20, 23-25
Sports activities: 19-20
Marriage for happiness: 17
End a romance or file for divorce: 25-27
Cut hair to increase growth: 16-18, 25
Cut hair to retard growth: None
Cut hair for added thickness: 25
Permanents and hair coloring: None
Start a weight loss program: 1, 3-6, 9-10, 27-28
Stop a bad habit: None
See dentist for fillings: 4, 6, 26
See dentist for extractions: 15, 22
Consult physician: 1-3, 9-11, 16-18, 23-25, 28-30
Purchase major appliances: None
Buy a car or have repairs done: 5
Purchase electronic equipment: 14
Buy antiques or jewelry: 18
Buy real estate for speculation: 1-3, 9-11, 16-18, 23-25, 28-30
Buy permanent home: 3-6, 11-14, 18-20, 25-27
Sell home, property or possessions: 2-3, 7-8, 17, 19-20, 25, 29
Sign important papers: 20
Building: 12
Ask for credit or loan: 7
Start new ventures or advertise: 12-13, 17-18
Apply for job: 21
Ask for raise or promotion: 8, 20, 29
Collect money: 2, 17-18, 29
Move into new home: None
Painting or roofing: 3-6, 25-27
Cut timber: 2-6, 9-10
Travel for business: 2-3, 17, 20, 29
Travel for pleasure: 2, 5, 17-18, 29
Air travel: 14
Buy animals: 11, 13, 15
Neuter or spay an animal: 7-9, 11-13
Dock or dehorn animals: 3-6, 14-17
Brewing: 6-9, 25
Canning: 6-9, 25-27
Mow lawn to retard growth: 1-10, 25-30

•MAY•

Entertain: 1-3, 11-13, 15-18, 20-22, 28-30
Sports activities: 16-18
Marriage for happiness: 14, 22
End a romance or file for divorce: None
Cut hair to increase growth: 13-15, 22-24
Cut hair to retard growth: None
Cut hair for added thickness: 24
Permanents and hair coloring: None
Start a weight loss program: 1-3, 5-8, 24-26, 28-30
Stop a bad habit: None
See dentist for fillings: 3, 10, 30
See dentist for extractions: 13, 20
Consult physician: 1, 5-8, 13-15, 20-22, 26-28
Purchase major appliances: 2
Buy a car or have repairs done: 29
Purchase electronic equipment: None
Buy antiques or jewelry: 15, 22
Buy real estate for speculation: 1, 5-8, 13-15, 20-22, 26-28
Buy permanent home: 1-3, 8-11, 15-18, 22-24, 28-30
Sell home, property or possessions: 2, 4-5, 7, 11, 13-14, 17-18, 23, 26-27, 31
Sign important papers: 11, 17
Building: 9, 23
Ask for credit or loan: 4
Start new ventures or advertise: 11, 14
Apply for job: 19
Ask for raise or promotion: 5, 11, 17, 22
Collect money: 7, 14, 27
Move into new home: 2, 18
Painting or roofing: 1-3, 8-10, 28-30
Cut timber: 2-3, 5-10
Travel for business: 5, 14, 17, 27, 31
Travel for pleasure: 2, 5, 14, 18, 20, 27, 31
Air travel: None
Buy animals: 12, 16
Neuter or spay an animal: 7-9, 11-13
Dock or dehorn animals: 11-17
Brewing: 3-5, 24, 31
Canning: 3-5, 30-31
Mow lawn to retard growth: 1-10, 24-31

•JUNE•

Entertain: 7-10, 12-14, 16-19, 25-27
Sports activities: 14
Marriage for happiness: 10, 17
End a romance or file for divorce: None
Cut hair to increase growth: 10-12, 19-21
Cut hair to retard growth: 7-8
Cut hair for added thickness: 23
Permanents and hair coloring: None
Start a weight loss program: 2-5, 25-27, 29-30
Stop a bad habit: 7-8
See dentist for fillings: 6-7, 26
See dentist for extractions: 9, 16, 23
Consult physician: 2-5, 10-12, 16-19, 22-25, 29-30
Purchase major appliances: None
Buy a car or have repairs done: 14, 27
Purchase electronic equipment: 27
Buy antiques or jewelry: 17, 18
Buy real estate for speculation: 2-5, 10-12, 16-19, 22-25, 29-30
Buy permanent home: 5-7, 12-14, 19-21, 25-27
Sell home, property or possessions: 5, 10-11, 16, 19, 23-24, 29
Sign important papers: 5
Building: 6, 19
Ask for credit or loan: 1
Start new ventures or advertise: 10-12, 22
Apply for job: 15-16, 23
Ask for raise or promotion: 5, 10, 15, 27
Collect money: 10, 17, 23
Move into new home: 6
Painting or roofing: 5-7, 25-27
Cut timber: 2-8, 30
Travel for business: 10, 19, 23
Travel for pleasure: 3, 6, 10, 14, 17-18, 23
Air travel: None
Buy animals: 8, 13, 16
Neuter or spay an animal: 5-7, 9-11
Dock or dehorn animals: 7-15
Brewing: 1-2, 23
Canning: 1-2, 27-29
Mow lawn to retard growth: 1-8, 23-30

•JULY•

Entertain: 4-7, 9-11, 13-15, 22-24, 31
Sports activities: 10-11
Marriage for happiness: None
End a romance or file for divorce: None
Cut hair to increase growth: 8-9, 15-18
Cut hair to retard growth: 4-7, 31
Cut hair for added thickness: 22
Permanents and hair coloring: None
Start a weight loss program: 1-2, 23-24, 27-29
Stop a bad habit: 4-7, 31
See dentist for fillings: 3-4, 24, 31
See dentist for extractions: 13, 21-22
Consult physician: 1-2, 7-9, 13-15, 20-22, 27-29
Purchase major appliances: 23
Buy a car or have repairs done: 18
Purchase electronic equipment: None
Buy antiques or jewelry: None
Buy real estate for speculation: 1-2, 7-9, 13-15, 20-22, 27-29
Buy permanent home: 2-4, 9-11, 15-18, 22-24, 29-31
Sell home, property or possessions: 2, 7, 10, 14, 16, 20, 23, 25, 28, 31
Sign important papers: 16, 31
Building: 3, 17, 30
Ask for credit or loan: None
Start new ventures or advertise: 9, 20
Apply for job: 12
Ask for raise or promotion: 2, 7, 12, 16, 26, 31
Collect money: 1, 21
Move into new home: 16, 31
Painting or roofing: 2-4, 23-24, 29-31
Cut timber: 1-7, 30-31
Travel for business: 2, 7, 16, 20, 31
Travel for pleasure: 1, 3, 7, 13, 16, 18, 20-21, 27, 31
Air travel: 7
Buy animals: 9-11, 14-15
Neuter or spay an animal: 5-7, 9-10
Dock or dehorn animals: 4-15, 31
Brewing: 7-8, 22
Canning: 7-8, 24-27
Mow lawn to retard growth: 1-8, 23-31

•AUGUST•

Entertain: 1-3, 6-8, 10-12, 18-21, 28-31
Sports activities: 6-8
Marriage for happiness: 8
End a romance or file for divorce: None
Cut hair to increase growth: 12-14
Cut hair to retard growth: 1-3, 6, 28-31
Cut hair for added thickness: 21
Permanents and hair coloring: None
Start a weight loss program: 6, 21, 23-26
Stop a bad habit: 1-3, 6, 28-31
See dentist for fillings: 21, 27-28
See dentist for extractions: 17-18
Consult physician: 3-6, 10-12, 16-18, 23-26, 31
Purchase major appliances: 21
Buy a car or have repairs done: None
Purchase electronic equipment: 11
Buy antiques or jewelry: 11
Buy real estate for speculation: 3-6, 10-12, 16-18, 23-26, 31
Buy permanent home: 6-8, 12-14, 18-21, 26-28
Sell home, property or possessions: 4, 6-8, 11-13, 17, 21,
    26-27, 31
Sign important papers: 6, 27
Building: 13
Ask for credit or loan: None
Start new ventures or advertise: 19-20
Apply for job: 17
Ask for raise or promotion: 6, 11, 16, 27
Collect money: 4-5, 17, 31
Move into new home: 19
Painting or roofing: 6, 21, 26-28
Cut timber: 1-3, 6, 29-31
Travel for business: 4, 8, 11, 17, 27
Travel for pleasure: 4-5, 8, 11, 17, 19, 26, 30
Air travel: 11
Buy animals: 8-9, 12
Neuter or spay an animal: 3-5, 7
Dock or dehorn animals: 1-13, 29-31
Brewing: 3-6, 21, 31
Canning: 3-6, 21-23, 31
Mow lawn to retard growth: 1-6, 21-31

•SEPTEMBER•

Entertain: 2-4, 6-8, 14-17, 24-27, 29-30
Sports activities: 3-4, 30
Marriage for happiness: 18
End a romance or file for divorce: None
Cut hair to increase growth: 8-10, 17-19
Cut hair to retard growth: 2-4, 24-27, 29-30
Cut hair for added thickness: 19
Permanents and hair coloring: None
Start a weight loss program: 2-5, 19-22, 29-30
Stop a bad habit: 2-5, 24-27, 29-30
See dentist for fillings: 4, 24
See dentist for extractions: 6, 13, 18-19
Consult physician: 1-2, 6-8, 13-14, 19-22, 27-29
Purchase major appliances: None
Buy a car or have repairs done: 10, 30
Purchase electronic equipment: 16, 27
Buy antiques or jewelry: 14
Buy real estate for speculation: 1-2, 6-8, 13-14, 19-22, 27-29
Buy permanent home: 2-4, 8-10, 14-17, 22-24, 29-30
Sell home, property or possessions: 2, 9, 13, 16, 18-19, 24, 27-29
Sign important papers: 16
Building: None
Ask for credit or loan: None
Start new ventures or advertise: 12, 15-17
Apply for job: 13
Ask for raise or promotion: 2, 7, 11, 16, 27
Collect money: 13, 28
Move into new home: 4
Painting or roofing: 2-4, 22-24, 29-30
Cut timber: 2-5, 29-30
Travel for business: 2, 13, 16, 27-28
Travel for pleasure: 4, 10, 13, 28, 30
Air travel: 27
Buy animals: 6, 12
Neuter or spay an animal: 2-3, 8
Dock or dehorn animals: 1-12, 27-30
Brewing: 1-2, 19, 27-29
Canning: 1-2, 27-29
Mow lawn to retard growth: 1-5, 19-30

•OCTOBER•

Entertain: 1-2, 4-5, 12-14, 21-24, 26-29, 31
Sports activities: 1, 28
Marriage for happiness: None
End a romance or file for divorce: None
Cut hair to increase growth: 5-8, 14-16
Cut hair to retard growth: 1-2, 21-24, 26-29
Cut hair for added thickness: 18
Permanents and hair coloring: None
Start a weight loss program: 1-4, 18-19, 26-31
Stop a bad habit: 1-4, 21-24, 26-31
See dentist for fillings: 1, 27
See dentist for extractions: 11, 15-16
Consult physician: 4-5, 10-12, 16-19, 24-26, 31
Purchase major appliances: None
Buy a car or have repairs done: 14, 29
Purchase electronic equipment: 24
Buy antiques or jewelry: 11
Buy real estate for speculation: 4-5, 10-12, 16-19, 24-26, 31
Buy permanent home: 1-2, 5-8, 12-14, 19-21, 26-29
Sell home, property or possessions: 3-4, 7, 10-11, 15-17, 23-24, 26, 28, 31
Sign important papers: 6
Building: 6, 20
Ask for credit or loan: None
Start new ventures or advertise: 9-10, 13-14
Apply for job: 11
Ask for raise or promotion: 2, 15, 24, 28
Collect money: 11, 25-26
Move into new home: None
Painting or roofing: 1-2, 19-21, 26-29
Cut timber: 1-4, 27-31
Travel for business: 3, 10-11, 16, 24, 26, 31
Travel for pleasure: 3, 9, 11, 14, 16, 24-26, 30-31
Air travel: 24
Buy animals: 5, 8
Neuter or spay an animal: 1
Dock or dehorn animals: 1-11, 27-31
Brewing: 18
Canning: 24-26
Mow lawn to retard growth: 1-4, 18-31

•NOVEMBER•

Entertain: 1-2, 8-11, 18-20, 23-25, 28-30
Sports activities: 24-25
Marriage for happiness: 11
End a romance or file for divorce: 2-3, 30
Cut hair to increase growth: 3-4, 11-13
Cut hair to retard growth: 18-20, 23-25
Cut hair for added thickness: 18
Permanents and hair coloring: 9
Start a weight loss program: 23-28
Stop a bad habit: 18-20, 23-28
See dentist for fillings: 24, 30
See dentist for extractions: 7-8, 11-13
Consult physician: 1-2, 6-8, 13-15, 20-23, 28-30
Purchase major appliances: None
Buy a car or have repairs done: None
Purchase electronic equipment: None
Buy antiques or jewelry: None
Buy real estate for speculation: 1-2, 6-8, 13-15, 20-23, 28-30
Buy permanent home: 2-4, 8-11, 15-18, 23-25, 30
Sell home, property or possessions: 1-2, 5-6, 8, 11-12, 15,
    20, 22-23, 25, 27, 29
Sign important papers: None
Building: 3, 16, 30
Ask for credit or loan: None
Start new ventures or advertise: 5, 6, 9, 16
Apply for job: 8
Ask for raise or promotion: 2, 6, 11, 22, 27
Collect money: 7-8, 21, 23
Move into new home: 25
Painting or roofing: 2-3, 18, 23-25, 30
Cut timber: 1-2, 26-30
Travel for business: 6, 8, 12, 22-23, 27
Travel for pleasure: 7-8, 12, 21, 23, 27-28
Air travel: None
Buy animals: 4-5, 8-9
Neuter or spay an animal: 6
Dock or dehorn animals: 1-10, 25,30
Brewing: 2-3,18, 30
Canning: 2-3, 20-23, 30
Mow lawn to retard growth: 1-3, 18-30

•DECEMBER•

Entertain: 6-8, 15-18, 20-23, 25-27
Sports activities: 21-22
Marriage for happiness: None
End a romance or file for divorce: 1-2, 27-29
Cut hair to increase growth: 8-10
Cut hair to retard growth: 17-18, 20-23
Cut hair for added thickness: 17
Permanents and hair coloring: 6-7
Start a weight loss program: 2, 20-25, 29-31
Stop a bad habit: 17-18, 20-25
See dentist for fillings: 21-22, 28
See dentist for extractions: 4-5, 9-10, 17
Consult physician: 4-6, 10-12, 18-20, 25-27
Purchase major appliances: None
Buy a car or have repairs done: 7
Purchase electronic equipment: 6
Buy antiques or jewelry: None
Buy real estate for speculation: 4-6, 10-12, 18-20, 25-27
Buy permanent home: 1-2, 6-8, 12-15, 20-23, 27-29
Sell home, property or possessions: 3, 6, 10, 12-13, 18, 20,
    25, 27-28, 31
Sign important papers: 6, 28
Building: 28
Ask for credit or loan: 2, 31
Start new ventures or advertise: 3, 6-7, 13-14
Apply for job: 13
Ask for raise or promotion: 2, 6, 12, 23
Collect money: 4, 19-20
Move into new home: None
Painting or roofing: 1-2, 20-23, 27-29
Cut timber: 2, 25-27, 29-31
Travel for business: 6, 10, 12, 20, 25, 28
Travel for pleasure: 4, 6-7, 10, 12, 19-20, 24-25, 27
Air travel: None
Buy animals: 3, 5, 9
Neuter or spay an animal: 4-5
Dock or dehorn animals: 1-8
Brewing: 1-2, 17, 27-29
Canning: 1-2, 18-20, 27-29
Mow lawn to retard growth: 1-2, 17-31

MOON VOID OF COURSE

Just before the Moon enters a new sign it will have one last aspect with one of the planets. Between that last major aspect and the entrance of the Moon into the next sign, it is said to be "void of course."

Decisions made while the Moon is void of course don't come to fruition in the way intended, and sometimes not at all. Decisions that are made during that time are usually later seen to be based on delusion, or an unrealistic presumption. When the Moon is void of course, try to carry on activities that previously had been planned.

Often purchases made during this time turn out to be poorly made, left unused, plagued with mechanical problems, or simply a bad investment.

It is nearly impossible in today's world to put off all decisions every time the Moon is void, but try to avoid this period for the most important ones. Or try to make the decision before the Moon is void, and then act on the decision at this time.

•JANUARY•

Last Aspect	Moon Enters New Sign
1 10:15 AM	1 Virgo 3:15 PM
3 1:42 PM	3 Libra 6:31 PM
5 5:13 PM	5 Scorpio 9:29 PM
7 8:39 PM	8 Sagittarius 12:34 AM
10 12:40 AM	10 Capricorn 4:16 AM
12 4:45 AM	12 Aquarius 9:25 AM
14 2:03 PM	14 Pisces 5:03 PM
16 10:47 PM	17 Aries 3:42 AM
19 3:27 PM	19 Taurus 4:22 PM
22 3:05 AM	22 Gemini 4:35 AM
24 1:02 PM	24 Cancer 1:56 PM
26 6:01 PM	26 Leo 7:39 PM
28 6:57 PM	28 Virgo 10:39 PM
30 8:57 PM	31 Libra 12:34 AM

•FEBRUARY•

Last Aspect	Moon Enters New Sign
1 3:47 PM	2 Scorpio 2:49 AM
4 2:35 AM	4 Sagittarius 6:14 AM
5 7:31 PM	6 Capricorn 11:02 AM
8 1:31 PM	8 Aquarius 5:17 PM
10 9:53 PM	11 Pisces 1:23 AM
13 7:52 AM	13 Aries 11:50 AM
15 6:21 PM	16 Taurus 12:20 AM
18 12:48 PM	18 Gemini 1:06 PM
20 12:37 AM	20 Cancer 11:28 PM
23 2:25 AM	23 Leo 5:48 AM
25 5:17 AM	25 Virgo 8:27 AM
27 6:01 AM	27 Libra 9:06 AM

•MARCH•

Last Aspect	Moon Enters New Sign
1 1:47 AM	1 Scorpio 9:43 AM
3 8:37 AM	3 Sagittarius 11:54 AM
5 2:04 PM	5 Capricorn 4:25 PM
7 10:10 PM	7 Aquarius 11:15 PM
10 4:25 AM	10 Pisces 8:10 AM
12 3:05 PM	12 Aries 6:59 PM
15 1:36 AM	15 Taurus 7:28 AM
17 7:34 PM	17 Gemini 8:29 PM
20 7:14 AM	20 Cancer 7:54 AM
22 11:59 AM	22 Leo 3:39 PM
24 3:47 PM	24 Virgo 7:14 PM
26 4:26 PM	26 Libra 7:47 PM
28 12:44 PM	28 Scorpio 7:15 PM
30 4:08 PM	30 Sagittarius 7:42 PM

•APRIL•

Last Aspect	Moon Enters New Sign
1 4:36 AM	1 Capricorn 10:38 PM
4 12:37 AM	4 Aquarius 4:46 AM
6 9:25 AM	6 Pisces 1:51 PM
8 11:30 PM	9 Aries 1:09 AM
11 6:03 AM	11 Taurus 1:47 PM
14 2:06 AM	14 Gemini 2:48 AM
16 7:24 AM	16 Cancer 2:41 PM
18 9:35 PM	18 Leo 11:46 PM
21 12:31 AM	21 Virgo 4:59 AM
23 2:24 AM	23 Libra 6:41 AM
25 5:12 AM	25 Scorpio 6:19 AM
27 1:25 AM	27 Sagittarius 5:49 AM
27 10:33 PM	29 Capricorn 7:05 AM

•MAY•

Last Aspect	Moon Enters New Sign
1 6:25 AM	1 Aquarius 11:35 AM
3 2:10 PM	3 Pisces 7:47 PM
6 1:02 AM	6 Aries 7:01 AM
8 12:21 PM	8 Taurus 7:50 PM
11 2:26 AM	11 Gemini 8:44 AM
13 4:48 AM	13 Cancer 8:28 PM
15 11:52 PM	16 Leo 5:59 AM
18 7:51 AM	18 Virgo 12:32 PM
20 3:31 PM	20 Libra 3:55 PM
22 3:33 PM	22 Scorpio 4:51 PM
24 11:09 AM	24 Sagittarius 4:43 PM
26 1:53 PM	26 Capricorn 5:17 PM
28 2:01 PM	28 Aquarius 8:19 PM
30 8:10 PM	31 Pisces 3:03 AM

•JUNE•

Last Aspect	Moon Enters New Sign
2 6:06 AM	2 Aries 1:31 PM
4 5:49 PM	5 Taurus 2:14 AM
7 7:18 AM	7 Gemini 3:04 PM
9 3:27 AM	10 Cancer 2:23 AM
12 5:09 AM	12 Leo 11:29 AM
14 11:02 AM	14 Virgo 6:17 PM
16 3:47 PM	16 Libra 10:48 PM
18 9:22 PM	19 Scorpio 1:20 AM
20 7:43 PM	21 Sagittarius 2:32 AM
21 10:46 PM	23 Capricorn 3:37 AM
24 10:49 PM	25 Aquarius 6:10 AM
27 3:49 AM	27 Pisces 11:45 AM
29 3:24 PM	29 Aries 9:07 PM

•JULY•

Last Aspect	Moon Enters New Sign
1 11:09 PM	2 Taurus 9:24 AM
4 1:16 PM	4 Gemini 10:13 PM
7 8:14 AM	7 Cancer 9:18 AM
9 9:24 AM	9 Leo 5:43 PM
11 3:44 PM	11 Virgo 11:48 PM
13 8:20 PM	14 Libra 4:15 AM
15 10:05 PM	16 Scorpio 7:35 AM
18 2:33 AM	18 Sagittarius 10:09 AM
19 6:02 AM	20 Capricorn 12:31 PM
22 3:16 PM	22 Aquarius 3:39 PM
24 12:26 PM	24 Pisces 8:57 PM
26 8:26 PM	27 Aries 5:31 AM
29 4:52 AM	29 Taurus 5:13 PM
31 9:35 PM	

•AUGUST•

Last Aspect	Moon Enters New Sign
	1 Gemini 6:05 AM
3 9:08 AM	3 Cancer 5:22 PM
5 10:44 PM	6 Leo 1:31 AM
7 10:30 PM	8 Virgo 6:42 AM
10 2:52 AM	10 Libra 10:07 AM
12 8:13 AM	12 Scorpio 12:56 PM
14 7:53 AM	14 Sagittarius 3:54 PM
16 3:20 PM	16 Capricorn 7:18 PM
18 3:21 PM	18 Aquarius 11:34 PM
21 1:48 AM	21 Pisces 5:28 AM
23 5:01 AM	23 Aries 1:55 PM
25 11:04 AM	26 Taurus 1:13 AM
28 4:50 AM	28 Gemini 2:07 PM
30 12:11 PM	31 Cancer 1:59 AM

•SEPTEMBER•

Last Aspect	Moon Enters New Sign
2 5:31 AM	2 Leo 10:37 AM
4 11:06 AM	4 Virgo 3:34 PM
6 10:36 AM	6 Libra 5:57 PM
8 7:16 AM	8 Scorpio 7:26 PM
10 2:06 PM	10 Sagittarius 9:26 PM
12 6:35 AM	13 Capricorn 12:45 AM
14 10:05 PM	15 Aquarius 5:42 AM
17 4:42 AM	17 Pisces 12:31 PM
19 3:00 PM	19 Aries 9:29 PM
21 9:47 PM	22 Taurus 8:47 AM
24 1:29 PM	24 Gemini 9:41 PM
25 12:30 PM	27 Cancer 10:12 AM
29 2:47 PM	29 Leo 7:56 PM

•OCTOBER•

Last Aspect	Moon Enters New Sign
1 7:02 PM	2 Virgo 1:40 AM
4 3:41 AM	4 Libra 3:57 AM
5 4:10 PM	6 Scorpio 4:22 AM
7 10:52 PM	8 Sagittarius 4:47 AM
9 7:08 AM	10 Capricorn 6:44 AM
12 4:54 AM	12 Aquarius 11:09 AM
14 11:53 AM	14 Pisces 6:18 PM
16 9:25 PM	17 Aries 3:56 AM
19 2:16 PM	19 Taurus 3:35 PM
21 10:01 PM	22 Gemini 4:28 AM
24 4:59 AM	24 Cancer 5:16 PM
26 10:23 PM	27 Leo 4:05 AM
29 6:12 AM	29 Virgo 11:22 AM
31 10:06 AM	31 Libra 2:46 PM

•NOVEMBER•

Last Aspect	Moon Enters New Sign
2 3:52 AM	2 Scorpio 3:19 PM
4 10:34 AM	4 Sagittarius 2:46 PM
6 7:04 PM	6 Capricorn 3:01 PM
8 1:54 PM	8 Aquarius 5:48 PM
10 7:35 PM	11 Pisces 12:04 AM
13 5:12 AM	13 Aries 9:44 AM
15 8:02 AM	15 Taurus 9:45 PM
18 6:24 AM	18 Gemini 10:42 AM
20 9:20 AM	20 Cancer 11:21 PM
23 6:52 AM	23 Leo 10:33 AM
25 3:49 PM	25 Virgo 7:09 PM
27 9:25 PM	28 Libra 12:22 AM
29 8:37 PM	30 Scorpio 2:22 AM

•DECEMBER•

Last Aspect	Moon Enters New Sign
1 11:45 PM	2 Sagittarius 2:13 AM
3 10:08 PM	4 Capricorn 1:43 AM
6 1:43 AM	6 Aquarius 2:52 AM
8 7:03 AM	8 Pisces 7:25 AM
10 1:40 PM	10 Aries 4:04 PM
12 4:40 PM	13 Taurus 3:56 AM
15 2:54 PM	15 Gemini 4:59 PM
18 2:24 AM	18 Cancer 5:25 AM
20 2:34 PM	20 Leo 4:13 PM
22 11:35 PM	23 Virgo 1:01 AM
25 6:14 AM	25 Libra 7:28 AM
27 3:12 AM	27 Scorpio 11:18 AM
29 11:53 AM	29 Sagittarius 12:46 PM
30 1:27 AM	31 Capricorn 12:58 PM

RETROGRADES

When the planets cross the sky, they occasionally appear to move backwards as seen from Earth. When a planet turns "backwards" it is said to be *retrograde*. When it turns forward again it is said to go *direct*. The point at which the movement changes from one direction to another is called a *station*.

When a planet is retrograde its expression is delayed or out of kilter with the normal progression of events. Generally, it can be said that whatever is planned during this period will be delayed, but usually it will come to fruition when the retrograde is over. Of course, this only applies to activities ruled by the planet which is retrograde.

Although retrogrades of all the planets are of significance, those involving Mercury and Venus are particularly easy to follow and of a personal use.

Mercury Retrograde

Mercury rules informal communications—reading, writing, speaking and short errands. Whenever Mercury goes retrograde, personal communications get fouled up or misunderstood more often. Letters get lost, more misspellings occur and so on. So the rule astrologers have developed is, *when Mercury is retrograde, avoid means of communication of an informal nature.*

Venus Retrograde

This is the planet of love, affection, friendship and marriage, so the retrograde is an unreliable time for these activities. Misunderstandings and alienations of an affectional nature are more common.

PLANETARY STATIONS FOR 1994
(Eastern Standard Time)

Planet	Begin		End	
Mercury	02/11/94	3:24 AM	03/05/94	12:44 AM
Jupiter	02/28/94	7:52 AM	07/01/94	10:08 PM
Pluto	03/01/94	12:15 AM	08/05/94	10:10 AM
Neptune	04/25/94	12:23 AM	10/01/94	8:47 AM
Uranus	04/30/94	1:07 AM	10/01/94	6:23 PM
Mercury	06/12/94	12:43 PM	07/06/94	2:39 PM
Saturn	06/22/94	8:28 PM	11/09/94	1:54 AM
Mercury	10/09/94	1:38 AM	10/28/94	11:00 PM
Venus	10/13/94	12:38 AM	11/23/94	11:57 AM

BEST DAYS FOR YOUR
SPECIAL PURPOSES

When you wish to choose a favorable day for something other than matters governed by your own ruling planet, read the following list and note the planet which rules the matter in question. Turn to the list of Favorable and Unfavorable Days in the Moon Tables section. Choose a date for the activity listed below that is both marked favorable (F or f) for your Sun sign and one that is marked with an X or T in the Lunar Aspectarian under the planet described. Never choose a date for any of these activities which is marked with an O or Q under Saturn, Mars or Uranus, as these are negative aspects. They tend to counteract good results.

The more good aspects in operation on the date you choose, the better the outlook for your affairs. *The better the day the better the deed.* To recapitulate: Choose a date from the proper lists of dates marked X or T under the planet ruling the activity and also marked F or f in your own sign, but never a date marked O or Q in the Lunar Aspectarian to Mars, Saturn or Uranus.

Moon
For housecleaning or baking, putting up preserves, washing, using liquids or chemicals, for matters connected with babies or small children, and to deal with the public in general, choose the good aspects of the Moon.

Sun
To gain favors of persons of high rank, title or prominent social standing, or those in government office, to make a change or try for promotion, choose the good dates of the Sun.

Mercury
For writing or signing an important document, seeking news or information, shopping, studying, dealing with literary matters, choose the good dates of Mercury.

Venus
To give a successful party, ball or entertainment, to marry, for matters of courtship, art, beauty, adornment, to cultivate the friendship of a woman, choose the good dates of Venus.

Mars
For dealing with surgeons, dentists, hair stylists, assayers, contractors, mechanics, lumber workers,

police officers, army or navy personnel, choose the good dates of Mars.

Jupiter
To deal with physicians, educators, sportspeople, bankers, brokers, philanthropists, to collect money or make important changes, choose the good dates of Jupiter.

Saturn
For dealing with plumbers, excavators or miners, for starting a new building, leasing a house or dealing in land, choose the good dates of Saturn.

Uranus
For successful work on an invention, for dealing with inventors, metaphysicians, astrologers or new thought people, for new methods, or starting a journey, choose the good dates of Uranus.

Neptune
For affairs connected with the deep sea or liquids in general, for practicing psychometry or developing mediumship, photography, tobacco and drugs, choose the good dates of Neptune.

Pluto
For uncovering errors, overcoming habits, healing, fumigation, pasteurizing, pest control, also for matters related to the affairs of the dead, taxes, inheritance, etc., choose the good dates of Pluto.

TABLE OF TERMS REFERRING TO LUNAR QUARTERS (PHASES)

Sun-Moon Angle	Moon Sign Book Term	Common Terms	Division by:		
		2	4	8	
0-90° after Conjunction	First Quarter	Increasing Waxing Light New	New Moon	New Moon	
				Crescent	
90-180°	Second Quarter		First Quarter	First Quarter	
				Gibbous	
180-270°	Third Quarter	Decreasing Waning Dark Old	Full Moon	Full Moon	
				Disseminating	
270-360°	Fourth Quarter		Last Quarter	Last Quarter	
				Balsamic	

HOME & FAMILY

HOME & FAMILY

Automobiles
Choose a favorable date for your Sun sign, when the Moon is in a fixed sign (Taurus, Leo, Scorpio, Aquarius), well-aspected by the Sun (X or T) and not aspected by Mars and Saturn (the planets of accidents).

Automobile Repair
Repair work is more successful when begun with the Moon in a fixed sign (Taurus, Leo, Scorpio, Aquarius), and well-aspected to the Sun. First and second quarters are the best Moon phases. Avoid unfavorable aspects (Q or O) with Mars, Saturn, Uranus, Neptune or Pluto.

Baking
Baking should be done when the Moon is in a cardinal sign (Aries, Cancer, Libra, Capricorn). Bakers who have experimented with these rules say that

dough rises higher and bread is lighter during the increase of the Moon (first or second quarter).

Brewing
It is best to brew during the Full Moon and the fourth quarter. Plan to have the Moon in a water sign (Cancer, Scorpio, Pisces).

Building
Turning the first sod for the foundation of a home or laying the cornerstone for a public building marks the beginning of the building. Excavate, lay foundations, and pour cement when the Moon is full and in a fixed sign (Taurus, Leo, Aquarius). Saturn should be aspected but not Mars, for Mars aspects may indicate accidents.

Canning
Can fruits and vegetables when the Moon is in either the third or fourth quarter, and when it is in one of the water signs (Cancer, Scorpio, Pisces). For preserves and jellies, use the same quarters but see that the Moon is in one of the fixed signs (Taurus, Scorpio, Aquarius).

Cement and Concrete
Pour cement for foundations and concrete for walks and pavements during the Full Moon. It is best, too, for the Moon to be in one of the fixed signs (Taurus, Leo, Aquarius).

Dressmaking

Design, cut, repair or make clothes during the first and second quarters on a day marked favorable for your Sun sign. Venus, Jupiter and Mercury should be aspected, but avoid Mars or Saturn aspects.

Williams Lily wrote in 1676, "make no new clothes, or first put them on when the Moon is in Scorpio or afflicted by Mars, for they will be apt to be torn and quickly worn out." (Also see *Buying Clothing* in the Business Section.)

Fence Posts and Poles

Set the posts or poles when the Moon is in the third or fourth quarter. The fixed signs (Taurus, Leo, Aquarius) are best for this.

House

If you desire a permanent home, buy when the Moon is in one of the fixed signs (Taurus, Leo, Scorpio, Aquarius). If you're buying for speculation and a quick turnover, be certain that the Moon is not in a fixed sign, but in one of the cardinal signs (Aries, Cancer, Libra, Capricorn).

House Furnishings

Follow the same rules for buying clothing, avoiding days when Mars is aspected. Days when Saturn is aspected make things wear longer and tend to a more conservative purchase. Saturn days are good for buying, and Jupiter days are good for selling.

Lost Articles
Search for lost articles during the first quarter and when your Sun sign is marked favorable. Also check to see that the planet ruling the lost item is trine, sextile or conjunct the Moon. The Moon governs household utensils, Mercury letters and books, and Venus clothing, jewelry and money.

Marriage
As a general rule, the best time for marriage to take place is during the increase of the Moon, just past the first quarter. Such marriages will bear a higher tendency towards optimism. Good signs for the Moon to be in are Taurus, Cancer, Leo, Libra and Pisces. The Moon in Taurus produces the most steadfast marriages, but if the partners later want to separate they may have a very difficult time. Avoid Aries, Gemini, Virgo, Scorpio and Aquarius. Make sure that the Moon is well-aspected (X or T), especially to Venus or Jupiter. Avoid aspects to Mars, Uranus or Pluto.

Moving into a House or Office
Make sure that Mars is not aspected to the Moon. Try to move on a day which is favorable to your Sun sign, or when the Moon is conjunct, sextile or trine the Sun.

Mowing the Lawn
Mow the lawn in the first or second quarter to increase growth. If you wish to retard growth, mow in the third or fourth quarter.

Painting
The best time to paint buildings is during the decrease of the Moon (third and fourth quarter).

If the weather is hot, do the painting while the Moon is in Taurus; if the weather is cold, paint while the Moon is in Leo. By painting in the fourth quarter, the wood is dryer and the paint will penetrate; painting around the New Moon the wood is damp and the paint is subject to scalding when hot weather hits it. It is not advisable to paint while the Moon is in a water sign if the temperature is below 70 degrees, as it is apt to creep, check or run.

Pets
Take home new pets when the date is favorable to your Sun sign, or the Moon is well-aspected by the Sun, Venus, Jupiter, Uranus or Neptune. Avoid days when the Moon is afflicted by the Sun, Mars, Saturn, Uranus, Neptune or Pluto.

When selecting a new pet it is good to have the Moon well-aspected by the planet which rules the animal. Cats are ruled by the Sun, dogs by Mercury, birds by Venus, horses by Jupiter, and fish by Neptune.

Train pets starting when the Moon is in Taurus. Neuter them in any sign but Virgo, Libra, Scorpio or Sagittarius. Avoid the week before and after the Full Moon. Declaw cats in the dark of the Moon. Avoid the week before and after the Full Moon and the sign of Pisces.

Predetermining Sex

Count from the last day of menstruation to the day next beginning, and divide the interval between the two dates into halves.

Pregnancy occurring in the first half produces females, but copulation should take place when the Moon is in a feminine sign.

Pregnancy occurring in the later half, up to within three days of the beginning of menstruation, produces males, but copulation should take place when the Moon is in a masculine sign. This three-day period to the end of the first half of the next period again produces females.

Romance

The same principles hold true for starting a relationship as for marriage. However, since there is less control over when a romance starts, it is sometimes necessary to study it after the fact. Romances begun under an increasing Moon are more likely to be permanent, or at least satisfying. Those started on the waning Moon will more readily transform the participants. The general tone of the relationship can be guessed from the sign the Moon is in. For instance, those begun when the Moon is in Capricorn will take greater effort to bring to a desirable conclusion, but may be very rewarding. Those begun when the Moon is in Aries may be impulsive and quick to burn out. Good aspects between the Moon and Venus are excellent influences. Avoid Mars, Uranus and Pluto aspects. Ending relationships is facilitated by a decreasing

Moon, particularly in the fourth quarter. This causes the least pain and attachment.

Sauerkraut
The best sauerkraut is made just after the Full Moon in a fruitful sign (Cancer, Scorpio, Pisces).

Shingling
Shingling should be done in the decrease of the Moon (third or fourth quarter) when it is in a fixed sign (Taurus, Leo, Scorpio, Aquarius). If shingles are laid during the New Moon, they have a tendency to curl at the edges.

Weaning Children
This should be done when the Moon is in Sagittarius, Capricorn, Aquarius or Pisces. The child should nurse the last time in a fruitful sign. Venus should then be trine, sextile or conjunct the Moon.

Wine and Drinks Other Than Beer
It is best to start when the Moon is in Pisces or Taurus. Good aspects (X or T) with Venus are favorable. Avoid aspects with Mars or Saturn.

MAKE MONEY BY GROWING PLANTS

by Carly Wall

If you enjoy gardening and growing things, you can make it pay off with a little mini-business that comes from your very own garden. It can be as simple or as involved as you want it to be, something that brings in a couple thousand dollars a year with part-time effort, or a full-time income that takes over your lifestyle. The choice is up to you. All you need is the interest, a good idea, and the right type of advertising to bring in customers willing to pay for your product.

SEEING IS BELIEVING

You may love to wander where wildflowers and butterflies mingle, and the stone walkways lead you to interesting and lovely scented plants. There really are places like that, places where you can lose yourself in the beauty and pastoral delights of nature. One such place is Mary's Apple Tree Herb Garden, located in southern Ohio along a tree-lined road at Mary's Plant Farm—a small farm where the owner, Mary Harrison, grows and provides a wide selection of plants that are hard to find elsewhere. It's a business that was 40 years in the making, if not more.

"It began when I was a child, my parents loved plants and flowers, so of course, I took a special interest in them. I love them. I don't think anyone can go into this business without that love."

She's been collecting new and unusual plants over the years and markets all types of perennials, both woody and herbacious.

"I got into this business because I needed certain plants and nobody had them. Fifteen years ago, who had the Japanese lilac? If you wanted one, how would you get it? I started collecting tiny starts and plants of all different species. People would come over—gardening club friends and others—and they would be begging me for starts. My business grew from that. You see, it takes years of growth if plants are to be big and productive perennials. Commercial growers aren't that patient. It takes someone with that special love to care for and grow the starts up to a size suitable for sale. I've always tried to offer people a place to come, that I had always dreamed of myself. I'm always on the lookout for new plants. I think my farm is a success because even if I didn't make money doing this, I'd still be doing it. Your goals have to be in the right place. If I were to give advice on going into business, I'd have to say you have to have an interest in it first. Then learn all you can and study—from books and other people. That way you will be able to let your customers know what is used for cooking, what type plant is what, where you should plant it, etc. It's a long learning process, but it is fun."

DIGGING UP MORE INFORMATION

Before you do anything about starting your mini-business, you might want to learn more about specific how-to's and talk to others who have already done it. You can learn from their mistakes and their successes. The Small Business Administration (SBA) can help by connecting you with someone in your field of interest. You might also want to get in touch with one or all of the following:

INTERNATIONAL HERB GROWERS AND MARKETERS ASSOCIATION, P.O. Box 281, Silver Spring, Pennsylvania 17575.

MICHIGAN HERB BUSINESS ASSOCIATION, Gloria Rodammer (Herbally Yours), 8600 State St., Millington, Michigan 48764.

THE BUSINESS OF HERBS, Northwind Farm, Route 2, Box 246, Shevelin, Minnesota 56676. This is a bimonthly journal (sample issue $3.00). For a brochure send a self-addressed stamped envelope.

THE HERB SOCIETY OF AMERICA, P.O. Box 162, Rumson, New Jersey 07760.

LET THE IDEAS GROW

Your particular interests will lead you to developing a business that is all your own. Here's a list of ideas others have used successfully. You can use these as a launching point for your own creativity.

Herbs for Sale

Herbs are useful plants and quite in demand—whether for culinary, medicinal, aromatic, or magical purposes. Raising plants to sell retail or wholesale to greenhouses and nurseries can bring in good money. If selling from your home, an ad in the local newspaper or a small sign out front may bring in customers. If marketing your product wholesale, approach owners of nurseries with a sampling of what you have to offer. Kitchen herbs sell pretty well, but you may want to try the more unusual or hard-to-find herbs as well. Also, you can specialize with specific types of herbs or a wide variety. For a catalog of herb and rare seeds write :

NICHOLS GARDEN NURSERY, 1190 North Pacific Highway, Albany, Oregon 97321.

PARK SEED COMPANY, Cokesbury Road, Greenwood, South Carolina 29647-0001.

Crafts

One extraordinary thing about herbs is that they're so versatile. Herbal crafts are "in" now, and there are literally hundreds of items you can produce: potpourris, sachets, wreaths, dried floral arrangements, catnip toys for cats. These items move well at flea markets, craft shops and gift shops (approach managers with your product at times when the shop is not busy).

Your best bet is to find books on herbs in your library or at the local bookstore to get some ideas and how-to's. Several good books to look for on crafting are: *Earth Presents: How to Make Beautiful Gifts from Nature's Bounty* by Beverly Plummer (A & W Visual Library), *Herbal Treasures: Inspiring Month-by-Month Projects for Gardening, Cooking, and Crafts* by Phillis V. Shaudys (Garden Way Publishing), and *Profitable Herb Growing* by N.P. Nichols of Nichols Garden Nursery (see address on previous page). It gives loads of tips including mail-order marketing and profit angles.

Dried Arrangements

Wildflowers, weeds, grasses, pods and branches make delightful natural dried arrangements that are snapped up by those looking for decorative home accents. Long walks in the summer can yield a year's worth of "raw" materials to work with all winter. Bunches of lavender, yarrow, or other aromatic flowers dried and tied in small bundles can also be sold. You'll need a good-sized growing spot and a good drying shed or attic.

Specialize with Groupings

Many people that aren't acquainted with herbs can be attracted by groupings of useful herbs: a pot of kitchen herbs containing chives, tarragon and basil; a tea garden with lemon verbena, peppermint and catnip; even a potpourri garden package with lavender, sweet woodruff and lemon balm. These groupings can be packaged attractively and offered for sale along with printed pamphlets containing the information on growing and using them.

Landscape and Garden Work

Busy people may want a beautiful formal or informal herb garden but may not have the time or energy to create it. That's where you come in. With an ad in the local paper you're sure to land plenty of business. And don't forget big businesses. Many want to spruce up their entrances and walkways and you can convince them that an herbal theme is the best way to go.

Classes

Your herb expertise or creative craft ideas are valuable. Offer classes by tacking up ads in laundromats, grocery stores and on college bulletin boards.

Pretty Pots

Here's something that doesn't deal directly with herbs but is a fun business for the "arty" types. Use your talents to create pretty pots by decorating them with ribbons, paints and appliques. Or grow gourds, cut off the top or side and remove the pulp and seeds, sand the outside smooth, coat the inside with paraffin and then drill holes in the top edges to make hanging planters. Decorate them attractively and sell them anywhere that plants are sold. You can even plant them with attractive greenery and price accordingly.

Terrariums

A gift of herbs is especially appreciated and makes an economical choice. Terrariums are excellent products to offer during holidays when jars are decorated with ribbons and such.

Picture This

Dry flowers and stems or pretty weeds by pressing them between paper towels and weighting them down with a heavy object. Let this dry about four weeks and then use mats and frames to create beautiful, artistic pictures of nature. Everyone will want them to hang on their walls.

Creative Muses

For some, writing is a good way to let others in on your gardening techniques, while adding income to your pocket. Each plant you buy, every garden grown or investigated, all garden club meetings attended, any new idea or bits of information can be used to create articles, books, or pamphlets to sell. *The Writer's Market* (published by *Writer's Digest*) lists thousands of markets for writers, with a special listing of home and garden markets. *The Writer's Handbook* (from *The Writer*) lists buyers of manuscripts. Information on starting a writing career is available at the library or bookstore.

With a little effort, you may soon find yourself with a successful little business. And when friends ask how your garden is growing, you can honestly answer, PROFITABLY!

THE SHAKER LEGACY
by Jude Williams

The Shakers of yesterday are best remembered for their furniture style and unparalleled craftsmanship. They were instrumental in introducing the flat broom, wooden clothes pins, the washing machine and the circular saw. Today the objects they manufactured are highly prized collectibles.

Conservation was introduced through their farming practices. Their articles regarding conservation, composting and other farming methods were given to customers along with the purchase of seeds. They strove for a utopian community here on Earth. Their goal was to create a self-sustaining healthful life compatible with their religious beliefs. They were successful in this endeavor until shortly after the Civil War.

I recently visited Shaker Village of Pleasant Hill near Lexington, Kentucky and came away with a new respect for the early group. I learned that they were a branch of the Quaker religion and founder Ann Lee came to America from England with a group of devoted followers. From this small group many communities were formed and ran successfully through the sale of agricultural products. A Shaker from the New Lebanon community summed it up when he stated that "To prosper, every commune must be founded, so far as its

industry goes, on agriculture. Only the simple labors and manners of a farming people can hold a community together." They soon amassed large amounts of acreage to till and use for the support of the communities. As converts were enlisted into the faith, they donated the farms and land. The large farms were combined and this composed a "family." The group had two Deacons and two Deaconesses that served as spiritual leaders. All the

communities were under control of the Church
Family Ministry. The lead Ministry was situated in
New Lebanon, New York. The "Families" helped
each other whenever the need arose for seasonal
activities such as haying, sugaring, gathering or
planting. Money was also extended to the families
most in need. It is amazing to me that such a large
group of people could live in harmony. The hold-
ings of the Shakers was quite extensive and they
formed their own methods of meeting the needs of
all in their communities. The communities sur-
vived for over 200 years.

The herb trade in this country can be traced
directly to the Shaker communities. The business
began modestly enough by collecting the herbs
from the surrounding woods and fields. Native
Americans were soon asked to help identify and
supply the wild starts. The early herbalists of the
communities were also familiar with the Doctrine
of Signatures attributed to the herbs. They were
aware that many different conditions affected the
potency of the plants. The weather and growing
conditions, soil identification, growing needs of
specific plants, identification of the herbs and uses
were all studied by the physicians who were expert
botanists as well. Soon their herbal remedies were
in demand all over the world. They became expert
at the proper gathering and drying of the plants.
Because they were practiced horticulturists they
had a reputation for excellence in the preparations
of the herbs as well as the vegetable seeds that were
packaged and sold. Eventually the species grown

and sold by the communities were numbered in the thousands. Pharmaceutical companies worldwide bought the herbs in bulk and this necessitated the formation of large gardens for the wild herbs that were hard to find or gather. The gardens insured that they had a ready supply for their own use as well as to sell, as this was a major means of support for the communities.

They devised a method that enabled them to press large amounts of herbs. The first year they processed 5500 pounds of herbs. The following year over eighteen tons went through the hydraulic press process. They invented a machine that not only dried the herbs but also heated the buildings and water. The herbs were pressed into solid bricks, wrapped and packed in tin boxes, and then placed in wooden boxes ready to be shipped. Soon the herbs were put in glass containers and sold to pharmacies. The medical society was more willing to accept herbs prepared in this method. By 1826 the demand exceeded the supply and the Shaker community began to purchase some of the herbs from all over the country. They soon had a catalog listing the herbs and extract products for sale along with vegetable seeds and brooms made in the community. With the Civil War came demands for the herbs that could not be met. The plants were sold for medicinal purposes, as well as for dyes, cosmetics, culinary and other household uses.

The Shakers had extensive recipes for preparing perfumes and other cosmetics and this aspect of their history certainly should catch our interest—

society as a whole has always had an appreciation for fragrances. This is an art in which we can participate, along with gardening and learning to use the natural gifts from Mother Earth.

Here is a recipe for preparing the rose water for which the communities were so famous. Because the process of obtaining rose oil is not feasible for everyone, this recipe has been simplified using oils that you purchase from your pharmacy. Place 2 1/2 teaspoons of rose soluble in 1 pint of distilled water. Color with a few drops of food coloring if desired. You can use this recipe to prepare many different distilled waters for use as fragrances. To extract your own rose oil, start with a large jar of rose petals. Cover with spring water and set in a sunny window for a week. When the oil floats to the top, remove it with a cotton ball. Squeeze this into a vial and close tightly. Repeat until desired amount of oil is extracted.

An old Shaker recipe for men's cologne consists of 1 pint of vodka, $1/4$ ounce each of lemon oil, rosemary oil, lavender, and $1/8$ ounce jasmine. Add 15 drops of clove oil and mix well.

The Shakers' study and use of herbs is fascinating, as is the formation and operation of the communities. Many areas are realizing that the contributions from the Shaker communities to our society were worth saving and many of the communities are being preserved as historical sites. After visiting one of the historical communities you may feel a little guilty. We have laborsaving devices and we don't do half the good that these communities did. We need to take a second look at the farming methods of the Shakers and relearn how to care for the earth. We need to take a look at the way they proposed equality for all and perhaps put that into practice. They maintained a natural, simple life that we all could try to emulate.

The Shaker communities that I have listed feature artists that demonstrate how the different products were created. The making of brooms, buckets, soap, blankets, clothing, kitchen utensils and furniture, herb, wool and silk preparation, animal husbandry, cooking skills and other self-sustaining arts are all on display. Young and old alike learn while they are having the time of their life.

The Shaker Village at Pleasant Hill offers boat trips as well rooming for overnight guests. The food is delicious and plentiful (absolutely no tipping is allowed!). There are gift shops that carry the crafts made by the artisans (all the products in the gift shops are inexpensive). Tours with groups as well as self-guided tours are available. You can take the tour in several hours or become so fascinated that it could take a week. Once you have visited, you make plans to return again and again.

There are five communities that are open to the public as museums. These are located in New Lebanon, New York; Hancock, Massachusetts; Enfield, New Hampshire; and Shaker Village of Pleasant Hill in Harrodsburg, Kentucky. Pleasant Hill is the only community that offers guest rooms. They are open to the public year round (with the exception of Christmas Eve and Day). The communities in Canterbury, New Hampshire and Sabbathday Lake, Maine have museums and are the only active communities.

LEISURE &
RECREATION

LEISURE & RECREATION

The best time to perform an activity is when its ruling planet is in favorable aspect to the Moon or when the Moon is in its ruling sign—that is, when its ruling planet is trine, sextile or conjunct the Moon (marked T, X or C in the Lunar Aspectarian or when its ruling sign is marked F in the Favorable and Unfavorable Days tables).

Animals and Hunting
Animals in general: Mercury, Jupiter, Virgo, Pisces
Animal training: Mercury, Virgo
Cats: Leo, Sun, Virgo, Venus
Dogs: Mercury, Virgo
Fish: Neptune, Pisces, Moon, Cancer
Birds: Mercury, Venus
Game animals: Sagittarius
Horses, trainers, riders: Jupiter, Sagittarius
Hunters: Jupiter, Sagittarius

Arts
Acting, actors: Neptune, Pisces, Sun, Leo
Art in general: Venus, Libra
Ballet: Neptune, Venus
Ceramics: Saturn
Crafts: Mercury, Venus
Dancing: Venus, Taurus, Neptune, Pisces
Drama: Venus, Neptune
Embroidery: Venus
Etching: Mars
Films, filmmaking: Neptune, Leo, Uranus, Aquarius
Literature: Mercury, Gemini
Music: Venus, Libra, Taurus, Neptune
Painting: Venus, Libra
Photography: Neptune, Pisces, Uranus, Aquarius
Printing: Mercury, Gemini
Theaters: Sun, Leo, Venus

Fishing
During the summer months the best time of the day for fishing is from sunrise to three hours after, and from about two hours before sunset until one hour after. In cooler months, the fish are not biting until the air is warmed. At this time the best hours are from noon to 3 PM. Warm and cloudy days are good. The most favorable winds are from the south and southwest. Easterly winds are unfavorable. The best days of the month for fishing are those on which the Moon changes quarters, especially if the change occurs on a day when the Moon is in a watery sign (Cancer, Scorpio, Pisces). The best period in any month is the day after the Full Moon.

Friends

The need for friendship is greater when Uranus aspects the Moon, or the Moon is in Aquarius. Friendship prospers when Venus or Uranus is trine, sextile or conjunct the Moon. The chance meeting of informed acquaintances and friends is facilitated by the Moon in Gemini.

Parties (Hosting or Attending)

The best time for parties is when the Moon is in Gemini, Leo, Libra or Sagittarius with good aspects to Venus and Jupiter. There should be no aspects to Mars or Saturn.

Sports

Acrobatics: Mars, Aries
Archery: Jupiter, Sagittarius
Ball games in general: Venus
Baseball: Mars
Bicycling: Uranus, Mercury, Gemini
Boxing: Mars
Calisthenics: Mars, Neptune
Chess: Mercury, Mars
Competitive sports: Mars
Coordination: Mars
Deep-sea diving: Neptune, Pisces
Exercising: Sun
Football: Mars
Horse racing: Jupiter, Sagittarius
Jogging: Mercury, Gemini
Physical vitality: Sun
Polo: Uranus, Jupiter, Venus, Saturn

Racing (other than horse): Sun, Uranus
Ice skating: Neptune
Roller skating: Mercury
Sporting equipment: Jupiter, Sagittarius
Sports in general: Sun, Leo
Strategy: Saturn
Swimming: Neptune, Pisces, Moon, Cancer
Tennis: Mercury, Venus, Uranus, Mars
Wrestling: Mars

Travel
Air travel: Mercury, Sagittarius, Uranus
Automobile travel: Mercury, Gemini
Boating: Moon, Cancer, Neptune
Camping: Leo
Helicopters: Uranus
Hotels: Cancer, Venus
Journeys in general: Sun
Long journeys: Jupiter, Sagittarius
Motorcycle travel: Uranus, Aquarius
Parks: Sun, Leo
Picnics: Venus, Leo
Rail travel: Uranus, Mercury, Gemini
Restaurants: Moon, Cancer, Virgo, Jupiter
Short journeys: Mercury, Gemini
Vacations, holidays: Venus, Neptune

Long trips which threaten to exhaust the traveler
are best begun when the Sun is well-aspected to the
Moon and the date is favorable for the traveler. If
traveling with others, good aspects from Venus are
desirable. For enjoyment, aspects to Jupiter are

preferable; for visiting, aspects to Mercury. To prevent accidents, avoid squares or oppositions to Mars, Saturn, Uranus or Pluto.

For air travel, choose a day when the Moon is in Gemini or Libra, and well-aspected by Mercury and/or Jupiter. Avoid adverse aspects of Mars, Saturn or Uranus.

Writing
Write for pleasure or publication when the Moon is in Gemini. Mercury should be direct. Favorable aspects to Mercury, Uranus and Neptune promote ingenuity.

Other Entertainments
Barbecues: Moon, Mars
Casinos: Venus, Sun, Jupiter
Festivals: Venus
Parades: Jupiter, Venus

FISHING BY THE MOON
by Louise Riotte

Hundreds of books have been written about the art of fishing since Izaak Walton penned the first edition of the *Compleat Angler* in 1653. The serious fisherperson has probably read a number of these books, and most of us have studied something of the creature that we pursue. We know that fish are creatures of instinct and habit. The problem is that anglers, too, are creatures of habit. We also develop patterns of behavior, and most of us are painfully aware of how seldom our patterns coincide with the fish's pattern.

Owning the best equipment and reading the best books will not improve anyone's fishing skills unless that person knows how to use that equipment and knowledge. Most anglers need to *forget* some of their unproductive fishing habits and learn a variety of new approaches. In the final analysis, being successful means being versatile. You must adjust your techniques to fit the fish. Their pattern is not likely to change, so your pattern must.

As creatures captive to their environment, fish are closely attuned to changes in weather and water conditions, and they respond to these changes. Season, time of day, and many other factors have a bearing on whether or not you will catch fish at a particular time.

From sunset to one hour after during the summer months, fishing should be great. In the colder months, fishing is best from noon to three in the afternoon. The best day to fish is a warm, close and cloudy day that follows a bright moonlit night. This is because fish have no eyelids. On a cloudy day, there is no bright light to distress them, so they feed near the surface.

Wind, too, has a bearing on these matters with the most favorable winds from the south, southwest, and west. East winds are unfavorable.

The concept of fish movement is really very simple. Most game fish spawn in the spring, migrating into shallow waters. This migration is triggered by water temperature with each species responding to a different temperature. Each species also prefers a certain set of bottom conditions in which to spawn. Walleyes, for instance, like hard gravel bottoms while northern pike prefer shallow, weedy sloughs. After spawning, fish move into a summer location pattern, often choosing another area of the lake. Again, this movement is triggered by water temperature and is in response to locating prey that the game fish will feed on all summer long. Once this pattern is established, fish location will be fairly predictable throughout the summer.

With the arrival of the first cold nights that come in the fall, lakes and rivers cool off rather quickly, and once more the fish move to a new location. In the north where lakes and rivers ice over, ice fishers usually find a gradual movement of game fish from shallow to deeper waters as the winter progresses. In southern waters fish also move deeper and become less active, but daily weather conditions can make dramatic changes if a warm spell sends the water temperature soaring.

There are many who believe that fish can sense weather changes and are particularly active three days before a storm. But on the day of the actual weather change, the fish will not bite. This may be because the winds often stir up the water, inducing the smaller fish to come out. And small fish are considered the lawful prey of big fish.

A wise old fisherman once told me to watch out for storm if insects were flying low and fish were jumping out of the water to catch them. Insects fly lower to avoid the thin atmosphere above due to the lowering air pressure. He also said to take note of the variety of insect that was flying and to set flies for bait accordingly.

After heavy rains fish may not bite since plenty of food has been washed into the lake. They are also hard to catch when fresh snow water is in a stream. Generally speaking, June is usually the best fishing month and July the worst.

It is often conceded that the best days of the month for fishing are those on which the Moon changes quarters (plus the day before and day after), especially if the change occurs on a day when the Moon is in a water sign (Cancer, Scorpio, Pisces). The best period in any month is the day after the Full Moon. Three days before and after the Full Moon are also favorable.

And which water sign is the best? An experienced fisherman took a day off from work, and it happened to fall under the sign of Scorpio. He caught the fish he had been after for so long but was so delighted to win the fight of wills that he put it back and gave it its freedom. His theory is that fish are hungrier, less cautious and more likely to be caught in the sign of Scorpio.

He also told me that he had his best luck when using an active lure. "With live bait," he said, "attach the hook so the bait will have natural movements. With artificial lures, jig or pop the bait and vary the pace of the retrieve. Present the lure to the water in a manner that will be interesting to fish both in location and in action. Fish the shady sides of logs and rocks, the down-current sides of boulders and large stumps, and the windless side of ledges and cliffs. Let the bait sink and keep it moving all the time."

Although they don't have eyelids, fish possess remarkable sight. Sensitive to light, they adjust their eyesight to the rhythms of the natural night and day cycle. Any sudden light thrown on them will cause them to quit the area rapidly. Because of the placement of their eyes, it is impossible for them to see objects on their level or directly below. However, they can see all that is occurring above and around them for distances of 50 feet or more.

They also have a keen sense of smell and don't like strong aromas. Certain odors can be attractive, however. Many fisherpersons believe that bait rubbed with oil of anise will draw the fish. Others swear by the juice of smallage of lovage.

According to Clarence Meyer in *The Herbalist Almanac*, the Chinese use the following method for catching fish: "Take *Cocculus indicus*, pulverize and mix with dough, then scatter it broadcast over the water, as you would with seed. The fish will seize it with great avidity, and they will instantly become so intoxicated that they will turn belly up on top of the water by dozens, hundreds or even thousands, as the case may be. All that you have to do is to have a boat, gather them up and put them in a tub of clean water, and presently they will be as lively and healthy as ever." Some American Indian tribes similarly used herbs, such as blue-curls, camphorweed, vinegarweed, wild cucumber and marsh.

Remember that fish have very good hearing as evidenced by their sensitivity to vibrations. Be as quiet in your movements as possible—talking does not seem to bother them as much as walking about or dropping something heavy.

As previously indicated, fish usually reside in fresh water on three levels. Some, according to season, time of day, etc., are near the surface, some mid-water, and some on the bottom. Work the various levels to find the area of biting fish. Trolling enables you to cover large or otherwise inaccessible areas to locate fish. Furthermore, you learn more about the water you are working.

Position yourself with your back to the wind, and don't let your shadow fall on the water. If fishing in moving water, cast upstream and let your bait drift down with the flow.

Fish are greedy by nature. They also have a built-in sense as to the size of an object they can swallow and will go for larger baits up to their maximum swallowing capacity.

Fishing for an abundant catch will be most rewarding in the sign of Cancer. Big ones may be caught in the sign of Scorpio, but they tend to slack off a bit when the Moon is in Pisces, although this is still a good fishing sign. Other possibilities are the moist signs of Taurus, Virgo, Libra and Capricorn.

A fishing guide states: "The best time to catch fish is when the Moon is directly overhead and the two hours before and after. The next best time is the hour before and after the Moon is straight down on the other side of the Earth." The author insists that these periods work every time.

Fish usually feed on a regular time schedule. If they feed in the early morning, they will be likely to feed again in the late afternoon and again early the next morning. Night feeders are just as regular.

Often fish will feed on only one insect or food for quite lengthy periods. When this happens, it is almost impossible to lure them with any other bait.

Before and after spawning season, fish eagerly

take a variety of baits. Brook trout and many other species absolutely refuse food during spawning.

The larger the fish, the better its swimming ability. It has been calculated that fish can swim about eight miles per hour for each foot of body length. But after striking bait or making any other sudden move, a fish can accelerate up to about 50 percent over its usual cruising speed.

During the summer months black bass go in pairs—if you catch one, try for its mate. Don't try to catch black bass when the water is perfectly smooth, it's a waste of time.

There are other water creatures besides fish that deserve mention. When the Moon is full, residents of Chatham on Cape Cod head for the beach where they dig up bushels of giant sea clams, which are about four times as big as the quahogs favored by most New Englanders. Clams are ruled by the Moon. An experienced clam digger says they should be dug at the entrance of the wet Sun sign of Libra—its first week, September 22 to 29, is thought to be the best time. She says she marks special spots that look good for digging and then uses this Libra week for harvesting. She, too, thinks they are best and most plentiful during the Full Moon.

According to Louisiana folk, crabs, ruled by the Moon and Cancer, are best caught when the Moon is full. They use a chicken neck for bait, and the crabs bite quickly. They claim the meat at this time is full and juicy, but at other times the crabs are mostly shell.

FISHING AND HUNTING DATES

Jan. 5, 9:29 PM-Jan. 8, 12:34 AM (Sco./4th qtr.)

Jan. 14, 5:03 PM-Jan. 17, 3:42 AM (Pis./1st qtr.)

Jan. 24, 1:56 PM-Jan. 26, 7:39 PM (Can./2nd qtr.)

Jan. 27, 8:23 AM (Leo/Full Moon)

Feb. 2, 2:49 AM-Feb. 3, 6:14 AM (Sco./3rd qtr.)

Feb. 11, 1:23 AM-Feb. 13, 11:50 AM (Pis./1st qtr.)

Feb. 20, 11:28 PM-Feb. 23 , 5:48 AM (Can./2nd qtr.)

Feb. 25, 8:15 PM (Vir./Full Moon)

Mar. 1, 9:43 AM-Mar. 3, 11:54 AM (Sco./3rd qtr.)

Mar. 10, 8:10 AM-Mar. 12, 6:59 PM (Pis./4th qtr.)

Mar. 20, 7:54 AM-Mar. 22, 3:39 PM (Can./1st, 2nd qtr.)

Mar. 27, 6:10 AM (Lib./Full Moon)

Mar. 28, 7:15 PM-Mar. 30, 7:42 PM (Sco./3rd qtr.)

Apr. 6, 1:51 PM-Apr. 9, 1:09 AM (Pis./4th qtr.)

Apr. 16, 2:41 PM-Apr. 18, 11:45 PM (Can./1st qtr.)

Apr. 25, 6:19 AM-Apr. 27, 5:49 AM (Sco./2nd, 3rd qtr.)

Apr. 25, 2:46 PM (Sco./Full Moon)

May 3, 7:47 PM-May 5, 7:01 AM (Pis./4th qtr.)

May 13, 8:28 PM-May 15, 5:59 AM (Can./1st qtr.)

May 22, 4:51 PM-May 24, 4:43 PM (Sco./2nd qtr.)

May 24, 10:39 PM (Sag./Full Moon)

May 30, 3:03 AM-Jun. 2, 1:31 PM (Pis./3rd, 4th qtr.)

Jun. 10, 2:23 AM-Jun. 12, 11:29 AM (Can./1st qtr.)

Jun. 19, 1:20 AM-Jun. 21, 2:32 AM (Sco./2nd qtr.)

Jun. 23, 6:33 AM (Cap./Full Moon)

Jun. 27, 11:45 AM-Jun. 29, 9:07 PM (Pis./3rd qtr.)

Jul. 7, 9:18 AM-Jul. 9, 5:43 PM (Can./4th qtr.)

Jul. 16, 7:35 AM-Jul. 18, 10:09 AM (Sco./1st, 2nd qtr.)

Jul. 22, 3:16 PM (Cap./Full Moon)

Jul. 24, 8:57 PM-Jul. 27, 5:31 AM (Pis./3rd qtr.)

Aug. 3, 5:22 PM-Aug. 6, 1:31 AM (Can./4th qtr.)

Aug. 12, 12:56 PM-Aug. 14, 3:54 PM (Sco./1st qtr.)

Aug. 21, 1:47 AM (Aqu./Full Moon)

Aug. 21, 5:28 AM-Aug. 23, 1:55 PM (Aqu./3rd qtr.)

Aug. 31, 1:59 AM-Sep. 2, 10:37 AM (Can./4th qtr.)

Sep. 8, 7:26 PM-Sep. 10 , 9:26 PM (Sco./1st qtr.)

Sep. 17, 12:31 PM-Sep. 19, 9:29 PM (Pis./2nd qtr.)

Sep. 19, 3:00 PM (Pis./Full Moon)

Sep. 27, 10:12 AM-Sep. 29, 7:56 PM (Can./3rd, 4th qtr.)

Oct. 6, 4:22 AM-Oct. 8, 4:47 AM (Sco./1st qtr.)

Oct. 14, 6:18 PM-Oct. 16, 3:56 AM (Pis./2nd qtr.)

Oct. 19, 7:18 AM (Ari./Full Moon)

Oct. 24, 5:16 PM-Oct. 26, 4:05 AM (Can./3rd qtr.)

Nov. 2, 3:19 PM-Nov. 4, 2:46 PM (Sco./4th qtr.)

Nov. 11, 12:04 AM-Nov. 13, 9:44 AM (Pis./2nd qtr.)

Nov. 18, 1:58 AM (Tau./Full Moon)

Nov. 20, 11:21 PM-Nov. 23, 10:33 AM (Can./3rd qtr.)

Nov. 30, 2:22 AM-Dec. 1, 2:46 PM (Sco./4th qtr.)

Dec. 8, 7:25 AM-Dec. 10, 4:04 PM (Pis./1st qtr.)

Dec. 17, 9:17 PM (Gem./Full Moon)

Dec. 18, 5:25 AM-Dec. 20, 4:13 PM (Can./3rd qtr.)

Dec. 27, 11:18 AM-Dec. 29, 12:46 PM (Sco./4th qtr.)

MOON GUIDE TO GAMBLING
by Ralph Jordan Pestka

Astrology and gambling have one important thing in common. Both are concerned with the probable outcome of events. For example, in the game of poker you can expect to be dealt a full house in the first five cards once in 693 deals. The number of times a person can expect to hold the winning number for a lottery drawing is once in millions of drawings. Astrologers also work probabilities. Particular types of events are more likely to occur under particular astrological influences. The ancients said, "To every thing there is a season, and a time to every purpose under the heaven." That is pure astrological insight. My own study of astrology and gambling has proven to me there is definitely a time to take a chance and a time to minimize your risk.

I have been interested in probabilities, speculation and gambling for over twenty-five years. I have known all kinds of gamblers, card room operators and bookies. They bet on sports, horses, dogs, lotteries, dice, casino games and every type of card game. I have spent thousands of hours gambling in Las Vegas, in casinos in Michigan, and in poker clubs in the midwest. I have asked hundreds of people their birth dates, and then watched when they have won or lost. I have also examined the detailed horoscopes of hundreds of gamblers, and come to understand many of the astrological factors that point to winning at gambling. I specialize in poker, as it is a game that combines pure chance with a degree of decision making and skill. But most gamblers rely on luck and some rely on systems. I know gamblers that thought they had discovered *the* system for beating the dice or roulette table—they all went broke. Others say that winning is "all luck." But winning at gambling is more than skill, systems or pure luck. It is, above all else, a matter of timing. You can have your skill, your system, and the mathematical laws of probability can be functioning (pure luck), but the one thing you must have in addition to these is timing.

The Sun and the Moon are the great timekeepers of astrology. Together they mark the days, months and years. The Moon is considered the greatest trigger. Its fast moving aspects to the other planets trigger the many events we see around us. The Sun rules the sign of Leo and the Fifth House, which rule speculation, games of chance and gambling in the individual horoscope. The aspects that the transiting Moon makes to your Sun sign reveal when your timing is right for winning at gambling. The transits also show when the timing is not right. A good aspect from the Moon to your Sun can trigger good fortune in games of chance. A difficult aspect can trigger difficulties and losses. The following delineations tell you when to gamble, when to wait, and give you particular hints on your gambling activities for the Moon in each of the signs. Follow the transits of the Moon through the signs. Gamble on your best days, hold off on your less fortunate days, and you will be using the most basic and dependable astrological factor for timing and winning at gambling.

ARIES SUN SIGN
Moon Transiting In:

Aries—Can produce wins, but don't get egotistical and think you have a license to win.

Taurus—Winning is possible, but you may have the urge to splurge; control your spending.

Gemini—A neutral influence, but can stimulate your mind for numbers, memorization and problem solving.

Cancer—Better hold back and save your money for a more fortunate day.

Leo—You could be fired up to gamble. Others are too. Control your impulses and you can win. Lose control and you can lose big!

Virgo—Good for the professional gambler. The average gambler is better off holding back.

Libra—Competitive sports or games in which you directly compete can attract your betting dollars. Keep self-control. Avoid impulse or emotional betting and you could come out ahead.

Scorpio—You may borrow to gamble, go into debt, or gamble with the bill money. If you avoid these pitfalls you have a chance to win.

Sagittarius—Impulse and risk abound, so don't take any crazy chances. You could win, but control yourself.

Capricorn—Your wins may be small most of the time, but if you're going to hit the lottery, this could be the time.

Aquarius—You can win among friends or a friend can give you a winning tip. Surprises abound.

Pisces—If you're even in the mood to gamble, you may be uncertain, indecisive or distracted. Stay conservative if you are in the action.

TAURUS SUN SIGN
Moon Transiting In:

Taurus—If you risk your money now you will probably play the favorites. Look for the long shot that pays big. Your financial intuition is sharp.

Gemini—You can be fascinated by numbers games and by the numbers that have dollar signs in front of them. Keep your investment small and you may multiply your resources.

Cancer—Security concerns can dominate your thinking. Winning is possible, but if you start losing don't be stubborn; learn when to quit.

Leo—Others around you may be stimulated to gamble. Your own chances of winning are not that great. Bet small.

Virgo—Your best laid plans and systems can now be put to the test. Stay alert, analyze things, watch the details and you can come out ahead.

Libra—You spend best by studying, planning and organizing your gambling activities. Wait for a better period to put down your cash.

Scorpio—You may feel the challenge to hit it big. Sports and competitions you bet on or participate in are most likely to win you money.

Sagittarius—You have to spend it to make it, and bet it to win it, but if you borrow it you'll most likely lose it. You can win, but don't let your blind optimism cause you to gamble with more than you can afford.

Capricorn—You could be ready for some serious speculation. Depend on your experience and expertise in financial matters and you can find the winning bets.

Aquarius—Lotteries, sweepstakes and electronic gambling machines may be fortunate now. You may hit a big payoff that makes you famous among your friends.

Pisces—Your intuition is heightened, but make sure it's not just wishful thinking. Winning is possible. Don't loan money to gambling friends.

Aries—You are better off holding back now. Events may be too fast breaking or too anxious and distracting for you to use your best judgment.

GEMINI SUN SIGN
Moon Transiting In:

Gemini—You naturally thrive on action and you can be ready to gamble big. Self-control is essential to end up in the winner's circle.

Cancer—Your better money-making instincts dominate now. Winning is possible. Memory serves you well.

Leo—You may get carried away by the gambling fever surrounding you. Lotteries, number games and casinos can hold winning opportunities, but don't risk it all.

Virgo—This transit favors detailed analysis, looking over forms, refining your systems. Don't bet yet, however; save your cash for a better transit.

Libra—Many opportunities for speculative gains. You can apply what you have learned and test your skills and systems.

Scorpio—Not a fortunate period. You may be better off reviewing your wins and losses, refining your techniques and investigating new strategies.

Sagittarius—Sports and racing competitions can attract your attention. Winning is possible, but remain objective and reserved. Don't let optimism carry you away.

Capricorn—You may have visions of scoring big. There is money to be won, and you may get a piece of it now.

Aquarius—Friends could be a part of your gambling scene. You may think you finally have the perfect system; be cautious. Winning is possible, but don't lose more than you can afford.

Pisces—Draw on your sixth sense and gain the intuitive insights that lead to winning. Remain sensitive to your inner promptings.

Aries—Your mind may be too fast for your pocketbook. Winning is possible, but you had better set your budget before you begin to gamble.

Taurus—This period is better used for socializing, entertainment or relaxation. Wins may be small or you may risk more than you should.

CANCER SUN SIGN
Moon Transiting In:

Cancer—Security interests can dominate now. Winning is possible.

Leo—This can be fortunate. You will know how to get the most out of your gambling dollars.

Virgo—A generally neutral influence with a down tendency. You may be better off saving your money now.

Libra—You are not likely to win big now, although you may win the door prize.

Scorpio—Your instincts and intuition are sharp for risky business. You can turn a small bet into a big payoff. Draw on your memory and remain sensitive to your psychic promptings.

Sagittarius—If you make a living through speculation, this transit could produce a tidy profit. The average gambler may be swept away by visions of riches and should remain conservative.

Capricorn—You are inclined to bet on the favorites or stay conservative. You'd be smart to keep your bets small as wins can be meager.

Aquarius—Your brain may be working overtime, trying to figure out how to win big. Number games can be lucky. Do not lend money to gambling friends.

Pisces—A fortunate time. Stay in touch with your feelings and intuitions. They can lead you to a big winner.

Aries—You may win in competition or sports. Maintain composure and self-control or you can gamble fast and lose.

Taurus—Sweepstakes and contests may be lucky now. The lotteries may produce a winner. Remain conservative, as this is not your best time.

Gemini—You would do just as well to save your money under this transit. Distractions, indecision or anxieties can keep you from using your best judgment.

LEO SUN SIGN
Moon Transiting In:

Leo—Your time to shine! Good fortune will usually come your way, but don't think you can do no wrong or you can lose everything you've won.

Virgo—You are more pragmatic and perhaps even nervous about taking risks. Be particular about your bets.

Libra—You may gain by mixing social activities with your gambling. A neighbor or relative may prove a fortunate influence.

Scorpio—This is a less fortunate period. It may produce some wins, but you should remain conservative in the amount you risk.

Sagittarius—You may really want to gamble, especially if you like sports or races. You can win big if you are smart, but don't let your enthusiasm cause you to lose too much if you see that it's not your day.

Capricorn—You are probably better off tending to more serious business. Winning is not that likely and you will really hate yourself if you lose.

Aquarius—You think you have it all figured out, ready to battle the bookies or casinos, but it's not a very fortunate time. Keep your eyes on the competition.

Pisces—Winning is possible. Depend on your best financial instincts and intuition.

Aries—Sports, competitions and contests are strongly favored. Your tendency is to gamble too much, so keep self-control.

Taurus—Get the most value from your betting dollar. Stick with your most dependable gambles. A big win from a small bet is possible.

Gemini—Picking numbers may prove surprisingly profitable. Lotteries, bingo and keno games give you a big chance on a small investment.

Cancer—Not very fortunate. You are better off renewing your inner resources in preparation for a new cycle of excitement and risk.

VIRGO SUN SIGN
Moon Transiting In:

Virgo—Luck through wagering in very particular and limited ways. Bet one horse out of ten races or buy only one lottery ticket.

Libra—Winning is possible, but you may be indecisive or influenced by others' opinions. Keep your risk small if you gamble.

Scorpio—Your skill with numbers and odds can serve you well. This may not produce a big win but it can be profitable.

Sagittarius—You are better off holding back. If you do gamble, keep it small.

Capricorn—Your instincts for finding the best bet will come now, though your winnings may be modest.

Aquarius—If you are numbers crazy this transit may be lucky. Others are better off studying forms and systems and saving their bets for another day.

Pisces—You are not at your best for picking the winners. Confusion or indecision can cost you.

Aries—Decisive and exacting application of your best gambling instincts may produce a big win on a small investment.

Taurus—This transit could produce winners. Take your time to find the very best odds for your money.

Gemini—You should have at least one lottery ticket, as you can achieve public recognition for numbers games.

Cancer—Don't let feelings cloud your thinking or you may imagine you have the perfect system. Winning is possible, but bet conservatively.

Leo—You could get caught up in an urge to gamble. Keep it at the level of entertainment. Lose control and you can lose big.

LIBRA SUN SIGN
Moon Transiting In:

Libra—Winning is possible if you keep your balance. Don't let the lure of luxury cause you to risk too much.

Scorpio—You may know just how to extract the cash. Your sense of values serves you well.

Sagittarius—Numbers games or racing events may be fortunate. Maintain your self-control. You could lose much if not lucky, and lose your winnings if too self-confident.

Capricorn—Forget this transit for winning. If you do win, it could be small, and a loss will leave you very sour.

Aquarius—A most fortunate transit. You can win in social settings, numbers games and electronic gambling.

Pisces—Not that fortunate. Relax and take care of yourself. Save your betting dollars for a better time.

Aries—Competition of every type can attract your bets. You can pick the winners. Stay in touch with your intuitive/psychic impulses.

Taurus—A lottery ticket may be a good idea. If you are destined to win a massive sum, this could be the time.

Gemini—Big numbers attract you. You understand the patterns behind numbers. You can win now, but don't risk more than you can afford.

Cancer—Winning is possible, but security matters may occupy your attention. Remain realistic, as your emotions could hinder smart betting.

Leo—Electronic games, lotteries and casinos could be profitable. A generally favorable transit.

Virgo—Get in touch with facts and real figures. You could be too confused, distracted or undecided to be right. Proceed cautiously.

SCORPIO SUN SIGN
Moon Transiting In:

Scorpio—Your desire for gain could be great. Draw on your deep insights and intuition.

Sagittarius—Maintain self-control and remain realistic and this can produce some wins.

Capricorn—Tends toward the down side. It may be better to wait, learn and plan.

Aquarius—Unusual or surprising events could surround your gambling and end up costing you money. Remain conservative.

Pisces—Your insight and intuition serve you well. Winning could be easy, almost like magic!

Aries—If you dig in and work at it you may come up a winner. Pace yourself and maintain your discipline or you may end up losing.

Taurus—Don't let feelings cause you to take a poor risk. Winning is possible, but this is not your best time.

Gemini—You have a chance to win if you use your head. You may tend to bet too often or stay in the action long after you have gotten ahead. Learn to quit a winner.

Cancer—Your intuitive knowledge of gambling can make you a winner. Definitely one of your better periods.

Leo—You could strike it rich under this transit! If you are going to achieve fame for winning, this is when it could happen, but don't get carried away.

Virgo—Adept with numbers, you may want to play the lottery, bingo or keno. Not your most fortunate time, but it can produce some wins.

Libra—You could bet emotionally, be undecided or not get the best value for your dollar. You should probably wait for a more fortunate transit.

SAGITTARIUS SUN SIGN
Moon Transiting In:

Sagittarius—You can be off and running, ready for action and willing to gamble big. Maintain perspective and self-control and you can cash in a winner.

Capricorn—You could have one eye on your bank book and one on the racing form. Betting the favorites or remaining conservative would be wise.

Aquarius—Gambling among friends, neighbors or in social settings may prove favorable. Electronic and numbers games are possible winners.

Pisces—Subconscious desires for grandeur and great wealth may cloud your betting choices. Not your most fortunate transit. Bet small if at all.

Aries—You can put your natural instincts for gambling and risk to good use. Depend on your intuition.

Taurus—If you work at it, this can produce some winners. Try to get a big payoff for a small investment. Not very fortunate, so be prudent.

Gemini—You may want to "show 'em" and prove you are a winner. Maintain your perspective and composure. Winning in competitive events is possible, but remain conservative.

Cancer—Don't let your feelings or sentiments cause you to bet more than you can afford. Winning is possible, but you should look for small bets that pay big.

Leo—You could be too willing to gamble; you'll lose big if you lose self-control. Depend on your experience and common sense.

Virgo—Numbers games may be lucky. Watch out for races, sports and competitions, as these could go against you.

Libra—Groups and social settings can be favorable. You can be good at picking the winners in competitions.

Scorpio—A time for caution. Your desire to gamble can overcome your best judgment and cause you to lose more than you can afford. It wouldn't hurt to wait.

CAPRICORN SUN SIGN
Moon Transiting In:

Capricorn—You are inclined to limit your bets. Bet on the favorites. Don't risk much money. Your gambling forte is your conservative and realistic approach.

Aquarius—Gambling among friends, in groups, or on electronic and numbers games can turn a profit.

Pisces—A dream or your intuition may lead you to pick winning numbers. This transit is a neutral influence so you should not risk a lot.

Aries—Emotion and impulse could get the best of you and cause losses.

Taurus—Your heightened sense of values can lead you to get good odds. Definitely one of your better times to risk your resources.

Gemini—Worry, indecision or mental irritations may get in the way of your winning. You should probably save your money for a more fortunate time.

Cancer—Cautions against emotional betting. Keep in touch with your intuition and competitive events could produce winners.

Leo—A strong transit for the urge to win big. Research or inside information could mean big gains. Maintain self-control.

Virgo—Pay attention to details, examine records, tables, charts. Possible wins.

Libra—You can pick between individuals or teams in competitions. You can evaluate the important factors for winning.

Scorpio—You can profit among friends or by pooling a great deal of money. Your mind is sharp for gambling with multiple numbers.

Sagittarius—This is not the time to get carried away by the gambling fever surrounding you. Control yourself and you can win. Blind faith could cost you.

AQUARIUS SUN SIGN
Moon Transiting In:

Aquarius—Gambling among friends, with groups or in social settings is favored now. Stay in tune to ingenious bets; they could surprise you with a winner.

Pisces—Subtle and intuitive insight can lead to winning, but don't risk everything.

Aries—Using your computer brain is a good idea, but guard against impulse betting.

Taurus—Tough to win under this transit. Winnings small and slow to come. Minimize risk.

Gemini—This transit could produce wins. Don't go off on a tangent, betting too much or too often. Control your betting with your mind and you can win.

Cancer—If you work with a gambling system, this is a good time to apply what you have learned. Remain sensitive to your intuitive impulses. Not your most fortunate time, but winning is possible.

Leo—You can place your gambling in perspective now. Casino gambling and gambling among friends or in groups could be productive. Remain reserved.

Virgo—Maintain your mental balance, don't risk more than you can afford to lose. Investigation and detailed digging could reveal winners.

Libra—A fortunate influence in general. Numbers games or competitions could bring winners. Remain in control, as you are more willing to risk a great deal.

Scorpio—Past research and experience can lead you to winners. Gains come through hard work, but the possibility for success is present.

Sagittarius—You can win big among friends, groups or in social settings. Lotteries and numbers games are also favored. Stay within a budget, as you are more inclined to risk too much.

Capricorn—If you have a hidden advantage you may be able to profit in speculation. Proceed with caution and you may show a small profit.

PISCES SUN SIGN
Moon Transiting In:

Pisces—Intuition is your guide. Remain sensitive to dreams, visions, larger concepts and you can find winners.

Aries—A willingness to risk your resources boldly. You can win, but don't let impulse masquerade as courage. Stay within a budget.

Taurus—A rather neutral influence. You may have intuitive insight into numbers. Modest wagering could be worth it.

Gemini—You may be too distracted, bet emotionally or rely too much on the opinions of others. You might want to skip it during this transit.

Cancer—Your psychic and intuitive insight could pay big dividends in risk and speculation. This is definitely the time to have a bet in.

Leo—A willingness to risk too much could cost you dearly. Others may be eager to gamble, but this may not be your time. Keep wages small if you do bet.

Virgo—Good fortune will not fall now. You need to be very alert to come out ahead.

Libra—You may receive a tip or be directed to a winning bet by someone else. This could produce winners, but remember you are responsible for the final decisions.

Scorpio—Your desire to win could overcome your best judgment. Winning is possible, but you will do best by risking little.

Sagittarius—A profitable transit for you. You know how to take advantage of others' willingness to take big risks. Maintain your self-control.

Capricorn—People, places and things from the past could produce winners now. Gambles sponsored by governments, institutions or organizations contain special promise.

Aquarius—Lotteries and electronic gambles could produce a winner. Strong intuition directs your winning choices. Protect yourself by remaining on a budget, or you could go into debt.

HEALTH & BEAUTY

HEALTH & BEAUTY

Beauty Care
For beauty treatments, skin care and massage, the Moon should be in Taurus, Cancer, Leo, Libra, Scorpio or Aquarius and sextile, trine or conjunct Venus and/or Jupiter.

Fingernails should be cut when the Moon is not in any aspect with Mercury or Jupiter. Saturn and Mars must not be marked Q or O because this makes the nails grow slowly or thin and weak. The Moon should be in Aries, Taurus, Cancer or Leo. For toenails, the Moon should not be in Gemini or Pisces. Corns are best cut when the Moon is in the third or fourth quarter.

Dental Work
Pick a day that is marked favorable for your Sun sign. Mars should be marked X, T or C and Saturn, Uranus and Jupiter should not be marked Q or O.

Teeth are best removed during the increase of the Moon in the first or second quarter in Gemini, Virgo, Sagittarius, Capricorn or Pisces. The day should be favorable for your lunar cycle, and Mars and Saturn should be marked C, T or X.

Fillings should be done when the Moon is in a fixed sign (Taurus, Leo, Scorpio, Aquarius) and decreasing in light. The same applies for having impressions made for plates.

Dieting
Weight gain occurs more readily when the Moon is in a water sign (Cancer, Scorpio, Pisces). Experience has shown that weight may be lost if a diet is started when the Moon is decreasing in light (third or fourth quarter) and when it is in Aries, Leo, Virgo, Sagittarius or Aquarius. The lunar cycle should be favorable on the day you wish to begin your diet.

Eyeglasses
Eyes should be tested and glasses fitted on a day marked favorable for your Sun sign and on a day which falls during your favorable lunar cycle. Mars should not be in aspect with the Moon. The same applies for any treatment of the eyes, which should also be started during the increase of the Moon (first or second quarter).

Habits
To end any habit, start on a day when the Moon is in the third or fourth quarter and in a barren sign.

Gemini, Leo or Virgo are the best times, while Aries and Capricorn are suitable too. Make sure your lunar cycle is favorable. Avoid lunar aspects to Mars or Jupiter. Aspects to Neptune or Saturn are helpful. These rules apply to smoking and will produce a good start.

Hair Care
Haircuts are best when the Moon is in a mutable sign (Gemini, Sagittarius, Pisces) or earthy sign (Taurus, Capricorn), well-placed and aspected, but not in Virgo, which is barren. For faster growth, the Moon should be in a water sign (Cancer, Scorpio, Pisces). To make hair grow thicker, cut it when the Moon is full or in opposition to the Sun (marked O in the Lunar Aspectarian). However, if you want your hair to grow more slowly, the Moon should be in Gemini or Leo in the third or fourth quarter with Saturn square or opposite the Moon.

Permanents, straightening and hair coloring will take well if the Moon is in Aquarius and Venus is marked T or X. You should avoid doing your hair if Mars is marked Q or O, especially if heat is to be used. For permanents, a trine to Jupiter is helpful. The Moon also should be in the first quarter and at the same time check the lunar cycle for a favorable day in relation to your Sun sign.

Health
Diagnosis is more likely to be successful when the Moon is in a cardinal sign (Aries, Cancer, Libra, Capricorn) and less so when in a mutable sign.

Begin a program for recuperation or recovery when the Moon is in a cardinal or fixed sign and the day is favorable to your sign. Enter hospitals at these times. For surgery, see *Surgical Procedures*. Buy medicines when the Moon is in Scorpio if they are made from natural substances.

Surgical Procedures

The flow of blood appears to be related to the Moon's phases. *Time* magazine reported on 1,000 tonsillectomy case histories analyzed by Dr. Edson J. Andrews—only 18 percent of associated hemorrhaging occurred in the fourth and first quarters. Thus, an astrological rule: To reduce the hazard of hemorrhage after a surgical procedure, plan to have the surgery within one week before or after the Full Moon. Also select a date when the Moon is not in the sign governing the part of the body involved in the operation. The farther removed the Moon sign from the sign ruling the afflicted part of the body, the better for healing. There should be no lunar aspects to Mars, and favorable aspects to Venus and Jupiter should be present.

Cosmetic surgery should be done in the increase of the Moon, when the Moon is not in square or opposition to Mars. Avoid days when the Moon is square or opposite Saturn or the Sun.

For more information, read the following article on medical astrology.

MEDICAL ASTROLOGY

by Louise Riotte

In his book *Powerful Planets*, Llewellyn George, one of the most respected astrologers of all time, stated, "Medical astrology in its relation to diagnosis and the prevention and cure of disease is a valuable adjunct to metaphysicians, doctors, surgeons and dentists." What he said in 1931 is just as true today.

Physicians such as Hippocrates, "the Father of Medicine," used a knowledge of planetary influences to perform their wonders. They knew sympathy and antipathy; they knew that the angle of crystallization at sixty degrees, called sextile, was creative; they knew that bodies in opposite points of the zodiac were disintegrative in their effects. They knew that sulphur corresponds to the planet Mercury and they knew many other facts that will not be clear to modern scientists until they, too, take up a serious study of planetary influences.

So it may be seen that the subject of medical astrology takes in much more than the title implies. This is readily evidenced by the physicians, surgeons, holistic practitioners, and dentists who *are* using knowledge of astrology to enhance their skills and to assure more definite and satisfactory results by acting in harmony with the duly timed workings of nature.

By examining a person's natal chart, the physician skilled in medical astrology can see what disorders the patient is predisposed to at birth; by examining the progressed horoscopes he or she can see which tendencies are now coming into expression, whether complications are about to set in, or whether the sickness is about to break up. The physician can calculate the time of crisis in advance, for he or she knows that in acute situations the crises come about on the 7th, 14th, 21st and 28th days from the time the patient was taken sick. The Moon makes a revolution in her orbit in about 28 days, and the 7th, 14th and 21st days and her return to her place at the time of the New Moon correspond to the quarters, adverse aspects and crisis times in the illness. Therefore, the first, second and third quarters of the Moon from the time the illness began are crisis days in diseases.

If the patient lives through these crises, and until the Moon returns to her place, the disease will dissolve itself. The crisis days are the dangerous ones. As a rule, the most serious crisis day is the 14th when the Moon arrives at the opposite aspect to her place at the beginning of the illness. This crisis day is called the *Criticus Primus*, the "one of prime importance." More patients usually die on the 14th day of a serious illness than on the other crisis days; if they survive, their chances for recovery are usually good.

One simple but potent rule that is interesting to surgeons is: "Pierce not with steel that part of the body represented by the sign which the Moon occupies on that day." Another astrological rule is: "To reduce the hazard of hemorrhage after a surgical operation, plan to have the surgery occur within one week before or after the New Moon; avoid, whenever possible, submitting to surgery within one week before or after the Full Moon."

These rules are best applied to cases where one can "elect" whether or not to have surgery at a given time; in emergency cases, of course, they cannot be applied, as the delay of one or two weeks might prove fatal.

Dr. H.L. Cornell, author of the *Encyclopedia of Medical Astrology*, has stated that statistics show that surgical operations, including operations on the eyes, are apt to be most successful when the Moon is increasing in light, that is, between the New and Full Moons, and that the patients heal more rapidly and have fewer complications than when the Moon is decreasing.

During the decrease of the Moon vitality is usually less, and the bodily fluids at low ebb; these fluids rise and fill the vessels of the body to a greater fullness when the Moon is increasing.

ASTROLOGICAL GUIDELINES
FOR OPERATIONS

- Operate in the increase of the Moon if possible.

- Do not operate at the exact time of the Full Moon, as the fluids in the body are running high at this time.

- Never operate when the Moon is in the same sign as the patient's birth (Sun sign).

- Never operate upon that part of the body ruled by the sign through which the Moon is passing at the time. Wait a day or two until the Moon passes into the next sign—this rule is of great importance in major operations.

- The Moon should be in a fixed sign, but not in the sign ruling the part of the body which is to be operated on; such sign of the Moon should not be on the ascendant.

- Do not operate when the Moon is applying to (moving toward) any aspect of Mars, as such tends to promote inflammation and complications after the operation.

- There should be good aspects to Venus and Jupiter (sextile or trine).

- Avoid, when possible, operations when the Sun is in the sign ruling the part upon which the operation is to be performed.

- The Moon should be free from all manner of impediment.

- Fortify the sign ruling the part of the body to be operated upon.

- Avoid Mars aspects when planning surgery.

- Do not cut a nerve when Mercury is afflicted (square or opposition).

- When the Moon is under the Sun's beams and opposed by Mars, it is considered a dangerous time for amputations.

- Avoid abdominal operations when the Moon is passing through Virgo, Libra or Scorpio. Good times are when the Moon is passing through Sagittarius, Capricorn or Aquarius.

Consideration of the Moon's phases is no less important in the practice of dentistry. Teeth should be extracted in either the first or second quarter—waxing Moon—which promotes healing.

Best signs for extraction are Gemini, the arms; Virgo, the bowels; Sagittarius, the thighs; Capricorn, the knees; and Pisces, the feet. Note that all these signs are some distance from the head. Mars and Saturn should be marked C, T or X.

Avoid extractions when the Moon is passing through Aries, Cancer, Libra, Taurus, Leo, Scorpio or Aquarius.

Fillings should be done when the Moon is waning in the third and fourth quarters, in a fixed sign such as Taurus, the neck; Leo, the heart; Scorpio, the genitals; or Aquarius, the legs.

AN A-Z OF FOLK MEDICINE
by Mary Brown

In spite of the many inaccuracies in the work of the early botanist/doctors of the 15th and 16th centuries, with their belief in the "Doctrine of Signatures"—which stated that plants resembled the disease they were supposed to cure—they did chance upon some important discoveries. As scientific medicine developed in the last two hundred years, it has been found that in many cases there was more than a grain of truth in the old beliefs.

The folk medicine practiced by the ordinary people evolved by trial and error, with snippets of information from actual medical sources, plus the lore of the local "cunning man" or herb woman. These primitive practitioners used common plants found on any roadside or in the woods and fields. This at least made it easy for the patient to gather more plants for a repeat prescription.

In the following A-Z guide, note that an infusion is made by using 1 ounce of the dried or fresh flowers or leaves to 1 pint of boiling water (like making tea). The tea or tisane is left to stand for 5 minutes, then strained and taken in doses of 2 or 3 tablespoons at a time. It can be sweetened with honey if desired. For a decoction, use 1 ounce of the scrubbed root. Cover with 1 pint of water and boil for 20 minutes. Allow to stand until cool, then strain and take in doses of 1 tablespoon at a time.

 is for alkanet, said to be good for "old ulcers," hot inflammations and St Anthony's fire (erysipelas). Made into a vinegar, it would help leprosy. The ancient Greeks believed that eating the leaves or placing them on the wound would cure the bite of poisonous snakes. As an ointment, it cured bruises and open wounds. Modern day uses include cough syrup and use as a dyeing plant.

 is for bay, an old-time "wonder plant," used against jaundice, dropsy, rheumatism, consumption, cramps, convulsions, palsy and many more complaints. Seven berries would bring the speedy delivery of a child, and the berries were also believed to be effective against poisons and the plague. Bay is not used by herbalists now, except as an oil for treating rheumatism. The leaves are a useful kitchen herb.

 is for comfrey, another "wonder plant," well-known for its medicinal properties, especially as a chest medicine. It was thought to actually heal broken bones, and was called "knitbone" by country folk. It was used widely as a general medicine for almost any ailment. It is still valued today by herbalists, who sell skin preparations made from comfrey for psoriasis. It also is used for peptic ulcers, colitis and hiatus hernia, and is recommended for use in the treatment of wounds, either using the plain leaves or an ointment. A decoction of the root is used for tonsillitis, bronchitis and coughs. In addition to its medicinal properties, comfrey is a useful green fertilizer for the garden.

 is for dill, which provides relief from swelling and pain by boiling the seeds and then drinking the liquid. It also is said to stop hiccups and prevent vomiting. Dill seed oil was useful in easing pain. Today dill-water is a well-known digestive aid, especially for babies with wind.

is for elecampane, or "wild sunflower," a valuable medicinal plant in times gone by—good for all fevers and chest complaints and thought to be the very best cure for whooping cough, when all other medicines failed. Good for the kidneys and "waterworks," it also prevented the spread of "pestilential fevers" and the plague. Today it is recognized that the plant has value as an insulin or diabetic sugar source. A decoction is taken, usually in combination with coltsfoot or horehound, for coughs, asthma or bronchitis. Herbalists sell a liquid extract of the root.

is for fennel, which the ancients used with vinegar and rose water to help "lethargy, frenzy, giddiness of the head, the falling-sickness, palsy, sciatica and cramp." It also is thought to be good for relieving the pains of childbirth. In some parts of the world it is still used as a remedy for epilepsy.

is for goldenrod, once used in a distillation as a diuretic and for kidney stones. Also excellent for wound healing and for mouth and throat ulcers. A tea can be made from the young leaves and is useful for menstrual bleeding, arthritis and eczema. A powder of the dried leaves will help heal ulcers and sores.

 is for horehound (white), a favorite of old-time herbalists who used it as a decoction, or the fresh juice with honey, for coughs and consumption. It was also used as an antidote to poison. The juice taken with wine and honey was said to "clear the eyesight and purge away the yellow jaundice." The decoction or a powder made from the dried plant was used to cure worms. Today horehound is still valuable for making cough medicines and asthma remedies. A syrup is made by adding honey or sugar to an ordinary infusion. Taken hot, the herb reduces temperature and in larger doses can be a laxative.

 is for ivy, once used to cure ulcers, burns and scalds and as a remedy for the plague. It is not recommended for home use, but the leaves can be used in a poultice for boils and abscesses.

is for juniper—the berries of which were thought to be an antidote to poison and good for dropsy, fits, dysentery, coughs, consumption, rupture and cramps. The berries also were said to strengthen the brain and fortify the sight. Modern uses include an infusion of the berries for cystitis and the oil, taken on a lump of sugar, is a remedy for indigestion and flatulence.

 is for kidneywort, also known as pennywort, which was said to help "sore kidneys torn by the stones." The juice was used for inflammation, "unnatural heats," pimples, piles and chilblains. Last century, this was a popular remedy for epilepsy, but now is used only as a poultice to cure hemorrhoids.

 is for lily of the valley, once used for inflammation of the eyes, palsy, apoplexy and for the heart. It was said to be of use in all disorders of the nervous system, including "swimming in the head." Today the plant is recognized as an important cardiac tonic, but home use is inadvisable. Although a tincture can be obtained from herbalists, use with caution for it can affect the heart adversely.

 is for marsh mallow, a mild and soothing remedy for many ailments, once given to nursing mothers to increase their milk supply. The leaves rubbed on stings will soothe and take away inflammation. It was used as a gargle for sore throats and as a remedy for coughs and wheezing (in boiled root form). The oil was applied to rough and cracked skin. Still well-known as an emollient, marsh mallow is used for internal inflammations and can be obtained in several forms from herbalists. An infusion of the leaves is a useful home medicine.

 is for nettle, "nature's doctor," which was a safe and sure medicine to open the passages of the lungs, and was also used as a gargle to cure swelling in the mouth and throat. It was believed to be effective against dog bites and deadly poisons. The leaves are still used today, in infusion as a diuretic which also helps high blood pressure. Nettles are high in iron content and good for anemia, while a decoction of the root will cure diarrhea. You can eat the young leaves cooked like spinach.

is for orach, once gathered to make a tincture from the seeds. When just ripe, the seeds were bruised and placed in alcohol for a time, then the tincture was used as an aperient. Today the plant is more commonly used in salads or boiled like greens.

 is for pennyroyal, of the mint family. Once a common herbal remedy, the plant was used for steadying the stomach, fainting, headaches, jaundice, dropsy, and especially whooping cough. Like all the mints, pennyroyal is an excellent remedy still used today for digestive problems and stomach upsets. It can also ease the symptoms of fever and should be taken as an infusion.

 is for quince, which was grown in most gardens in former times. The juice was popular as a stomach medicine and would also cure sore throats and fever. The mucilage from the seeds is still used today to treat dysentery and diarrhea.

is for rosemary, once said to help "cold diseases of the head and brain such as giddiness and swimmings, drownings, loss of speech and lethargy." It was also said to stop toothache and to be good for the stomach. A rosemary comb was used to prevent falling hair. The herb is still very popular in hair preparations and cosmetics.

 is for sage, so highly thought of that the philosophers used to say that correct use of the herb could render humankind immortal! Once used for all manner of ailments, especially pains in the head and joints, the falling-sickness, palsy and cramps. Nowadays it is still known as an effective remedy for laryngitis and tonsillitis. Use the infusion as a gargle. A sweetened infusion is a mild laxative.

 is for thyme, a popular plant in healing and cooking. In olden times, the infusion was used for all kinds of nervous disorders, and would also cure headaches, giddiness, hangovers and nightmares. Thyme is known to modern herbalists as a natural antiseptic, and is also good for relieving coughs and sore throats. An infusion will relieve all chest and cough symptoms. Thyme contains thymol, which is used as an antiseptic, as a preservative, and in perfumery.

 is for the umbrella plant or galingale, good for the "swimming of the head." It could also cure giddiness, dropsy, and would "expel wind and strengthen the bowels." Though now less widely available, it is used today to treat water retention.

 is for violet, often used long ago to treat eye inflammation and other inflamed conditions. The powdered leaves were said to relieve quinsy and the falling-sickness. It was thought to be good for diseases of the lungs and pains in the back. Modern uses include application of the leaves, which are naturally antiseptic, for pain relief. The flowers made into an infusion with honey added is a good expectorant cough medicine.

 is for wormwood, once said to be excellent for gout and for "gravel" (sediment in the urine). Nowadays it is known as a fine remedy for dyspepsia, stomach pains and worms. A natural antiseptic, it can deter some pests in the garden.

 is for yarrow, good for inflammation and for curing wounds. It was said to be an excellent remedy for hemorrhoids, and a poultice of toadflax and yarrow would "induce sleep and ease pain." It is still an important ingredient in herbal medicine, as a remedy for the common cold made with elderflowers and peppermint. It also speeds up blood clotting and can reduce blood pressure.

 is for zea mays (Indian corn or maize), which is useful for urinary infections and bladder stones. The beard of corn silk is an excellent diuretic and can lower blood pressure.

NATURAL HEALTH AND BEAUTY AIDS

In a modern society with countless synthetic drugs, the question may be asked: Why use herbs? After witnessing the side effects of medicines artificially prepared, people are turning again to the valuable properties of herbs, fruits and vegetables. Nature's remedies are the plants that have grown naturally for centuries all over the earth.

Herbs are food for the human body and mind. They contain the vitamins and minerals necessary to the balance of the body's systems, as do the other natural foods we eat (vegetables, fruits, grains, etc.).

The purpose of a remedy is to help the body cure itself. When certain necessary organic minerals and vitamins are lacking in our diet, disease results. Therefore, the body must be supplied with the essential elements it needs to rebuild the areas weakened or damaged by disease.

HOW TO PREPARE HERBAL REMEDIES

Infusions are made as is regular tea, by pouring one pint of boiling water over half an ounce of herb flowers or leaves and steeping for a few minutes. Honey is sometimes added as a sweetener.

Decoctions are made of the hard parts of the herb—the stems, roots, bark, seeds—and they have to boil for some time to extract their full value.

To make a fomentation, dip a cloth or heavy towel into a decoction or an infusion. Wring out the excess moisture and apply to the affected area.

For salves, mix eight parts petroleum jelly or lard with two parts herbal and stir well while hot. Use when the mixture is cool.

To make a poultice, put the herbs loosely in a flannel bag large enough to cover the area. Pour boiling water over the bag and then wring out the extra moisture inside a towel. Use the poultice as hot as possible. It is good for nerve pains, painful joints and muscles, and promotes restful sleep when applied to the abdomen.

Backache
Exercise is important. Lie on the floor on your back with your legs up and make bicycling motions. Teas of nettle and rosinweed are also helpful.

Bites (Insect)
Apply eucalyptus oil, thyme oil or distilled witch hazel extract to the affected area.

Boils and Blisters
Make a poultice of lobelia and slippery elm, hops, skunk cabbage, or Solomon's sea. For blisters apply onion juice and salt.

Burns
Use a poultice of yarrow, comfrey, or mustard. Particularly good salves are made from elderberry blossom, golden seal, or red clover. You may also use wheat germ oil.

Colds
Drink teas of balsam, catnip, elderberry and peppermint, golden seal, mellein, rosemary, or sarsaparilla. Try a hot epsom salts foot bath for 20 minutes. For quick recovery, drink two teaspoons of honey and two teaspoons of cider vinegar in a glass of water, or eat raw or cooked onions.

Constipation
Teas of blue flag, cascara sagrada, or red clover are the best known remedies.

Corns
Tie lemon slices over the corns overnight. Apply this fluid extract morning and night, or tie a cloth soaked in turpentine around them overnight.

Dandruff
Rinse your hair and massage well into the scalp oils of rosemary and eucalyptus or a tea made of willow leaves and bark. A very successful remedy is a

tea made of one ounce of rosemary steeped in a pint of boiling water. (Be sure to let the mixture cool before you use it!)

Diarrhea
Eat raw apples and bananas or drink crowfoot, peppermint, red raspberry, or slippery elm tea.

Eczema
Make an ointment of apple cider vinegar or boric acid and use in place of soap and water. Internally, you daily can take lecithin, spikenard, valerian, or plantain.

Eyes (Black or Sore)
If the skin isn't broken, use arnica in water. If it is broken, use witch hazel in water. A poultice made of scraped raw potato is also effective.

Fevers
Drink teas of chamomile, sweet cicely, catnip, elderberry, peppermint and honey, or yarrow (said to relieve fever in 24 hours if taken every 30 minutes). Spearmint tea is particularly good for children. Also sponge the patient with common baking soda water.

Frostbite
Paint the affected area with friar's balsam and gently rub olive oil onto it after a few minutes.

Gums (Tender)
Try a mixture of orris root, myrrh and borax.

Headache
The most important thing is to rest where there is quiet and fresh air. Hot teas of peppermint, catnip, spearmint, or chamomile are useful. One table-spoon of mustard added to a very hot five- to ten-minute foot bath is known to work. Drink hot water with lemon juice or eat onions with honey.

Hiccoughs
The most popular and effective remedies are drink-ing orange or pineapple juice, sipping peppermint tea, or swallowing very cold or hot water (please take necessary precautions to avoiding burning your throat). A more unorthodox remedy consists of holding cold water in your mouth, placing the middle fingers of each hand in both ears, swallow-ing the water and then removing your fingers after a moment.

Insomnia
Drink teas of chamomile, catnip, hops, or lady's slipper. Also said to help are sleeping on a pillow stuffed with hops, eating raw onions, taking a very hot foot bath before bed, or using a heated com-press of rose leaves with mint.

Irritations (Skin)
Ingest citrus fruits, teas of balsam root, yarrow, or red clover blossoms and chickweed.

Pains (Menstrual)

Pennyroyal, chamomile, catnip, or sweet cicely teas are helpful. For depression, drink black cohosh tea.

Sores, Cuts and Wounds

Try a poultice of grated raw carrots, comfrey, dandelion, juniper, red clover, sweet cicely, skunk cabbage, yarrow and yerba mansa, or cod-liver oil (prevents infection). A salve of elderberry blossom is effective, as is a grindelia decoction.

Stomachache

Try drinking a glass of milk two hours after each meal. Teas made of the following are good for relieving gas: caraway, sweet cicely, sage, golden seal, chamomile, marigold leaves, mint, peppermint, slippery elm, valerian, yarrow, or dandelion.

Sunburn

Make an ointment of glycerine, witch hazel and sunflower seed oil.

Sunstroke

Put your feet in a hot mustard bath and apply hot or cold cloths to the forehead and back of neck.

Swellings and Sprains

Effective are poultices of chamomile and hops, caraway and hyssop (alleviates black and blue marks), juniper, mullein and pennyroyal, sweet cicely, skunk cabbage, Solomon's seal, yarrow, or yerba mansa. You may also use a comfrey fomentation.

Toothache
The most liked remedies are poultices made of juniper, willow, or hops with coarse salt. Herbs that can be put directly into a cavity include yarrow, raw cow parsnip, grindelia, and sweet cicely. Yarrow, yerba mansa, and blue flag can be chewed. Hops tea can be given to teething babies.

Travel Sickness
Taking sips of hot water every 10 or 15 minutes will help, as will avoiding heavy meals before starting a trip. Ingest lemon juice with salt every few minutes at the first signs of illness.

Varicose Veins
Lie on your back and elevate your legs to relieve the pressure. Try bathing your legs with white oak bark. Sea salt baths are also effective. Overnight, apply cloths soaked in distilled witch hazel extract and cover with a dry towel. Stroke your legs upward, toward your hips, whenever possible. Drink tea made of golden seal, myrrh, tansy, or bran (helps strengthen the veins).

Hair Care
Baldness
Try massaging oils of clove and eucalyptus into your scalp, or, after washing, rinse your hair with marsh mallow tea. You might also drink sarsaparilla tea and eat more wheat germ, carrots, apples, bananas, tomatoes, strawberries, lettuce, cantaloupe, and dried peas.

Gray Hair
To darken hair, use a rinse made from a handful of stinging nettles boiled in a quart of water, or use an ounce of chamomile or sage boiled in a quart of water for 20 minutes.

Growth
To encourage growth, daily ingest wheat germ, cod-liver oil, or lecithin.

Texture
To brighten and improve the texture of your hair, use rinses of plantain and shepherd's-purse, any mixture of peppergrass, marsh mallow, mullein, nettle, sage, or burdock. Chamomile rinses are good for blondes.

Skin Care
Aging
Apply the leaves and roots of comfrey.

Dryness
The oldest known moisturizers are glycerine and honey, next to these is lecithin. Also useful are lanolin, natural menthol, and oils of quince, avocado, apricot kernel, almond, sesame, and wheat germ.

To soften your complexion, smooth mashed papaya on your face and rest with your feet up, then rinse.

Hang a bag of meadow sweet, rosemary, lavender, or comfrey in the bath. Combine a pint of vegetable oil, a small amount of shampoo and a few drops of perfume. Add two tablespoons of this mixture to your bath.

You can make a good hand lotion of glycerine and benzoin, or half an ounce each of glycerine and rosewater and one-quarter ounce of witch hazel. Mix the ingredients and shake well. If your hands are chapped after having been in water, rub dampened table salt on them and rinse.

Oiliness

Make an astringent of honey and glycerine, and place cucumber slices on the face daily, or put a cloth moistened with witch hazel over the eyes and rest for 15 minutes.

Texture

Try a cold friction bath in the morning to open the pores and improve skin texture. Wet your hands and body and slap yourself for a few moments. Dry yourself well and tenderly massage your skin with almond oil until it's all absorbed.

Wrinkles

Make a lotion of benzoin, glycerine and honey plus a few drops of cologne. You can also massage warm olive oil into the forehead. Barley water and a few drops of balm of gilead works, too.

Miscellaneous Beauty Treatments

Breath
Improve your breath by chewing anise seed, orris root, angelica root, cardamom seed, or nutmeg. Drinking chamomile tea may also help.

Eyes
For dark circles and faded eyes, try eating more blueberries, tomatoes, avocados, eggplant, and sunflower seeds.

Teeth
To whiten teeth, an old English recipe suggests a mixture of honey and vegetable charcoal.

THE ART OF HERBAL TINCTURING
by Maggie Houston

The art of tincturing is a remarkably old form of preserving the healing powers of herbs. The tinctures themselves are expensive to buy, but easy to manufacture. Except in a couple of cases, the commercial extracts you purchase may or may not be chemically potent. You stand as good a chance, probably even a better chance, at getting a bio-chemically potent extract from your own extraction methods than from what you can purchase at the store. So inexpensive are the home brews that it is amazing that more people do not do it. There are just a few simple steps to follow and, then, the sky is the limit.

To start a tincture you will need the freshest and most organic flowers, leaves and/or roots you can find. Finding the herbal products really evokes a creative process. That is, be open and ever aware of your needs. I have found the fresh produce section of natural food groceries, oriental groceries and even ordinary groceries to have products suitable for tincturing.

I live in a small town in North Carolina and have come to learn that in healing the body you cannot be hindered by any obstacles. You've heard "where there's a will there's a way"? That's what the creative spirit is about when healing yourself, so remain open and pluck your herbs from wherever they manifest.

The optimum is to gather the upper parts of the herbs during the Full Moon and the roots during the New Moon. Also, flowers and leaves are more potent when gathered at dawn, before the sun has had time to deplete their life force. Roots are most potent in the late fall to late winter. All the life force has moved to the root for storage and is very concentrated at this time.

Using common sense when collecting your herbs means respecting the life of the plant. Do not pick every plant of the type you need. Leave some to replenish the supply during the next growing season. Leave something natural behind to honor the plants for giving of themselves for your benefit. Some of the things I've left include strands of hair, bread crumbs and fruit. Native Americans traditionally leave tobacco or corn. The main thing here is to raise your consciousness concerning the value of all living things. When you strive for a symbiotic relationship with nature, the potency of your tinctures will increase and so will your overall health.

Therefore, gather as correctly as you can and be grateful for what you have gotten and go on. Something is still better than nothing.

Once you have gotten the herbs, you have done the hardest part. The next step is to go to the local liquor store. Tinctures can be made out of any liquor—vodka, brandy, wine, even everclear. I use any brand of vodka as it is almost tasteless and doesn't compete with the taste of the herbs. The Native American medicine man I go to makes Swedish bitters out of everclear diluted with distilled water. Ho!

The main reason for tincturing in alcohol is that if the biochemically active constituents are present in the plant and extracted properly then the alcohol provides a stable environment. I have seen bottles that were extracted over thirty years ago by a homeopathic doctor that still tested positive for chemical activity. These tinctures were stored in dark bottles in a cool cupboard and were found when the man died. This is important if you are tincturing to start a medicine chest of natural tonics which you may or may not need any time soon.

Now that you've gotten your herbs and your alcohol of choice, what's next? Depending on whether you think you are going to need lots of this particular extract or not, choose a jar with a tight fitting lid. I use clear Ball brand jars ranging in size from pints to large half gallon sizes. I prefer clear jars because I can see what is going on during the extraction process. So far that hasn't meant much, but it's my preference anyway. Please boil the jars or wash them in a dishwasher that has a "water heat" cycle that will take them above two hundred degrees. With all the alcohol you are going to put in the jar it's not likely anything would survive, but it's better to be careful.

Once you've gotten the jar picked out you are ready to shred the plant into it. Tear or cut with a serrated knife blade as the object here is to expose as much of the plant tissue as is possible to the osmotic action that will occur between the plant tissue and the fluid. Now stuff the bottle as full of the shredded plant as is possible. Push it down and compact it in the jar. After you have filled the jar, pour enough alcohol in to cover the plants, leaving no room for air as it will destroy the potency of your tincture. Cover tightly. As already noted, it's hard to produce high potency products to start with, so please take care along the way—"an ounce of prevention is worth a pound of cure." After going to all this trouble you want to have a tincture that is better than most store bought products and something that is just as good as the best.

The optimal time to do tincturing is at the New Moon. When you start your tincture batch at that time you have the gravitational pull of the Moon helping to move those "sedentary" biochemicals from the plant out into the liquid. Store your jars in a cool, dark place. There is a lower section of a cupboard in my kitchen that works perfectly. Storage needs to be some place relatively convenient and mindful because during the extraction cycle you will need to take the jar(s) out every day or two to turn them end over end. During this process also knock the jar against your hand. These disturbances knock air bells from the plant surface and allow fresh liquid to flow in contact with the plant tissue. The more you shake and rattle the jar(s) the more chemicals will move into the liquid.

Your extract will be ready to use in as little as six weeks, although you can extract longer if you would like. For example, I have let burdock root extract for three months. In the case of Swedish bitters, I have extracted for over a year. A friend and I have used this brew with great results on her 95-year-old grandmother who has suffered from fungus infections for many years.

Once necessity or desire determines that it is time to stop the extraction, the next step is to separate the plant from the liquid. Do not use a metal strainer, especially if it is aluminum, as the metal can leave toxic residues in the tincture. Instead, use unbleached cheesecloth or cotton fabric. This will ensure a clean extract and no nasty surprises.

Strain the extract into dark or amber colored bottles. I recycle all my glass supplement bottles. The labels come off by soaking the bottles overnight. I then sterilize them before use and make my own labels and put dates on them. Once capped, they are ready for use. I put these bottles in the refrigerator and pull them out as I run out of the bottles I have on the counter that are for my daily dosage.

Remember, though, that this is just a starting place. Be creative and learn what you need for your body. Pinpoint your body's weaknesses and keep ready the herbs that will make your immune system strong. If you do not already know, learn at what intervals during the year you are most susceptible to disease and use the plants to help you get stronger. Plant tinctures are more biochemically active and potent than infusions or decoctions. However, as with most plant products, they are gentle and work better for you if taken consistently. Combine them with your infusions for even more biochemical power.

THE SACRED TREES
by Carly Wall

Trees stand alone it seems as guardians of the Earth's atmosphere—saviors in more ways than we could have ever envisioned. As we slowly kill off the rain forests and our ozone wanes, the destruction of life as we know it is peering over our horizon. Other disasters roam freely: radiation, pesticide poisoning and plagues; there's AIDS, a resurgence of a hardy tuberculosis and killer bacterias, not to mention the cancer epidemic. It seems quite overwhelming, doesn't it? Is there nothing we can do?

"Yes, there is," states Jude Williams, herbologist and author of *Jude's Herbal Home Remedies* (Llewellyn Publications, 1992). "But only if we change our actions and our mindset."

"The trees have served us long and well. They've sheltered us by providing materials to build homes, and shading us from the hot sun.

We've burned the trees as fuel to cook and keep warm, we've used trees throughout history for food, medicines, dyes and clothing. The great trees have filtered the air we breathe, and sunk their roots into the ground to hold fast our precious topsoil; without which, we wouldn't be able to grow our food," she adds.

With that kind of history, it's no wonder ancient peoples worshiped the tree. Primitive man believed his creation originated from the "Tree of the Universe" in the myth of Yggdrasil (see Grimm's *Teutonic Mythology*). And in Genesis there is mention of the "Tree of Life" and "Tree of Knowledge." Sacred tree sculptures and paintings abound from the past and are found in Egypt, Assyria and the remote East. The Soma (or "Tree of Life" in Sanskrit) states the most ancient traditions of the Hindus: JUICE IMPARTS IMMORTALITY.

It seems that centered in every culture there is a sacred tree that imparts life and/or knowledge. Why is that so? Could there be a simple explanation behind these myths that we are just overlooking? Could the "juice" of our trees hold the keys to health? It would seem so.

Let us examine the clues. Both the Druids (who held trees as sacred) and the American Indians (who lived as one with nature) found special favor with the oak and the pine for their strength, durability, and ability to weather the elements. Both types of trees were used in healing rituals. It is evident today why these particular trees were admired by various cultures.

The leaves and bark of the oak are rich in tannin and very antiseptic, helping to stop bleeding and aiding in the healing process. In the nineteenth century, it was discovered that British tanners who inhaled the finely powdered bark of the oak as they cured hides, rarely suffered tuberculosis, as the drying effects helped keep the lungs clear.

As for the pine, the Indians chewed the needles as a source of vitamin C—something very necessary during long winters and food shortages. A mild laxative as well as a medicine used to treat malaria (quinine) can be made of the bark.

Today, more clues have been surfacing. Botanist Dr. James A. Duke, author of more than ten books on plants, has made clear that he is very upset about the decimation of the Pacific Northwest yew forests. It has been recently discovered that the bark of the yew contains a powerful chemical (taxol) that has demonstrated its role in helping to treat advanced ovarian cancer. Studies show it could even be used to cure lung and breast cancer. In the midst of these exciting discoveries, yew trees continue to be senselessly destroyed. When the yew species is wiped out, what will we turn to treat these diseases? Dr. Duke's advice is simple: all that need be done is prune the yew hedges. The doctor even sent the needles of the yew from trees at the Agricultural Department itself, over to the National Cancer Institute to be tested. These needles contained 80 parts per million of taxol, versus 100 parts per million from the average bark of a cut-down tree—a virtually negligible difference, and a difference between a continued supply of this chemical or the loss of a species of tree and certain loss of the chemical for future generations.

This isn't the only instance. Another tree has been discovered to be a powerful healer. It is called the papaw or the "Indiana banana," a tree that grows mainly over central North America. It is another cancer fighter, and a safe, natural pesticide has been created from this amazing tree. Does the future of the papaw now stand on shaky ground?

Jude Williams, a master herbalist who has worked with herbs and nature for over 25 years, states that we must understand how far-reaching our actions are and that we must learn to think before we act.

"Nature is there for our use, but we must not abuse the privilege. We are paying for our past mistakes now. But if we can open our eyes, if we make the effort to learn from nature, instead of use her, there is still a chance for us. I believe there's a cure for every disease on earth, and the secret is finding which plant or tree or shrub it is . . . and hoping that an important species which would have cured a terrible disease hasn't been destroyed already. We must act, we must act now."

Ms. Williams feels an urgency to get the word across. She wants to help teach people to return to the simpler, more natural way of life, so that ancient wisdom isn't lost, and with it, perhaps our destiny. Here is a list of a few of the most beneficial trees that we can learn to use in healing.

APPLE

The apple is a blood cleanser. It was offered by both Eve and Aphrodite and was the healing fruit of the Arabian tribes. We can use it to cleanse our body of toxins. The University of Texas Health Science Centers have found that the pectin in the apple outdid cellulose, a fiber in vegetables, in fighting certain diseases. Colon cancer is reduced, as well as cholesterol. Poisons and toxins have been found to be removed just by drinking apple juice.

CAMPHOR TREE

This tree is not native to the United States but has long been used medicinally in many cultures. The extraction of camphor from the tree has been done for over 1000 years, but only recently have the leaves alone been used for it. It is now cultivated as a cash crop and the leaves gathered three to four times yearly. There's no better treatment for sore muscles than a camphor rub. And it's good to use the fumes for respiratory ailments.

TREMBLING ASPEN

There is a long history behind this tree. Native Americans used the inner bark simmered in water as a spring tonic. The Cree made a cough syrup from the bark. The Delaware used the root as a tonic for debility. The Chippewa made a tea from the roots to stave off premature childbirth and heart remedies. In the 19th century, herbalists used tinctures made from the inner bark to treat arthritis, fever and other ailments. It was found to have properties similar to aspirin and was good as a pain reliever and a treatment for inflammations. It is economically valuable for use in reforestation because it feeds 500 different species of animals, fungi and other forms of life.

BLACK BIRCH

The black birch almost became extinct in the early 19th century when people of the Appalachian area found that selling the bark could become a source of income. The oil extracted from it is similar to wintergreen and is used in medications as a pain reliever. It is also a great disinfectant and can be used for kidney disorders and gout.

PRICKLY ASH

Called the toothache tree because the bark was chewed by the Indians to ease tooth pain, it also heals wounds and sores, and has been helpful in gonorrhea. It also improves blood circulation.

WHITE WILLOW

There are more than 300 species of the willow. The Greek physician Dioscorides was probably the first to prescribe a tea from the willow to treat pain. It was the first known aspirin. It has been used as a remedy for arthritis, colds, insomnia and many other maladies.

As history demonstrates, trees actually can be used to heal our ills. With our ever-increasing technology and daily advances in medical research, it seems pretty ironic that primitive humans were more sophisticated than we in having sense enough to regard trees as sacred.

BUSINESS, FINANCE
& LEGAL

BUSINESS, FINANCE & LEGAL

Advertising
Write advertisements when it is a favorable day for
your Sun sign and Mercury or Jupiter is conjunct,
sextile or trine the Moon. Mars and Saturn should
not aspect the Moon by square, opposition or conjunction. Begin ad campaigns when the Moon is in
Taurus, Cancer, Sagittarius or Aquarius, and well-
aspected. Advertise to give away pets when the
Moon is in Sagittarius or Pisces.

Business
As you begin any occupation, see that your lunar
cycle is favorable for that day and that the planet
ruling your occupation is marked C, T or X.

In starting a business of your own business,
see that the Moon is free of afflictions and that the
planet ruling the business is marked C, T or X.

When you take a new job, Jupiter and Venus
should be sextile, trine or conjunct the Moon.

To draw up contracts, see that the Moon is in a fixed sign and sextile, trine or conjunct Mercury.

Buying
For quality, buy during the third quarter when the Moon is in Taurus; for savings, buy in a mutable sign (Gemini, Virgo, Sagittarius, Pisces). Good aspects from Venus or the Sun (C, X, T) are desirable. If you are buying for yourself, it is good if the day is favorable to your Sun sign.

Clothes
There are several astrological guidelines for buying clothes. First, see that the Moon is sextile or trine to the Sun, and that the Moon is in the first or second quarter. When the Moon is in Taurus, buying clothes will bring pleasure and satisfaction. Do not buy clothing or jewelry or wear them for the first time when the Moon is in Scorpio or Aries. It is best to buy clothes on a favorable day for your Sun sign and when Venus or Mercury is well-aspected (T or X). Avoid aspects to Mars and Saturn.

Collections
Try to make collections on days when your Sun is well-aspected. Avoid days in which Mars or Saturn is aspected. If possible, the Moon should be in a cardinal sign (Aries, Cancer, Libra, Capricorn). It is more difficult to collect when the Moon is in Taurus and Scorpio.

Electronic Equipment
In purchasing electronics, choose a day when the Moon is in an air sign (Gemini, Libra, Aquarius) and well-aspected by Mercury and/or Uranus. A favorable Saturn aspect aids in buying sound equipment. See also *Machinery, Appliances and Tools.*

Employment (Promotions or Favors)
Choose a day when your Sun sign is favorable. Mercury should be marked C, T or X. Avoid days when Mars or Saturn is aspected.

Furniture
Follow the guidelines for *Machinery, Appliances and Tools,* but buy when the Moon is in Libra as well. Buy antique furniture when the Moon is in Cancer, Scorpio or Capricorn.

Legal Matters
In general, a good aspect between the Moon and Jupiter is the best influence for a favorable decision. If you are starting a lawsuit to gain damages, begin during the increase of the Moon (first and second quarters). If you are seeking to avoid payment, get a court date when the Moon is decreasing (third and fourth quarters). A good Moon-Sun aspect strengthens your chance of success. In divorce cases, a favorable Moon-Venus aspect may produce a more amicable settlement. The Moon in Cancer or Leo and well-aspected by the Sun brings the best results in custody cases.

Loans
The Moon in the first and second quarters favors the lender, in the third and fourth it favors the borrower. Good aspects of Jupiter and Venus to the Moon are favorable to both, as is the Moon in Leo, Sagittarius, Aquarius or Pisces.

Machinery, Appliances and Tools
Machinery, tools and other implements should be bought on days when your lunar cycle is favorable and when Mars and Uranus are trine, sextile or conjunct the Moon. Any quarter of the Moon is suitable. When buying gas or electrical appliances, the Moon should be in Aquarius. The same applies for electronic equipment.

Mailing
For best results, send mail on favorable days for your Sun sign. The Moon in Gemini is good, while Virgo, Sagittarius and Pisces are helpful, too.

Mining
Saturn rules drilling and mining. Begin this work on a day when Saturn is marked C, T or X. If mining for gold, pick a day in which the Sun is also marked C, T or X. Mercury rules quicksilver, Venus copper, Jupiter tin, Saturn lead and coal, Uranus radioactive elements, Neptune oil, and the Moon water. Choose a day when the planet ruling whatever is being drilled for is marked C, T or X.

New Ventures
Things usually get off to a better start during the increase of the Moon (first and second quarters). Impatience, anxiety or deadlocks often can be broken at the Full Moon and agreements reached.

News
Handling news is related to Uranus, Mercury and all of the air signs. When Uranus is aspected, there is always an increase in the spectacular side of the news. Collection of news is related to Saturn.

Photography, Radio, TV, Film and Video
For all these activities it is best to have Neptune, Venus and Mercury trine, sextile or conjunct the Moon. The act of taking a picture is not dependent on any particular phase of the Moon, but Neptune rules photography, while Venus is related to beauty in line, form and color.

Selling and Canvassing
Contacts for these activities will be better during a day favorable to your Sun sign. Otherwise, make strong efforts to sell when Jupiter, Mercury or Mars is trine, sextile or conjunct the Moon. Avoid days when Saturn is square or opposite the Moon.

Signing Important Papers
Sign contracts or agreements when the Moon is increasing (first and second quarters) in a fruitful sign, and on a day when Moon-Mercury aspects are operating. Avoid days when Mars, Saturn or

Neptune is square or opposite the Moon (Q or O). Don't sign anything if it is an unfavorable day.

Travel
Short journeys are ruled by Mercury, long ones by Jupiter. The Sun rules the actual journey itself. Long trips which threaten to exhaust the traveler are best begun when the Sun is well-aspected to the Moon and the date is favorable for the traveler. If traveling with other people, good aspects from Venus are desirable. For employment, aspects to Jupiter are profitable. For visiting, aspects to Mercury. To prevent accidents, avoid afflictions from Mars, Saturn, Uranus or Pluto, and again look for good aspects from the Sun.

For air travel, choose a day when the Moon is in Gemini or Libra, and well-aspected by Mercury and/or Jupiter. Avoid adverse aspects of Mars, Saturn or Uranus.

Writing
Writing for pleasure or publication is best done when the Moon is in Gemini. Mercury should be direct. Favorable aspects to Mercury, Uranus and Neptune promote ingenuity.

Writing a Will
The Moon should be in a fixed sign (Taurus, Leo, Scorpio, Aquarius) in the first or second quarter. There should be favorable aspects to Saturn, Venus and Mercury and no Pluto afflictions (Q or O).

USING THE MOON FOR BUSINESS AND LEGAL DECISIONS

by Bruce Scofield

When making a decision that pertains to business, legal, financial or real estate matters, attention to the phase of the Moon could prove a real benefit. Decisions made at the right time usually result in a neater, more efficient result than those made at less auspicious times. Fewer complications stemming from a decision means less time wasted—and time means money. Before you sign away your money or your property, read ahead and take the Moon into account.

Since ancient times, the cycle of the Moon from new to full to new has been observed and correlated with events on Earth. The earliest farmers learned that sowing seeds of above-ground plants before the Full Moon lead to a better harvest. Sailors learned to time their travels by the phases of the Moon, which everyone knows controls the tides. In many cultures, specific guidelines for activities on each day of the Moon cycle were given. Today much of this lore is lost to us or is irrelevant to our modern culture, but a few basic principles remain and continue to serve those who use them well.

In general, it is better to initiate a business deal or legal suit or make an offer as the Moon is increasing in light from New Moon to Full Moon. The object is to time your event when the Moon is on the upswing. As the Moon moves from new to full, it symbolizes the unfolding of a new cycle. Exactly what form it will take may not be known, but there is room to move and time to make adjustments. There are a few details that also should be taken into consideration as well. Do not initiate a process exactly (within 12 hours) at the time of the New Moon or the first quarter. An event started precisely at the New Moon may tend to be premature, while an event started exactly at the first quarter may be conflict-ridden.

It is best to culminate a business deal or a real estate transaction or sign legal agreements at the Full Moon. The Full Moon symbolizes the climax of the cycle that began two weeks earlier at the New Moon. In essence, the Full Moon sheds light on whatever is occurring, it symbolizes an objectivity that is not found during the previous two weeks. In practice, it may be best to avoid a business climax or agreement or other practical matter within 12 hours of the exact Full Moon. Some astrologers feel that conditions are best the day after the Full Moon when the second half of the lunar cycle has actually begun. Here, just past the exact opposition of the Sun and the Moon, the turning point which led to the agreement is seen in full perspective.

The sign that the New Moon falls in should also be taken into consideration. If the New Moon occurs in a sign that is square your Sun sign, then perhaps you should wait until the next lunar cycle to make your move. In real estate transactions, which often take months, making the first move just after a New Moon in a sign that favorably relates to your Sun sign is recommended. The culmination of the transaction should be timed for a Full Moon, even though it most likely won't be the one that occurs two weeks later. In astrology, the first step is the most important.

If one follows news events carefully, particularly bargaining sessions and political conflicts, the truth of these general rules will be apparent. Some years ago, President Carter negotiated with the leaders of Egypt and Israel in search of a peace treaty. Both the agreement and the signing of the Camp David Accords occurred on a Full Moon. Frequently, decisions made by world leaders are announced at the Full Moon. The astute observer will learn much by noting when public decisions are made, mindful of their ultimate outcomes.

STARTING A NEW BUSINESS OR BUSINESS VENTURE

When starting a new business or any type of new venture, check to make sure that the Moon is in the first or second quarter. You should also check the aspects of the Moon to the type of venture with which you are becoming involved. Look for positive aspects to the planet that rules the activity and avoid any dates marked Q or O, as you are sure to have trouble with the client or deal.

Activities and Occupations Ruled by the Sun
Advertising, executive positions, acting, finance, government, jewelry, law and public relations.

Activities and Occupations Ruled by Mercury
Accounting, brokerage, clerical, disc jockey, doctor, editor, inspector, librarian, linguist, medical technician, scientist, teaching, writing, publishing, communication and mass media.

Activities and Occupations Ruled by Venus
Architect, art and artisit, beautician, dance, design, fashion and marketing, music, poetry and chiropractor.

Activities and Occupations Ruled by Mars
Barber, butcher, carpenter, chemist, construction, dentist, metal worker, surgeon and the military.

Activities and Occupations Ruled by Jupiter
Counseling, horse training, judge, lawyer, legislator, minister, pharmacist, psychologist, public analyst, social clubs, research and self-improvement.

Activities and Occupations Ruled by Saturn
Agronomy, math, mining, plumbing, real estate, repairperson, printer, paper making and dealing with older people.

Activities and Occupations Ruled by Uranus
Aeronautics, broadcasting, electrician, inventing, lecturing, radiology and computers.

Activities and Occupations Ruled by Neptune
Photography, investigator, institutions, shipping, pets, movies, wine merchant, health foods, resorts, travel by water and welfare.

Activities and Occupations Ruled by Pluto
Acrobatics, athletic manager, atomic energy, research, speculation, sports, stockbroker and any purely personal endeavors.

FARM & GARDEN

GARDENING BY THE MOON

Today, we still find those who reject the notion of Moon gardening—the usual non-believer is not the scientist, but the city dweller who has never had any real contact with nature and no conscious experience of natural rhythms.

Cato wrote that "fig, apple, olive, and pear trees, as well as vines, should be planted in the dark of the Moon in the afternoon, when there is no south wind blowing."

Camille Flammarian, the French astronomer, also testifies to Moon planting. "Cucumbers increase at full Moon, as well as radishes, turnips, leeks, lilies, horseradish, saffron; but onions, on the contrary, are much larger and better nourished during the decline and old age of the Moon than at its increase; than during its youth and fullness, which is the reason the Egyptians abstained from onions, on account of their antipathy to the Moon. Herbs gathered while the Moon increases are of great efficiency. If the vines are trimmed at night when the Moon is in the sign of the Lion, Sagittarius, the Scorpion, or the Bull, it will save them from field-rats, moles, snails, flies, and other animals."

Dr. Clark Timmins is one of the few modern scientists to have actually conducted tests in Moon planting. The following is a summary of some of his experiments:

- Beets: When sown with the Moon in Scorpio, the germination rate was 71%; when sown in Sagittarius, the germination rate was 58%.
- Scotch Marigold: When sown with the Moon in Cancer, the germination rate was 90%; when sown in Leo, the germination rate was 32%.
- Carrots: When sown with the Moon in Scorpio, the germination rate was 64%; when sown in Sagittarius, the germination rate was 47%.
- Tomatoes: When sown with the Moon in Cancer, the germination rate was 90%; when sown in Leo, the germination rate was 58%.

Two things should be emphasized. First, remember that this is only a summary of the results of the experiments; the experiments themselves were conducted in a scientific manner to eliminate any variation in soil, temperature, moisture, etc., so that only the Moon's sign used in planting varied. Second, note that these astonishing results were obtained without regard to the phase of the Moon—the other factor we utilize in Moon planting, and which presumably would have increased the differential in germination rates.

Further experiments by Dr. Timmins involved transplanting Cancer- and Leo-planted tomato seedlings while the Moon was increasing and in Cancer. The result was 100% survival. When the transplanting was done with the Moon decreasing and in Sagittarius, there was 0% survival.

The results of Dr. Timmins' tests show that the Cancer-planted tomatoes had first blossoms 12 days earlier than those planted under Leo; that the Cancer-planted tomatoes had an average height of 20 inches at the same age when the Leo plants were only 15 inches high; the first ripe tomatoes were gathered from the Cancer plantings 11 days ahead of the Leo plantings; and finally, a count of the hanging fruit and comparison of size and weight shows an advantage to the Cancer plants over the Leo plants of 45%.

Dr. Timmins also observed that there have been similar tests that did not indicate results favorable to the Moon planting theory. As a scientist, he asked why one set of experiments indicated a positive verification of Moon planting, and others did not. He checked these other tests and found that the experimenters had not followed the *geocentric* system for determining the Moon sign positions, but the *heliocentric*. When the times used in these other tests were converted to the geocentric system, the dates chosen often were found to be in barren rather than fertile signs. Without going into the technical explanations, it is sufficient to point out that geocentric and heliocentric positions often vary by as much as *four days*. This is a large enough differential to place the Moon in Cancer, for example, in the heliocentric system, and at the same time in Leo by the geocentric system.

Most almanacs and calendars show the Moon's signs heliocentrically—and thus incorrectly for Moon planting—while the *Moon Sign Book* is calculated correctly for planting purposes, using the geocentric system.

Some readers are also confused because the *Moon Sign Book* talks of first, second, third and fourth quarters, while some almanacs refer to these same divisions as New Moon, first quarter, Full Moon and last quarter. Thus, the almanac says first quarter when the *Moon Sign Book* says second quarter. (Refer to the introductory material in this book for more information.)

There is nothing complicated about using astrology in agriculture and horticulture in order to increase both pleasure and profit, but there is one very important rule that is often neglected—*use common sense!* Of course this is one rule that should be remembered in every activity we undertake, but in the case of gardening and farming by the Moon it is not always possible to use the best dates for planting or harvesting, and we must select the next best and just try to do the best we can.

This brings up the matter of the other factors to consider in your gardening work. The dates we give you as best for a certain activity apply to the entire country (with slight time correction), but in your section of the country you may be buried under three feet of snow on a date we say is a good day to plant your flowers. So we have factors of weather, season, temperature and moisture variations, soil conditions, your own available time and opportunity, and so forth. And don't forget the matter of the "green thumb." Some astrologers like to think it is all a matter of science, but gardening is also an art. In art you develop an instinctive identification with your work so that you actually influence it with your feelings and visualization of what you want to accomplish.

The *Moon Sign Book* gives you the place of the Moon for every day of the year so that you can select the best times once you have become familiar with the rules and practices of lunar agriculture. We try to give you the most specific, easy-to-follow directions so that you can get right down to work.

We give you the best dates for planting, and also for various related activities, including cultivation, fertilizing, harvesting, irrigation, and getting rid of weeds and pests. But we cannot just tell you when it's good to plant at the particular time. Many of these rules were learned by observation and experience, but as our body of experience grew, we could see various patterns emerging which allow us to make judgments about new things. Then we test the new possible applications and learn still more. That's what you should do, too. After you have worked with lunar agriculture for a while and have gained a working background of knowledge, you will probably begin to try new things—and we hope you will share your experiments and findings with us. That's how the science grows.

Here's an example of what we mean. Years ago, Llewellyn George suggested that we try to combine our bits of knowledge about what to expect in planting under each of the Moon signs in order to benefit with several such lunar factors in one plant. From this came our rule for developing "thoroughbred seed." To develop thoroughbred seed, save the seed for three successive years from plants grown by the correct Moon sign and phase. You can plant in the first quarter phase and in the sign of Cancer for fruitfulness; the second year, plant seeds from the first year plants in Libra for beauty; and in the third year, plant the seeds from the second year plants in Taurus to produce hardiness. In a similar manner you can combine the fruitfulness of Cancer, the good root growth of Pisces, and the sturdiness and good vine growth of Scorpio. And don't forget the characteristics of Capricorn, hardy like Taurus, but drier and perhaps more resistant to drought and disease.

Unlike common almanacs, we consider both the Moon's phase and the Moon's sign in making our calculations for the proper timing of our work within nature's rhythm. It is perhaps a little easier to understand this if we remind you that we are all living in the center of a vast electromagnetic field that is the Earth and its environment in space. Everything that occurs within this electromagnetic field has an effect on everything else within the same field, but since we are living on the Earth we must relate these happenings and effects to our own health and happiness. The Moon and the Sun are the most important and dynamic of the rhythmically changing factors affecting the life of the Earth, and it is their relative positions to the Earth that we project for each day of the coming year.

Many people claim that not only do they achieve larger crops gardening by the Moon, but that their fruits and vegetables are much tastier and more healthful.

A number of organic gardeners have also become lunar gardeners using the natural growing methods within the natural rhythm of life forces that we experience through the relative movements of the Sun and Moon.

We provide a few basic rules and then give you month-by-month and day-by-day the guidance for your farming and gardening work. You will be able to choose the best dates to meet your own needs and opportunities.

PLANTING BY THE MOON'S PHASES

During the increasing light (from New Moon to Full Moon), plant annuals that produce their yield above the ground. (An annual is a plant that completes its entire life cycle within one growing season and has to be seeded anew each year.)

During the decreasing light (from Full Moon to New Moon), plant biennials, perennials, bulb and root plants. (Biennials include crops that are planted one season to winter over and produce crops the next, such as winter wheat. Perennials and bulb and root plants include all plants that grow from the same root year after year.)

A simple, though less accurate rule is to plant crops that produce above the ground during the increase of the Moon, and to plant crops that produce below the ground during the decrease of the Moon. This is the source of the old adage, "Plant potatoes during the dark of the Moon."

Llewellyn George went a step further and divided the lunar month into quarters. He called the first two from New Moon to Full Moon the first and second quarters, and the last two from Full Moon to New Moon the third and fourth quarters. Using these divisions, we can increase our accuracy in timing our efforts to coincide with natural forces.

First Quarter (Increasing)
Plant annuals producing their yield above the ground which are generally of the leafy kind that produce their seed outside the fruit. Examples are asparagus, broccoli, Brussels sprouts, cabbage, cauliflower, celery, cress, endive, kohlrabi, lettuce, parsley, spinach, etc. Cucumbers are an exception, as they do best in the first quarter rather than the second, even though the seeds are inside the fruit. Also in the first quarter, plant cereals and grains.

Second Quarter (Increasing)
Plant annuals producing their yield above the ground which are generally of the viney kind that produce their seed inside the fruit. Examples include beans, eggplant, melons, peas, peppers,

pumpkins, squash, tomatoes, etc. These are not hard and fast divisions. If you can't plant during the first quarter, plant during the second, and vice versa. There are many plants that seem to do equally well planted in either quarter, such as watermelon, garlic, hay, and the cereals and grains.

Third Quarter (Decreasing)
Plant biennials, perennials, and bulb and root plants. Also plant trees, shrubs, berries, beets, carrots, onions, parsnips, peanuts, potatoes, radishes, rhubarb, rutabagas, strawberries, turnips, winter wheat, grapes, etc.

Fourth Quarter (Decreasing)
This is the best time to cultivate, turn sod, pull weeds and destroy pests of all kinds, especially when the Moon is in the barren signs of Aries, Leo, Virgo, Gemini, Aquarius and Sagittarius.

PLANTING BY THE MOON'S SIGNS

The phases and signs of the Moon are combined in the dates we give you for various activities. However, we want to give you some general rules in relation to each of the signs so that you can make various individual decisions as the occasion may require. In each of the 12 zodiacal signs, the Moon reflects the special characteristics associated with the sign, and your activities should be coordinated to benefit from this natural cycle.

Moon in Aries
Barren and dry, fiery and masculine. Used for destroying noxious growths, weeds, pests, etc. and for cultivating.

Moon in Taurus
Productive and moist, earthy and feminine. Used for planting many crops, more particularly potatoes and root crops, and when hardiness is important. Also used for lettuce, cabbage, and similar leafy vegetables.

Moon in Gemini
Barren and dry, airy and masculine. Used for destroying noxious growths, weeds and pests, and for cultivation.

Moon in Cancer
Very fruitful and moist, watery and feminine. This is the most productive sign, used extensively for planting and irrigation.

Moon in Leo
Barren and dry, fiery and masculine. This is the most barren sign, used only for killing weeds and other noxious growths, and for cultivation.

Moon in Virgo
Barren and moist, earthy and feminine. Considered good for cultivation and destroying weeds and pests.

Moon in Libra
Semi-fruitful and moist, airy and masculine. Used for planting many crops and producing good pulp growth and roots. A very good sign for flowers and vines. Also used for seeding hay, corn fodder, etc.

Moon in Scorpio
Very fruitful and moist, watery and feminine. Very nearly as productive as Cancer, used for the same purposes. Especially good for vine growth and sturdiness.

Moon in Sagittarius
Barren and dry, fiery and masculine. Used for planting onions, seeding hay and for cultivation.

Moon in Capricorn
Productive and dry, earthy and feminine. Used for planting potatoes, tubers, etc.

Moon in Aquarius
Barren and dry, airy and masculine. Used for cultivation, and destroying noxious growths, weeds and pests.

Moon in Pisces
Very fruitful and moist, watery and feminine. Used along with Cancer and Scorpio, especially good for root growth.

GARDENING DATES

Jan. 1, 3:15 PM– Jan. 3, 6:31 PM Virgo, 3rd qtr.	Cultivate, especially medicinal plants. Destroy weeds and pests. Trim to retard growth.
Jan. 5, 9:29 PM– Jan. 8, 12:34 AM Scorpio, 4th qtr.	Plant biennials, perennials, bulbs and roots. Irrigate. Fertilize (organic). Prune.
Jan. 8, 12:34 AM– Jan. 10, 4:16 AM Sagit., 4th qtr.	Cultivate. Destroy weeds and pests. Harvest fruits and root crops. Trim to retard growth.
Jan. 10, 4:16 AM– Jan. 11, 6:10 PM Capri., 4th qtr.	Plant potatoes and tubers. Prune.
Jan. 11, 6:10 PM– Jan. 12, 9:25 AM Capri., 1st qtr.	Graft or bud plants. Trim to increase growth.

Jan. 14, 5:03 PM- Jan. 17, 3:42 AM Pisces, 1st qtr.	Plant annuals, grains. Irrigate. Fertilize (chemical). Trim to increase growth. Graft or bud plants.
Jan. 19, 3:27 PM- Jan. 19, 4:22 PM Taurus, 1st qtr.	Plant annuals for hardiness. Trim to increase growth.
Jan. 19, 4:22 PM- Jan. 22, 4:35 AM Taurus, 2nd qtr.	Plant annuals for hardiness. Trim to increase growth.
Jan. 24, 1:56 PM- Jan. 26, 7:39 AM Cancer, 2nd qtr.	Plant annuals, grains. Irrigate. Fertilize (chemical). Trim to increase growth. Graft or bud plants.
Jan. 27, 8:23 AM Leo, Full Moon	Gather mushrooms. Harvest root crops for seed.
Jan. 27, 8:23 PM- Jan. 28, 10:39 PM Leo, 3rd qtr.	Cultivate. Destroy weeds and pests. Harvest fruits and root crops. Trim to retard growth.
Jan. 28, 10:39 PM- Jan. 31, 12:34 AM Virgo, 3rd qtr.	Cultivate, especially medicinal plants. Destroy weeds and pests. Trim to retard growth.
Feb. 2, 2:49 AM- Feb. 2, 3:06 AM Scorpio, 3rd qtr.	Plant biennials, perennials, bulbs and roots. Irrigate. Fertilize (organic). Prune.

Feb. 2, 3:06 AM-
Feb. 4, 6:14 AM
Scorpio, 4th qtr.

Plant biennials, perennials, bulbs and roots. Irrigate. Fertilize (organic). Prune.

Feb. 4, 6:14 AM-
Feb. 6, 11:02 AM
Sagit., 4th qtr.

Cultivate. Destroy weeds and pests. Harvest fruits and root crops. Trim to retard growth.

Feb. 6, 11:02 AM-
Feb. 8, 5:17 PM
Capri., 4th qtr.

Plant potatoes and tubers. Prune.

Feb. 8, 5:17 PM-
Feb. 10, 9:30 AM
Aquar., 4th qtr.

Cultivate. Destroy weeds and pests. Harvest fruits and root crops. Trim to retard growth.

Feb. 11, 1:23 AM-
Feb. 13, 11:50 AM
Pisces, 1st qtr.

Plant annuals, grains. Irrigate. Fertilize (chemical). Trim to increase growth. Graft or bud plants.

Feb. 16, 12:20 AM-
Feb. 18, 12:48 PM
Taurus, 1st qtr.

Plant annuals for hardiness. Trim to increase growth.

Feb. 20, 11:28 PM-
Feb. 23, 5:48 AM
Cancer, 2nd qtr.

Plant annuals, grains. Irrigate. Fertilize (chemical). Trim to increase growth. Graft or bud plants.

Feb. 25, 8:27 AM- Feb. 25, 8:15 PM Virgo, 2nd qtr.	Plant annuals for fragrance and beauty. Trim to increase growth.
Feb. 25, 8:15 PM Virgo, Full Moon	Gather mushrooms. Harvest root crops for seed.
Feb. 25, 8:15 PM- Feb. 27, 9:06 AM Virgo, 3rd qtr.	Cultivate, especially medicinal plants. Destroy weeds and pests. Trim to retard growth.
Mar. 1, 9:43 AM- Mar. 3, 11:54 AM Scorpio, 3rd qtr.	Plant biennials, perennials, bulbs and roots. Irrigate. Fertilize (organic). Prune.
Mar. 3, 11:54 AM- Mar. 4, 11:54 AM Sagit., 3rd qtr.	Cultivate. Destroy weeds and pests. Harvest fruits and root crops. Trim to retard growth.
Mar. 4, 11:54 AM- Mar. 5, 4:25 PM Sagit., 4th qtr.	Cultivate. Destroy weeds and pests. Harvest fruits and root crops. Trim to retard growth.
Mar. 5, 4:25 PM- Mar. 7, 11:15 PM Capri., 4th qtr.	Plant potatoes and tubers. Prune.
Mar. 7, 11:15 PM- Mar. 10, 8:10 AM Aquar., 4th qtr.	Cultivate. Destroy weeds and pests. Harvest fruits and root crops. Trim to retard growth.

Mar. 10, 8:10 AM- Mar. 12, 2:05 AM Pisces, 4th qtr.	Plant biennials, perennials, bulbs and roots. Irrigate. Fertilize (organic). Prune.
Mar. 12, 2:05 AM- Mar. 12, 6:59 PM Aries, 1st qtr.	Plant annuals, grains. Irrigate. Fertilize (chemical). Trim to increase growth. Graft or bud plants.
Mar. 15, 7:28 AM- Mar. 17, 8:29 PM Taurus, 1st qtr.	Plant annuals for hardiness. Trim to increase growth.
Mar. 20, 7:14 AM- Mar. 20, 7:54 AM Cancer, 1st qtr.	Plant annuals, grains. Irrigate. Fertilize (chemical). Trim to increase growth. Graft or bud plants.
Mar. 20, 7:54 AM- Mar. 22, 3:39 PM Cancer, 2nd qtr.	Plant annuals, grains. Irrigate. Fertilize (chemical). Trim to increase growth. Graft or bud plants.
Mar. 24, 7:14 PM- Mar. 26, 7:47 PM Virgo, 2nd qtr.	Plant annuals for fragrance and beauty. Trim to increase growth.
Mar. 26, 7:47 PM- Mar. 27, 6:10 AM Libra, 2nd qtr.	Plant annuals for fragrance and beauty. Trim to increase growth.

Mar. 27, 6:10 AM Libra, Full Moon	Gather mushrooms. Harvest root crops for seed.
Mar. 28, 7:15 PM– Mar. 30, 7:42 PM Scorpio, 3rd qtr.	Plant biennials, perennials, bulbs and roots. Irrigate. Fertilize (organic). Prune.
Mar. 30, 7:42 PM– Apr. 1, 10:38 PM Sagit., 3rd qtr.	Cultivate. Destroy weeds and pests. Harvest fruits and root crops. Trim to retard growth.
Apr. 1, 10:38 PM– Apr. 2, 9:56 PM Capri., 3rd qtr.	Plant potatoes and tubers. Prune.
Apr. 2, 9:56 PM– Apr. 4, 4:46 AM Capri., 4th qtr.	Plant potatoes and tubers. Prune.
Apr. 4, 4:46 AM– Apr. 6, 1:51 PM Aquar., 4th qtr.	Cultivate. Destroy weeds and pests. Harvest fruits and root crops. Trim to retard growth.
Apr. 6, 1:51 PM– Apr. 9, 1:09 AM Pisces, 4th qtr.	Plant biennials, perennials, bulbs and roots. Irrigate. Fertilize (organic). Prune.
Apr. 9, 1:09 AM– Apr. 10, 7:17 PM Aries, 4th qtr.	Cultivate. Destroy weeds and pests. Harvest fruits and root crops. Trim to retard growth.

Apr. 11, 1:47 PM- Apr. 14, 2:48 AM Taurus, 1st qtr.	Plant annuals for hardiness. Trim to increase growth.
Apr. 16, 2:41 PM- Apr. 18, 9:35 PM Cancer, 1st qtr.	Plant annuals, grains. Irrigate. Fertilize (chemical). Trim to increase growth. Graft or bud plants.
Apr. 21, 4:59 AM- Apr. 23, 6:41 AM Virgo, 2nd qtr.	Plant annuals for fragrance and beauty. Trim to increase growth.
Apr. 23, 6:41 AM- Apr. 25, 6:19 AM Libra, 2nd qtr.	Plant annuals for fragrance and beauty. Trim to increase growth.
Apr. 25, 6:19 AM- Apr. 25, 2:46 PM Scorpio, 2nd qtr.	Plant annuals, grains. Irrigate. Fertilize (chemical). Trim to increase growth. Graft or bud plants.
Apr. 25, 2:46 PM Scorpio, Full Moon	Gather mushrooms. Harvest root crops for seed.
Apr. 25, 2:46 PM- Apr. 27, 5:49 AM Scorpio, 3rd qtr.	Plant biennials, perennials, bulbs and roots. Irrigate. Fertilize (organic). Prune.
Apr. 27, 5:49 AM- Apr. 28, 7.05 AM Sagit., 3rd qtr.	Cultivate. Destroy weeds and pests. Harvest fruits and root crops. Trim to retard growth.

Apr. 28, 7:05 AM– May 1, 11:35 AM Capri., 3rd qtr.	Plant potatoes and tubers. Prune.
May 1, 11:35 AM– May 2, 9:32 AM Aquar., 3rd qtr.	Cultivate. Destroy weeds and pests. Harvest fruits and root crops. Trim to retard growth.
May 2, 9:32 AM– May 3, 7:47 PM Aquar., 4th qtr.	Cultivate. Destroy weeds and pests. Harvest fruits and root crops. Trim to retard growth.
May 3, 7:47 PM– May 6, 7:01 AM Pisces, 4th qtr.	Plant biennials, perennials, bulbs and roots. Irrigate. Fertilize (organic). Prune.
May 6, 7:01 AM– May 8, 7:50 PM Aries, 4th qtr.	Cultivate. Destroy weeds and pests. Harvest fruits and root crops. Trim to retard growth.
May 8, 7:50 PM– May 10, 12:07 PM Taurus, 4th qtr.	Plant potatoes and tubers. Prune.
May 10, 12:07 PM– May 11, 8:44 AM Taurus, 1st qtr.	Plant annuals for hardiness. Trim to increase growth.
May 13, 8:28 PM– May 16, 5:59 AM Cancer, 1st qtr.	Plant annuals, grains. Irrigate. Fertilize (chemical). Trim to increase growth. Graft or bud plants.

May 18, 7:51 AM– May 18, 12:32 PM Virgo, 1st qtr.	Plant annuals for fragrance and beauty. Trim to increase growth.
May 18, 12:32 PM– May 20, 3:55 PM Virgo, 2nd qtr.	Plant annuals for fragrance and beauty. Trim to increase growth.
May 20, 3:55 PM– May 22, 4:51 PM Libra, 2nd qtr.	Plant annuals for fragrance and beauty. Trim to increase growth.
May 22, 4:51 PM– May 24, 4:43 PM Scorpio, 2nd qtr.	Plant annuals, grains. Irrigate. Fertilize (chemical). Trim to increase growth. Graft or bud plants.
May 24, 10:39 PM Sagit., Full Moon	Gather mushrooms. Harvest root crops for seed.
May 24, 10:39 PM– May 26, 5:17 PM Sagit., 3rd qtr.	Cultivate. Destroy weeds and pests. Harvest fruits and root crops. Trim to retard growth.
May 26, 5:17 PM– May 28, 8:19 PM Capri., 3rd qtr.	Plant potatoes and tubers. Prune.
May 28, 8:19 PM– May 31, 3:03 AM Aquar., 3rd qtr.	Cultivate. Destroy weeds and pests. Harvest fruits and root crops. Trim to retard growth.

May 31, 3:03 AM- May 31, 11:02 PM Pisces, 3rd qtr.	Plant biennials, perennials, bulbs and roots. Irrigate. Fertilize (organic). Prune.
May 31, 11:02 PM- Jun. 2, 1:31 PM Pisces, 4th qtr.	Plant biennials, perennials, bulbs and roots. Irrigate. Fertilize (organic). Prune.
Jun. 2, 1:31 PM- Jun. 5, 2:14 AM Aries, 4th qtr.	Cultivate. Destroy weeds and pests. Harvest fruits and root crops. Trim to retard growth.
Jun. 5, 2:14 AM- Jun. 7, 3:04 PM Taurus, 4th qtr.	Plant potatoes and tubers. Prune.
Jun. 7, 3:04 PM- Jun. 8, 3:27 AM Gemini, 4th qtr.	Cultivate. Destroy weeds and pests. Harvest fruits and root crops. Trim to retard growth.
Jun. 10, 2:23 AM- Jun. 12, 11:29 AM Cancer, 1st qtr.	Plant annuals, grains. Irrigate. Fertilize (chemical). Trim to increase growth. Graft or bud plants.
Jun. 14, 6:17 PM- Jun. 16, 2:57 PM Virgo, 1st qtr.	Plant annuals for fragrance and beauty. Trim to increase growth.
Jun. 16, 2:57 PM- Jun. 16, 10:48 PM Libra, 1st qtr.	Plant annuals for fragrance and beauty. Trim to increase growth.

Jun. 16, 10:48 PM- Jun. 19, 1:20 AM Libra, 2nd qtr.	Plant annuals for fragrance and beauty. Trim to increase growth.
Jun. 19, 1:20 AM- Jun. 21, 2:32 AM Scorpio, 2nd qtr.	Plant annuals, grains. Irrigate. Fertilize (chemical). Trim to increase growth. Graft or bud plants.
Jun. 23, 3:37 AM- Jun. 23, 6:33 AM Capri., 2nd qtr.	Graft or bud plants. Trim to increase growth.
Jun. 23, 6:33 AM Capri., Full Moon	Gather mushrooms. Harvest root crops for seed.
Jun. 23, 6:33 AM- Jun. 25, 6:10 AM Capri., 3rd qtr.	Plant potatoes and tubers. Prune.
Jun. 25, 6:10 AM- Jun. 27, 11:45 AM Aquar., 3rd qtr.	Cultivate. Destroy weeds and pests. Harvest fruits and root crops. Trim to retard growth.
Jun. 27, 11:45 AM- Jun. 29, 9:07 PM Pisces, 3rd qtr.	Plant biennials, perennials, bulbs and roots. Irrigate. Fertilize (organic). Prune.
Jun. 29, 9:07 PM- Jun. 30, 2:31 PM Aries, 3rd qtr.	Cultivate. Destroy weeds and pests. Harvest fruits and root crops. Trim to retard growth.

Jun. 30, 2:31 PM- Jul. 2, 9:24 AM Aries, 4th qtr.	Cultivate. Destroy weeds and pests. Harvest fruits and root crops. Trim to retard growth.
Jul. 2, 9:24 AM- Jul. 4, 10:13 PM Taurus, 4th qtr.	Plant potatoes and tubers. Prune.
Jul. 4, 10:13 PM- Jul. 7, 9:18 AM Gemini, 4th qtr.	Cultivate. Destroy weeds and pests. Harvest fruits and root crops. Trim to retard growth.
Jul. 7, 9:18 AM- Jul. 8, 4:38 PM Cancer, 4th qtr.	Plant biennials, perennials, bulbs and roots. Irrigate. Fertilize (organic). Prune.
Jul. 8, 4:38 PM- Jul. 9, 5:43 PM Cancer, 1st qtr.	Plant annuals, grains. Irrigate. Fertilize (chemical). Trim to increase growth. Graft or bud plants.
Jul. 11, 11:48 PM- Jul. 14, 4:15 AM Virgo, 1st qtr.	Plant annuals for fragrance and beauty. Trim to increase growth.
Jul. 14, 4:15 AM- Jul. 15, 8:12 PM Libra, 1st qtr.	Plant annuals for fragrance and beauty. Trim to increase growth.

Jul. 15, 8:12 PM– Jul. 16, 7:35 AM Libra, 2nd qtr.	Plant annuals, grains. Irrigate. Fertilize (chemical). Trim to increase growth. Graft or bud plants.
Jul. 16, 7:35 AM– Jul. 18, 10:09 AM Scorpio, 2nd qtr.	Plant annuals, grains. Irrigate. Fertilize (chemical). Trim to increase growth. Graft or bud plants.
Jul. 20, 12:31 PM– Jul. 22, 3:16 PM Capri., 2nd qtr.	Graft or bud plants. Trim to increase growth.
Jul. 22, 3:16 PM Capri., Full Moon	Gather mushrooms. Harvest root crops for seed.
Jul. 22, 3:39 PM– Jul. 24, 8:57 PM Aquar., 3rd qtr.	Cultivate. Destroy weeds and pests. Harvest fruits and root crops. Trim to retard growth.
Jul. 24, 8:57 PM– Jul. 27, 5:31 AM Pisces, 3rd qtr.	Plant biennials, perennials, bulbs and roots. Irrigate. Fertilize (organic). Prune.
Jul. 27, 5:31 AM– Jul. 29, 5:13 PM Aries, 3rd qtr.	Cultivate. Destroy weeds and pests. Harvest fruits and root crops. Trim to retard growth.
Jul. 29, 5:13 PM– Jul. 30, 7:40 AM Taurus, 3rd qtr.	Plant potatoes and tubers. Prune.

Jul. 30, 7:40 AM– Aug. 1, 6:05 AM Taurus, 4th qtr.	Plant potatoes and tubers. Prune.
Aug. 1, 6:05 AM– Aug. 3, 5:22 PM Gemini, 4th qtr.	Cultivate. Destroy weeds and pests. Harvest fruits and root crops. Trim to retard growth.
Aug. 3, 5:22 PM– Aug. 6, 1:31 AM Cancer, 4th qtr.	Plant biennials, perennials, bulbs and roots. Irrigate. Fertilize (organic). Prune.
Aug. 6, 1:31 AM– Aug. 6, 3:45 AM Leo, 4th qtr.	Cultivate. Destroy weeds and pests. Harvest fruits and root crops. Trim to retard growth.
Aug. 8, 6:42 AM– Aug. 10, 10:07 AM Virgo, 1st qtr.	Plant annuals for fragrance and beauty. Trim to increase growth.
Aug. 10, 10:07 AM– Aug. 12, 12:56 PM Libra, 1st qtr.	Plant annuals for fragrance and beauty. Trim to increase growth.
Aug. 12, 12:56 PM– Aug. 14, 12:58 AM Scorpio, 1st qtr.	Plant annuals, grains. Irrigate. Fertilize (chemical). Trim to increase growth. Graft or bud plants.

Aug. 14, 12:58 AM- Aug. 14, 3:54 PM Scorpio, 2nd qtr.	Plant annuals, grains. Irrigate. Fertilize (chemical). Trim to increase growth. Graft or bud plants.
Aug. 16, 7:18 PM- Aug. 18, 11:34 PM Capri., 2nd qtr.	Graft or bud plants. Trim to increase growth.
Aug. 21, 1:47 AM Aquar., Full Moon	Gather mushrooms. Harvest root crops for seed.
Aug. 21, 1:47 AM- Aug. 21, 5:28 AM Aquar., 3rd qtr.	Cultivate. Destroy weeds and pests. Harvest fruits and root crops. Trim to retard growth.
Aug. 21, 5:28 AM- Aug. 23, 1:55 PM Pisces, 3rd qtr.	Plant biennials, perennials, bulbs and roots. Irrigate. Fertilize (organic). Prune.
Aug. 23, 1:55 PM- Aug. 26, 1:13 AM Aries, 3rd qtr.	Cultivate. Destroy weeds and pests. Harvest fruits and root crops. Trim to retard growth.
Aug. 26, 1:13 AM- Aug. 28, 2:07 PM Taurus, 3rd qtr.	Plant potatoes and tubers. Prune.
Aug. 28, 2:07 PM- Aug. 29, 1:40 AM Gemini, 3rd qtr.	Cultivate. Destroy weeds and pests. Harvest fruits and root crops. Trim to retard growth.

Aug. 29, 1:40 AM– Aug. 31, 1:59 AM Gemini, 4th qtr.	Cultivate. Destroy weeds and pests. Harvest fruits and root crops. Trim to retard growth.
Aug. 31, 1:59 AM– Sep. 2, 10:37 AM Cancer, 4th qtr.	Plant biennials, perennials, bulbs and roots. Irrigate. Fertilize (organic). Prune.
Sep. 2, 10:37 AM– Sep. 4, 3:34 PM Leo, 4th qtr.	Cultivate. Destroy weeds and pests. Harvest fruits and root crops. Trim to retard growth.
Sep. 4, 3:34 PM– Sep. 5, 1:33 PM Virgo, 4th qtr.	Cultivate, especially medicinal plants. Destroy weeds and pests. Trim to retard growth.
Sep. 5, 1:33 PM– Sep. 6, 5:57 PM Virgo, 1st qtr.	Plant annuals for fragrance and beauty. Trim to increase growth.
Sep. 6, 5:57 PM– Sep. 8, 7:26 PM Libra, 1st qtr.	Plant annuals for fragrance and beauty. Trim to increase growth.
Sep. 8, 7:26 PM– Sep. 10, 9:26 PM Scorpio, 1st qtr.	Plant annuals, grains. Irrigate. Fertilize (chemical). Trim to increase growth. Graft or bud plants.
Sep. 13, 12:45 AM– Sep. 14, 5:42 AM Capri., 2nd qtr.	Graft or bud plants. Trim to increase growth.

Sep. 17, 12:31 PM- Sep. 19, 3:00 PM Pisces, 2nd qtr.	Plant annuals, grains. Irrigate. Fertilize (chemical). Trim to increase growth. Graft or bud plants.
Sep. 19, 3:00 PM Pisces, Full Moon	Gather mushrooms. Harvest root crops for seed.
Sep. 19, 9:29 PM- Sep. 22, 8:47 AM Aries, 3rd qtr.	Cultivate. Destroy weeds and pests. Harvest fruits and root crops. Trim to retard growth.
Sep. 22, 8:47 AM- Sep. 24, 9:41 PM Taurus, 3rd qtr.	Plant potatoes and tubers. Prune.
Sep. 24, 9:41 PM- Sep. 27, 10:12 AM Gemini, 3rd qtr.	Cultivate. Destroy weeds and pests. Harvest fruits and root crops. Trim to retard growth.
Sep. 27, 10:12 AM- Sep. 27, 7:24 PM Cancer, 3rd qtr.	Plant biennials, perennials, bulbs and roots. Irrigate. Fertilize (organic). Prune.
Sep. 27, 7:24 PM- Sep. 29, 7:56 PM Cancer, 4th qtr.	Plant biennials, perennials, bulbs and roots. Irrigate. Fertilize (organic). Prune.
Sep. 29, 7:56 PM- Oct. 2, 1:40 AM Leo, 4th qtr.	Cultivate. Destroy weeds and pests. Harvest fruits and root crops. Trim to retard growth.

Oct. 2, 1:40 AM– Oct. 4, 3:57 AM Virgo, 4th qtr.	Cultivate, especially medicinal plants. Destroy weeds and pests. Trim to retard growth.
Oct. 4, 10:56 PM– Oct. 6, 4:22 AM Libra, 1st qtr.	Plant annuals for fragrance and beauty. Trim to increase growth.
Oct. 6, 4:22 AM– Oct. 8, 4:47 AM Scorpio, 1st qtr.	Plant annuals, grains. Irrigate. Fertilize (chemical). Trim to increase growth. Graft or bud plants.
Oct. 10, 6:44 AM– Oct. 11, 2:17 PM Capri., 1st qtr.	Graft or bud plants. Trim to increase growth.
Oct. 11, 2:17 PM– Oct. 12, 11:09 AM Capri., 2nd qtr.	Graft or bud plants. Trim to increase growth.
Oct. 14, 6:18 PM– Oct. 17, 3:56 AM Pisces, 2nd qtr.	Plant annuals, grains. Irrigate. Fertilize (chemical). Trim to increase growth. Graft or bud plants.
Oct. 19, 7:18 AM Aries, Full Moon	Gather mushrooms. Harvest root crops for seed.
Oct. 19, 7:18 AM– Oct. 19, 3:35 PM Aries, 3rd qtr.	Cultivate. Destroy weeds and pests. Harvest fruits and root crops. Trim to retard growth.

Oct. 19, 3:35 PM– Oct. 22, 4:28 AM Taurus, 3rd qtr.	Plant potatoes and tubers. Prune.
Oct. 22, 4:28 AM– Oct. 24, 5:16 PM Gemini, 3rd qtr.	Cultivate. Destroy weeds and pests. Harvest fruits and root crops. Trim to retard growth.
Oct. 24, 5:16 PM– Oct. 27, 4:05 AM Cancer, 3rd qtr.	Plant biennials, perennials, bulbs and roots. Irrigate. Fertilize (organic). Prune.
Oct. 27, 4:05 AM– Oct. 27, 11:45 AM Leo, 3rd qtr.	Cultivate. Destroy weeds and pests. Harvest fruits and root crops. Trim to retard growth.
Oct. 27, 11:45 AM– Oct. 29, 11:22 AM Leo, 4th qtr.	Cultivate. Destroy weeds and pests. Harvest fruits and root crops. Trim to retard growth.
Oct. 29, 11:22 AM– Oct. 31, 2:46 PM Virgo, 4th qtr.	Cultivate, especially medicinal plants. Destroy weeds and pests. Trim to retard growth.
Nov. 2, 3:19 PM– Nov. 3, 8:35 AM Scorpio, 4th qtr.	Plant biennials, perennials, bulbs and roots. Irrigate. Fertilize (organic). Prune.
Nov. 3, 8:35 AM– Nov. 4, 2:46 PM Scorpio, 1st qtr.	Plant annuals, grains. Irrigate. Fertilize (chemical). Trim to increase growth. Graft or bud plants.

Nov. 6, 3:01 PM– Nov. 8, 5:48 PM Capri., 1st qtr.	Graft or bud plants. Trim to increase growth.
Nov. 11, 12:04 AM– Nov. 13, 9:44 AM Pisces, 2nd qtr.	Plant annuals, grains. Irrigate. Fertilize (chemical). Trim to increase growth. Graft or bud plants.
Nov. 15, 9:45 PM– Nov. 18, 1:58 AM Taurus, 2nd qtr.	Plant annuals for hardiness. Trim to increase growth.
Nov. 18, 1:58 AM Taurus, Full Moon	Gather mushrooms. Harvest root crops for seed.
Nov. 18, 1:58 AM– Nov. 18, 10:42 AM Taurus, 3rd qtr.	Plant potatoes and tubers. Prune.
Nov. 18, 10:42 AM– Nov. 20, 11:21 PM Gemini, 3rd qtr.	Cultivate. Destroy weeds and pests. Harvest fruits and root crops. Trim to retard growth.
Nov. 20, 11:21 PM– Nov. 23, 10:33 AM Cancer, 3rd qtr.	Plant biennials, perennials, bulbs and roots. Irrigate. Fertilize (organic). Prune.
Nov. 23, 10:33 AM– Nov. 25, 7:09 PM Leo, 3rd qtr.	Cultivate. Destroy weeds and pests. Harvest fruits and root crops. Trim to retard growth.

Nov. 25, 7:09 PM- Nov. 26, 2:04 AM Virgo, 3rd qtr.	Cultivate, especially medicinal plants. Destroy weeds and pests. Trim to retard growth.
Nov. 26, 2:04 AM- Nov. 28, 12:22 AM Virgo, 4th qtr.	Cultivate, especially medicinal plants. Destroy weeds and pests. Trim to retard growth.
Nov. 30, 2:22 AM- Dec 2, 2:13 AM Scorpio, 4th qtr.	Plant biennials, perennials, bulbs and roots. Irrigate. Fertilize (organic). Prune.
Dec. 2, 2:13 AM- Dec. 2, 6:54 PM Sagit., 4th qtr.	Cultivate. Destroy weeds and pests. Harvest fruits and root crops. Trim to retard growth.
Dec. 4, 1:43 AM- Dec. 6, 2:52 AM Capri., 1st qtr.	Graft or bud plants. Trim to increase growth.
Dec. 8, 7:25 AM- Dec. 9, 4:07 PM Pisces, 1st qtr.	Plant annuals, grains. Irrigate. Fertilize (chemical). Trim to increase growth. Graft or bud plants.
Dec. 9, 4:07 PM- Dec. 10, 4:04 PM Pisces, 2nd qtr.	Plant annuals, grains. Irrigate. Fertilize (chemical). Trim to increase growth. Graft or bud plants.

Dec. 13, 3:56 AM- Dec. 15, 4:59 PM Taurus, 2nd qtr.	Plant annuals for hardiness. Trim to increase growth.
Dec. 17, 9:17 PM Gemini, Full Moon	Gather mushrooms. Harvest root crops for seed.
Dec. 17, 9:17 PM- Dec. 18, 5:25 AM Gemini, 3rd qtr.	Cultivate. Destroy weeds and pests. Harvest fruits and root crops. Trim to retard growth.
Dec. 18, 5:25 AM- Dec. 20, 4:13 PM Cancer, 3rd qtr.	Plant biennials, perennials, bulbs and roots. Irrigate. Fertilize (organic). Prune.
Dec. 20, 4:13 PM- Dec. 23, 1:01 AM Leo, 3rd qtr.	Cultivate. Destroy weeds and pests. Harvest fruits and root crops. Trim to retard growth.
Dec. 23, 1:01 AM- Dec. 25, 7:28 AM Virgo, 3rd qtr.	Cultivate, especially medicinal plants. Destroy weeds and pests. Trim to retard growth.
Dec. 27, 11:18 AM- Dec. 29, 12:46 PM Scorpio, 4th qtr.	Plant biennials, perennials, bulbs and roots. Irrigate. Fertilize (organic). Prune.
Dec. 29, 12:46 PM- Dec. 31, 12:58 PM Sagit., 4th qtr.	Cultivate. Destroy weeds and pests. Harvest fruits and root crops. Trim to retard growth.

DATES TO DESTROY
WEEDS AND PESTS

The Moon's sign and phase indicate the best dates to eliminate weeds, pests, insects, etc. Following are dates for 1994 when this will be most effective.

Jan. 1, 3:15 PM-Jan. 3, 6:31 PM (Vir./3rd qtr.)
Jan. 8, 12:34 AM-Jan. 9, 4:16 AM (Sag./4th qtr.)
Jan. 26, 7:39 PM-Jan. 28, 10:39 PM (Leo/3rd qtr.)
Jan. 28, 10:39 PM-Jan. 31, 12:34 AM (Vir./3rd qtr.)
Feb. 3, 6:14 AM-Feb. 6, 11:02 AM (Sag./4th qtr.)
Feb. 25, 8:27 AM-Feb. 27, 9:06 AM (Vir./3rd qtr.)
Mar. 3, 11:54 AM-Mar. 5, 4:25 PM (Sag./3rd qtr.)
Mar. 7, 11:15 PM-Mar. 10, 8:10 AM (Aqu./4th qtr.)
Mar. 30, 7:42 PM-Apr. 1, 10:38 PM (Sag./3rd qtr.)
Apr. 4, 4:46 AM-Apr. 6, 1:51 PM (Aqu./4th qtr.)
Apr. 27, 5:49 AM-Apr. 29, 7:05 AM (Sag./3rd qtr.)
May 1, 11:35 AM-May 3, 7:47 PM (Aqu./3rd qtr.)

May 6, 7:01 AM-May 8, 7:50 PM (Ari./4th qtr.)
May 24, 4:43 PM-May 26, 5:17 PM (Sag./3rd qtr.)
May 28, 8:19 PM-May 30, 3:03 AM (Aqu./3rd qtr.)
Jun. 2, 1:31 PM-Jun. 5, 2:14 AM (Ari./4th qtr.)
Jun. 25, 6:10 AM-Jun. 27, 11:45 AM (Aqu./3rd qtr.)
Jun. 29, 9:07 PM-Jul. 2, 9:24 AM (Ari./3rd qtr.)
Jul. 4, 10:13 PM-Jul. 7, 9:18 AM (Gem./4th qtr.)
Jul. 22, 3:39 PM-Jul. 24, 8:57 PM (Aqu./3rd qtr.)
Jul. 27, 5:31 AM-Jul. 29, 5:13 PM (Ari./3rd qtr.)
Jul. 31, 6:05 AM-Aug. 3, 5:22 PM (Gem./4th qtr.)
Aug. 23, 1:55 PM-Aug. 26, 1:13 AM (Ari./3rd qtr.)
Aug. 28, 2:07 PM-Aug. 31, 1:59 AM (Gem./3rd, 4th qtr.)
Sep. 2, 10:37 AM-Sep. 4, 3:34 PM (Leo/4th qtr.)
Sep. 19, 9:29 PM-Sep. 22, 8:47 AM (Ari./3rd qtr.)
Sep. 24, 9:41 PM-Sep. 27, 10:12 AM (Gem./3rd qtr.)
Sep. 29, 7:56 PM-Oct. 2, 1:40 AM (Leo/4th qtr.)
Oct. 2, 1:40 AM-Oct. 4, 3:57 AM (Vir./4th qtr.)
Oct. 22, 4:28 AM-Oct. 24, 5:16 PM (Gem./3rd qtr.)
Oct. 27, 4:05 AM-Oct. 29, 11:22 AM (Leo/3rd, 4th qtr.)
Oct. 29, 11:22 AM-Oct. 31, 2:46 PM (Vir./4th qtr.)
Nov. 18, 10:42 AM-Nov. 20, 11:21 PM (Gem./3rd qtr.)
Nov. 23, 10:33 AM-Nov. 25, 7:09 PM (Leo/3rd qtr.)
Nov. 25, 7:09 PM-Nov. 28, 12:22 AM (Vir./3rd, 4th qtr.)
Dec. 20, 4:13 PM-Dec. 23, 1:01 AM (Leo/3rd qtr.)
Dec. 23, 1:01 AM-Dec. 25, 7:28 AM (Vir./3rd qtr.)
Dec. 29, 12:46 PM-Dec. 31, 12:58 PM (Sag./4th qtr.)

OTHER GARDEN-RELATED
ACTIVITIES

Animal Husbandry
Animals are easiest to handle when the Moon is in
Taurus, Cancer, Libra or Pisces. Avoid the Full
Moon. Buy animals during the first quarter. Cas-
trate animals in any sign except Leo, Scorpio or
Sagittarius. Avoid the Full Moon. Slaughter for
food in the first three days after the Full Moon in
any sign except Leo.

Composting
Start compost when the Moon is in the fourth quarter in a water sign, especially Scorpio.

Cultivating
Cultivate when the Moon is in a barren sign and
waning, ideally the fourth quarter in Aries, Gemini,
Leo, Virgo or Aquarius.

Cutting Timber
Cut timber during the third and fourth quarters while the Moon is not in a water sign. This will diminish the rotting.

Drying Crops
Dry crops in the third quarter when the Moon is in a fire sign.

Fertilizing
Fertilize when the Moon is in a fruitful sign (Cancer, Scorpio, Pisces). Organic fertilizers are best used when the Moon is in the third or fourth quarter. Chemical fertilizers are best used in the first or second quarter.

Grafting
Graft during Capricorn, Cancer or Scorpio while the Moon is in the first or second quarter.

Harvesting
Harvest root crops when the Moon is in a dry sign (Aries, Leo, Sagittarius, Gemini, Aquarius) and in the third or fourth quarter. Harvest root crops intended for seed during the Full Moon. Harvest grain which will be stored just after the Full Moon, avoiding the water signs (Cancer, Scorpio, Pisces). Fire signs are best for cutting down on water content. Harvest fruits in the third and fourth quarters in the dry signs.

Irrigation
Irrigate when the Moon is in a water sign.

Mowing the Lawn
Mow in the first and second quarters to increase growth and lushness, in the third and fourth quarters to decrease growth.

Picking Mushrooms
Gather mushrooms at the Full Moon.

Pruning
Prune during the third and fourth quarters in Scorpio to retard growth and to promote better fruit, and in Capricorn to promote better healing.

Spraying
Destroy pests and weeds during the fourth quarter when the Moon is in a barren sign.

Transplanting
Transplant when the Moon is increasing and preferably in Cancer, Scorpio or Pisces.

A GUIDE TO PLANTING USING
PHASE AND SIGN RULERSHIPS

PLANT	PHASE	SIGN
Annuals	1st or 2nd	
Apple trees	3rd or 4th	Sagittarius
Artichokes	1st	Cancer, Pisces, Virgo
Asparagus	1st	Cancer, Scorpio, Pisces
Asters	1st or 2nd	Virgo
Barley	1st or 2nd	Cancer, Scorpio, Pisces, Libra, Capricorn
Beans (bush & pole)	2nd	Cancer, Scorpio, Pisces, Libra, Taurus

PLANT	PHASE	SIGN
Beans (kidney, white & navy)	3rd or 4th	Leo
Beech trees	3rd	Capricorn
Beets	3rd	Cancer, Scorpio, Pisces, Libra, Capricorn
Biennials	3rd or 4th	
Broccoli	1st	Cancer, Scorpio, Pisces, Libra
Brussels sprouts	1st	Cancer, Scorpio, Pisces, Libra
Buckwheat	1st or 2nd	Capricorn
Bulbs	3rd	Cancer, Scorpio, Pisces
Bulbs for seed	2nd or 3rd	
Cabbage	1st	Cancer, Scorpio, Pisces, Libra, Taurus
Cactus		Taurus, Capricorn
Canes (raspberries, blackberries & gooseberries)	2nd	Cancer, Scorpio, Pisces, Sagittarius

PLANT	PHASE	SIGN
Cantaloupes	1st or 2nd	Cancer, Scorpio, Pisces, Libra, Taurus
Carrots	3rd	Taurus
Cauliflower	1st	Cancer, Scorpio, Pisces, Libra
Celeriac	3rd	Cancer, Scorpio, Pisces
Celery	1st or 2nd	Cancer, Scorpio, Pisces
Cereals	1st or 2nd	Cancer, Scorpio, Pisces, Libra
Chard	1st or 2nd	Cancer, Scorpio, Pisces
Chicory	3rd	Cancer, Scorpio, Pisces, Sagittarius
Chrysanthe-mums	1st or 2nd	Virgo
Clover	1st or 2nd	Cancer, Scorpio, Pisces
Corn	1st	Cancer, Scorpio, Pisces
Corn for fodder	1st or 2nd	Libra
Coryopsis	2nd or 3rd	Libra

PLANT	PHASE	SIGN
Cosmos	2nd or 3rd	Libra
Cress	1st	Cancer, Scorpio, Pisces
Crocus	1st or 2nd	Virgo
Cucumbers	1st	Cancer, Scorpio, Pisces
Daffodils	1st or 2nd	Libra, Virgo
Dahlias	1st or 2nd	Libra, Virgo
Deciduous trees	3rd	Cancer, Scorpio, Pisces
Eggplant	2nd	Cancer, Scorpio, Pisces, Libra
Endive	1st	Cancer, Scorpio, Pisces, Libra
Flowers for: beauty	1st	Libra
abundance	1st	Cancer, Pisces, Virgo
sturdiness	1st	Scorpio
hardiness	1st	Taurus
Garlic	3rd or 4th	Scorpio, Sagittarius
Gladiola	1st or 2nd	Libra, Virgo
Gourds	1st or 2nd	Cancer, Scorpio, Pisces, Libra

PLANT	PHASE	SIGN
Grapes	2nd or 3rd	Cancer, Scorpio, Pisces, Sagittarius
Hay	1st or 2nd	Cancer, Scorpio, Pisces, Libra, Taurus, Sagittarius
Herbs	1st or 2nd	Cancer, Scorpio, Pisces
Honeysuckle	1st or 2nd	Scorpio, Virgo
Hops	1st or 2nd	Scorpio, Libra
Horseradish	1st or 2nd	Cancer, Scorpio, Pisces
House plants	1st	Libra (flowering), Cancer, Scorpio (vines), Pisces
Hyacinths	3rd	Cancer, Scorpio, Pisces
Iris	1st or 2nd	Cancer, Virgo
Kohlrabi	1st or 2nd	Cancer, Scorpio, Pisces, Libra
Leeks	2nd	Sagittarius
Lettuce	1st	Cancer, Scorpio, Pisces, Libra, Taurus (late sowings)
Lilies	1st or 2nd	Cancer, Scorpio, Pisces

PLANT	PHASE	SIGN
Maple trees	3rd	Sagittarius
Melons	1st or 2nd	Cancer, Scorpio, Pisces
Moon vine	1st or 2nd	Virgo
Morning-glory	1st or 2nd	Cancer, Scorpio, Pisces, Virgo
Oak trees	3rd	Sagittarius
Oats	1st or 2nd	Cancer, Scorpio, Pisces, Libra
Okra	1st	Cancer, Scorpio, Pisces, Libra
Onion seeds	2nd	Scorpio, Sagittarius, Cancer
Onion sets	3rd or 4th	Libra, Taurus, Pisces
Pansies	1st or 2nd	Cancer, Scorpio, Pisces
Parsley	1st	Cancer, Scorpio, Pisces, Libra
Parsnips	3rd	Taurus, Capricorn, Cancer, Scorpio
Peach trees	3rd	Taurus, Libra
Peanuts	3rd	Cancer, Scorpio, Pisces
Pear trees	3rd	Taurus, Libra

PLANT	PHASE	SIGN
Peas	2nd or 3rd	Cancer, Scorpio, Pisces, Libra
Peonies	1st or 2nd	Virgo
Peppers	2nd	Scorpio, Sagittarius
Perennials	3rd	
Petunias	1st or 2nd	Libra, Virgo
Plum trees	3rd	Taurus, Libra
Poppies	1st or 2nd	Virgo
Portulaca	1st or 2nd	Virgo
Potatoes	3rd	Cancer, Scorpio, Taurus, Libra, Capricorn, Sagittarius (for seed)
Privet	1st or 2nd	Taurus, Libra
Pumpkins	2nd	Cancer, Scorpio, Pisces, Libra
Quinces	1st or 2nd	Capricorn
Radishes	3rd	Libra, Taurus, Pisces, Sagittarius, Capricorn
Rhubarb	3rd	Aries
Rice	1st or 2nd	Scorpio
Roses	1st or 2nd	Cancer

PLANT	PHASE	SIGN
Rutabagas	3rd	Cancer, Scorpio, Pisces, Taurus
Saffron	1st or 2nd	Cancer, Scorpio, Pisces
Sage	3rd	Cancer, Scorpio, Pisces
Salsify	1st or 2nd	Cancer, Scorpio, Pisces
Shallots	2nd	Scorpio
Spinach	1st	Cancer, Scorpio, Pisces
Squash	2nd	Cancer, Scorpio, Pisces, Libra
Strawberries	3rd	Cancer, Scorpio, Pisces
String beans	1st or 2nd	Taurus
Sunflowers	3rd or 4th	Libra
Sweet peas	1st or 2nd	Cancer, Scorpio, Pisces
Tomatoes	2nd, transplant in 3rd	Cancer, Scorpio, Pisces, Capricorn (if hot and dry)

PLANT	PHASE	SIGN
Trees: shade	3rd	Taurus, Capricorn
ornamental	2nd	Libra, Taurus
erosion control	3rd	Cancer, Scorpio, Pisces, Taurus, Capricorn
Trumpet vines	1st or 2nd	Cancer, Scorpio, Pisces
Tubers for seed	3rd	Cancer, Scorpio, Pisces, Libra
Tulips	1st or 2nd	Libra, Virgo
Turnips	3rd	Cancer, Scorpio, Pisces, Taurus, Capricorn, Libra
Valerian	1st or 2nd	Virgo, Gemini
Watermelons	1st or 2nd	Cancer, Scorpio, Pisces, Libra
Wheat	1st or 2nd	Cancer, Scorpio, Pisces, Libra

COMPANION PLANTING

PLANT	HELPERS	HINDERED BY
Asparagus	Tomatoes, parsley, basil	
Beans	Carrots, cucumbers, cabbage, beets, corn	Onions, gladiola
Bush beans	Cucumbers, cabbage, strawberries	Fennel, onions
Beets	Onions, cabbage, lettuce	Pale beans
Cabbage	Beets, potatoes, onions, celery	Strawberries, tomatoes

PLANT	HELPERS	HINDERED BY
Carrots	Peas, lettuce, chives, radishes leeks, onions	Dill
Celery	Leeks, bush beans	
Chives		Beans
Corn	Potatoes, beans, peas, melons, squash, pumpkins, cucumbers	
Cucumbers	Beans, cabbage radishes, sunflowers, lettuce	Potatoes, aromatic herbs
Eggplant	Beans	
Lettuce	Strawberries, carrots	
Melons	Morning-glories	
Onions, leeks	Beets, chamomile, carrots, lettuce	Peas, beans
Garlic	Summer savory	
Peas	Radishes, carrots, corn, cucumbers, beans, turnips	Onions
Potatoes	Beans, corn, peas, cabbage, hemp, cucumbers	Sunflowers

PLANT	HELPERS	HINDERED BY
Radishes	Peas, lettuce, nasturtium, cucumbers	Hyssop
Spinach	Strawberries	
Squash, pumpkins	Nasturtium, corn	Potatoes
Tomatoes	Asparagus, parsley, chives, onions, carrots, marigold, nasturtium	Dill, cabbage, fennel
Turnips	Peas, beans	

PLANT	COMPANIONS AND USES
Anise	Coriander
Basil	Tomatoes; dislikes rue; repels flies and mosquitoes
Borage	Tomatoes and squash
Buttercup	Clover; hinders delphiniums, peonies, monkshood, columbines and others of this family

PLANT	COMPANIONS AND USES
Chamomile	Small amounts help peppermint, wheat, onions and cabbage; destructive in large amounts; makes spray for damping off
Catnip	Repels flea beetles
Chervil	Radishes
Chives	Carrots; spray against apple scab and powdery mildew
Coriander	Hinders seed formation in fennel
Cosmos	Repels corn earworm
Dill	Cabbage; hinders carrots and tomatoes
Fennel	Disliked by all garden plants
Garlic	Aids vetch and roses; hinders peas and beans
Hemp	Beneficial as a neighbor to most plants
Horseradish	Repels potato bugs
Horsetail	Makes fungicide spray
Hyssop	Attracts cabbage fly away from cabbages; harmful to radishes
Lovage	Improves hardiness and flavor of neighbors
Marigold	Pest repellent; use against Mexican bean beetles and nematodes; makes spray

PLANT	COMPANIONS AND USES
Mint	Repels ants, flea beetles and cabbage worm butterflies
Morning-glory	Corn; helps melon germination
Nasturtium	Cabbage, cucumbers, squash and melons; deters aphids, squash bugs and pumpkin beetles
Nettles	Increase oil content in neighbors
Parsley	Tomatoes, asparagus
Purslane	Good ground cover
Rosemary	Cabbage, beans and carrots; repels cabbage moths, bean beetles and carrot flies
Sage	Repels cabbage moths and carrot flies
Summer savory	Deters bean beetles
Sunflower	Hinders potatoes; improves soil
Tansy	Roses; deters flying insects, Japanese beetles, striped cucumber beetles, ants and squash bugs
Thyme	Repels cabbage worm
Yarrow	Increases essential oils of neighbors

BREEDING ANIMALS AND
SETTING EGGS

Eggs should be set and animals mated so that the young will be born when the Moon is increasing and in a fruitful sign (Cancer, Scorpio and Pisces). Young born in a fruitful sign are generally healthier, mature faster and make better breeding stock. Those born during a semi-fruitful sign (Taurus and Capricorn) will generally still mature fast, but will produce leaner meat. The sign of Libra yields beautiful, graceful animals for showing and racing.

To determine the best date to mate animals or set eggs, subtract the number of days given for incubation or gestation from the fruitful dates given in the following tables. For example, cats and dogs are mated 63 days previous to the desired birth date; chicken eggs are set 21 days previous.

GESTATION AND INCUBATION

Animal	Number of Young	Gestation
Horse	1	346 days
Cow	1	283 days
Monkey	1	164 days
Goat	1-2	151 days
Sheep	1-2	150 days
Pig	10	112 days
Chinchilla	2	110 days
Fox	5-8	63 days
Dog	6-8	63 days
Cat	4-6	63 days
Guinea pig	2-6	62 days
Ferret	6-9	40 days
Rabbit	4-8	30 days
Rat	10	22 days
Mouse	10	22 days

Domestic Fowl	Number of Eggs	Incubation
Turkey	12-15	26-30 days
Guinea	15-18	25-26 days
Pea hen	10	28-30 days
Duck	9-12	25-32 days
Goose	15-18	27-33 days
Hen	12-15	19-24 days
Pigeon	2	16-20 days
Canary	3-4	13-14 days

BEST DATES FOR SETTING EGGS

Dates to be Born	Moon's Sign and Phase	Set Eggs
Jan. 14, 5:03 PM- Jan. 17, 3:42 AM	Pisces 1st qtr.	Dec. 24-27
Jan. 19, 4:22 PM- Jan. 22, 4:35 AM	Taurus 1st/2nd qtr.	Dec. 29-Jan. 1
Jan. 24, 1:56 PM- Jan. 26, 7:39 PM	Cancer 2nd qtr.	Jan. 3-5
Feb. 11, 1:23 AM Feb. 13, 11:50 AM	Pisces 1st qtr.	Jan. 21-23
Feb. 16, 12:20 AM Feb. 18, 1:06 PM	Taurus 1st qtr.	Jan. 26-28
Feb. 20, 11:28 PM Feb. 23, 5:48 AM	Cancer 2nd qtr.	Jan. 30-Feb. 2
Mar. 15, 7:28 AM Mar. 17, 8:29 PM	Taurus 1st qtr.	Feb. 22-24
Mar. 20, 7:54 AM Mar. 22, 3:39 PM	Cancer 1st/2nd qtr.	Feb. 27-Mar. 1
Apr. 11, 1:47 PM Apr. 14, 2:48 AM	Taurus 1st qtr.	Mar. 21-24
Apr. 16, 2:41 PM Apr. 18, 11:45 PM	Cancer 1st qtr.	Mar. 26-28
Apr. 23, 6:41 AM Apr. 25, 6:19 AM	Libra 2nd qtr.	Apr. 2-4

Dates to be Born	Moon's Sign and Phase	Set Eggs
May 13, 8:28 PM May 16, 5:59 AM	Cancer 1st qtr.	Apr. 22-25
May 20, 3:55 PM May 22, 4:51 PM	Libra 2nd qtr.	Apr. 29-May 1
May 22, 4:51 PM May 24, 4:43 PM	Scorpio 2nd qtr.	May 1-3
Jun. 10, 2:23 AM Jun. 12, 11:29 AM	Cancer 1st qtr.	May 20-22
Jun. 16, 10:48 PM Jun. 19, 1:20 AM	Libra 1st/2nd qtr.	May 26-29
Jun. 19, 1:20 AM Jun. 21, 2:32 AM	Scorpio 2nd qtr.	May 29-31
Jul. 14, 4:15 AM Jul. 16, 7:35 AM	Libra 1st qtr.	Jun. 23-25
Jul. 16, 7:35 AM Jul. 18, 10:09 AM	Scorpio 1st/2nd qtr.	Jun. 25-27
Jul. 20, 12:31 PM Jul. 22, 3:39 PM	Capricorn 2nd qtr.	Jun. 30-Jul. 2
Aug. 10, 10:07 AM Aug. 12, 12:56 PM	Libra 1st qtr.	Jul. 20-22
Aug. 12, 12:56 PM Aug. 14, 3:54 PM	Scorpio 1st qtr.	Jul. 22-24
Aug. 16, 7:18 PM Aug. 18, 11:34 PM	Capricorn 2nd qtr.	July 26-28

Dates to be Born	Moon's Sign and Phase	Set Eggs
Sep. 6, 5:57 PM Sep. 8, 7:26 PM	Libra 1st qtr.	Aug. 16-18
Sep. 8, 7:26 PM Sep. 10, 9:26 PM	Scorpio 1st qtr.	Aug. 18-20
Sep. 13, 12:45 AM Sep. 15, 5:42 AM	Capricorn 2nd qtr.	Aug. 23-25
Sep. 17, 12:31 PM Sep. 19, 9:29 PM	Pisces 2nd qtr.	Aug. 27-29
Oct. 6, 4:22 AM Oct. 8, 4:47 AM	Scorpio 1st qtr.	Sep. 15-17
Oct. 10, 6:44 AM Oct. 12, 11:09 AM	Capricorn 1st qtr.	Sep. 19-21
Oct. 14, 6:18 PM Oct. 17, 3:56 AM	Pisces 2nd qtr.	Sep. 23-26
Nov. 6, 3:01 PM Nov. 8, 5:48 PM	Capricorn 1st qtr.	Oct. 16-18
Nov. 11, 12:04 AM Nov. 13, 9:44 AM	Pisces 2nd qtr.	Oct. 21-23
Dec. 4, 1:43 AM Dec. 6, 2:52 AM	Capricorn 1st qtr.	Nov. 13-15
Dec. 8, 7:25 AM Dec. 10, 4:04 PM	Pisces 1st qtr.	Nov. 17-19
Dec. 12, 3:56 AM Dec. 15, 4:59 PM	Taurus 2nd qtr.	Nov. 21-24

ASTROLOGICAL
APHRODISIAC EDIBLES

by Louise Riotte

Here's flowers for you;
Hot lavender, mints, savory, marjoram;
The marigold, that goes to bed wi' the sun,
And with him rises weeping.
These are the flowers
Of middle summer, and I think they are given
To men of middle age.

—Shakespeare

Ancient Romans draped flowers around the idol of Priapus, the garden god. In addition, Priapus also reigned as a guardian of fertility. According to Robert Hendrickson, writing about vegetables, "Like most peoples, the Romans saw the connection between their agriculture sex-god and the value of fruits and vegetables in their amatory diet. Our word vegetable, for example, comes from the

251

Latin *vegetus*, 'active or lively', and both slave and patrician thought all food from the fertile earth was a spur to love."

The Hindus, as a rule a race of vegetarians, rarely drink stimulants, but venerate vegetables as love foods, even more than the people of Rome. Many fruits, herbs and vegetables are mentioned throughout their sex manual, the *Ananga Ranga*.

Historically there is a tremendous amount of literature regarding the amatory effects of various garden products in almost every culture—from Chinese sex books to the Elizabethan vegetable gardens in England where "sprouted all the instruments of debauchery." But overall there seems to be tacit agreement that the basis of having and keeping virility was good health.

Dr. H.L. Cornell, in his *Encyclopedia of Medical Astrology*, defines aphrodisiacs as remedies which increase passion and sex desire: "A therapeutic property of Mars and Mars remedies. Also love potions, ruled by Venus, are used for this purpose." In the following list of garden edibles notice how often rulership by Venus and Mars crops up!

Artichokes (Venus). According to Robert Hendrickson, almost three centuries ago Dr. Nicolas wrote that the artichoke "produces much semen and vigor." Catherine de Medici reportedly fed her lovers artichokes, perhaps inspired by the French adage "artichokes like wine, are good for ladies when gentlemen partake of them." Two chemicals contained in artichokes, cynarin and chlorogenic acid, are said to make wine taste sweeter.

Asparagus (Jupiter) has, historically, long been included in the list of all-around love foods. It is thought that the Phoenicians introduced this member of the lily family to the Greeks, who gathered it from the wild and "there have been nothing but raves about it as a love food ever since."

Beans (Venus). Long before it became known that beans are rich in iron, copper and phosphorus, they were believed to be highly effective in amatory pursuits, in particular the haricot bean, beloved of the French gourmet. A pinch of soda or a small amount of cooking oil added to the water in which beans are cooked is said to help to control the flatulence they sometimes cause.

Beets (Jupiter, Saturn) are highly nutritious, their greens being particularly rich in vitamin A, copper and iron. As with asparagus they are also rich in apartic acid. Pliny mentions beets as an aphrodisiac food and numerous references are made to them in love cookery.

Cabbage (Moon) has long been regarded by the Russians as a high vitality food. This member of the mustard family has been cultivated for more than 4000 years and is thought to be the most ancient of all vegetables. Cauliflower, kale, Brussels sprouts and broccoli are all forms of cabbage and have been esteemed as aphrodisiacs by Europeans.

Carrots (Mercury) are excellent sources of the so-called "sexuality vitamins," A and E, and carrots have been thought of as a "love food" ever since the Greeks extolled them and called them *philtron*, meaning "love medicine."

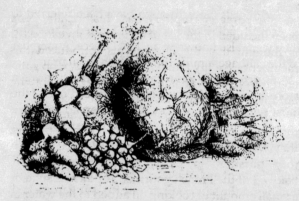

Celery—also celeriac and smallage (wild celery)—(Mercury) is praised by Charles Connell (*Aphrodisiacs in Your Garden*) as an aphrodisiac par excellence and he insists "no effort spared to produce a healthy crop." It is also thought to be helpful in cases of rheumatism and, as an extra bonus, its growth leaves the ground in first-class condition for another crop. Whether it is eaten raw, braised, curried, stewed, fried or pickled, the aphrodisiac effects of celery are said to be excellent. Celery soup, perhaps strengthened with truffles, is highly thought of by the French as a stimulating dish.

Chickpea (Venus), sometimes called garbanzo, is a favorite in southern Europe, dating back to earliest times. Its history as an aphrodisiac is similar to that of the pea, and the Romans doted on it as a "love food."

Cole (Moon) was held sacred by the Romans to the god Priapus, and childless couples were advised to eat it that they may become fecund.

Collards (Saturn) often have been referred to as "soul food" in the southern United States, but they were also known in ancient Greece. A member of the cabbage family, they are rich in vitamin A.

Corn (Sun). Few garden vegetables have a more fascinating history and it is indeed one of the most delicious foods that may be served at a love banquet. But to have it at its very best you must grow it in your own garden and pick it at the peak of perfection for the ears lose up to 90% of their sugar content an hour after harvesting. Have water boiling on the stove and go out to your garden and pick an armful. Invite a friend to share.

Cucumbers (Moon) as an aphrodisiac are not highly thought of, but we may simply enjoy them on a hot day to help us feel "cool as a cucumber." A tea-time favorite, cucumber sandwiches, sprinkled lightly with savory or marjoram, may be enjoyed with an aphrodisiac tea of mint or thyme.

Dandelion greens (Jupiter, Venus), rich in vitamin A, iron and copper, make an excellent salad. I also gather the unopened buds in spring, cook them with sliced leeks, and serve them with a light butter sauce seasoned with herbs.

Eggplant (Moon) is highly recommended by the Hindu love manual, the Kamasutra, and has been highly touted as an aphrodisiac all over the world. The French call it *aubergine*, the Spanish *berefina*, and the Italians *melanzana*.

Eryngoes and other sea vegetables (Neptune) are usually rich in iodine and have been favored by lovers for centuries. In *Your Astrological Guide to*

Health and Diet, Carroll Righter frequently recommends kelp. The sea cucumber, called *tripang* by the Chinese, is also said to be stimulating.

Fennel (Mercury, Leo)—actually an herb—has been used like a vegetable through the ages. Both fennel and its seed are still popular aphrodisiacs in Italy and other Mediterranean countries.

Garlic, chives, onions, leeks, shallots (Moon, Aries) are all love foods—garlic and onions being cited most often. According to Sybil Leek's *Astrological Cookbook*, these vegetables contain large quantities of sulphate of lime which has cleansing and antiseptic powers that help to maintain resisting forces of the body.

Lentils (Venus), rich in iron, copper and phosphorus, have enjoyed a reputation as a love food for centuries. Ann Mathers, author of *The Astrology Love Book*, speaks very highly of this member of the bean family.

Lettuce (Moon) has been rated both high and low by aphrodisiac food tasters. Perhaps it is most helpful in maintaining a trim figure!

Mushrooms (Moon) are thought to be surpassed as a love food only by "underground" truffles. A healthy food, it combines in its high percentages of glycogen and albumen all the benefits of meat without its indigestibility.

Peas (Venus), containing many of the same virtues as beans, have been favored by lovers since aphrodisiac foods were first mentioned in cookery.

Potatoes (Venus) once valued as amatory aids are now considered to be of little importance as a love food. But this versatile vegetable is very healthful and it may be enhanced with such amatory herbs as basil, parsley and thyme.

Radishes (Mars, Aries) were traditionally served at Greek weddings. Heliodorus is believed to have referred to a dish of radishes served at a marriage feast when he wrote, "Great deeds need great preparations."

Soybeans (Venus) are considered the "almost perfect food," as they contain high quantities of both vitamin B and the "sexuality vitamin," E, also present in parsley. The Chinese have valued them as a love food for centuries.

Spinach (Moon) has a reputation as a green powerhouse. Rich in vitamins and minerals, particularly vitamin E and the iron which supplies great vigor, its aphrodisiac value dates back 2000 years.

Squash (Moon, Libra) is nutritionally rich but as an aphrodisiac is not thought to have much clout. Which seems a pity as they are so delicious, baked, boiled, fried or steamed. The winter squashes do take kindly to spices however. Bake them, remove seeds, and fill the hollow with brown sugar, a dab of butter, and sprinkle with your choice of cinnamon, clove, ginger or nutmeg, all highly thought of as aphrodisiacs.

Tomatoes (Jupiter, Neptune and Mars), once called "love apples," are now generally scorned by researchers of vegetable aphrodisiacs. If not particularly stimulating on its own, America's favorite vegetable does contribute toward the general effect. Stuff it with chopped mushrooms, shallots, parsley, ham and bread-crumbs, top with a smidgen of butter and bake and you have an exciting dish guaranteed to invigorate.

Turnip roots (Moon) are rich in vitamin A, iron and copper, but the leaves are even more so and they are much relished by those who like the spicy "bite." The leaves may be mixed with radish greens and spinach.

Yams (Venus, Saturn) were held to be a highly aphrodisiac food by the Elizabethans. Though often mistaken for the sweet potato, they actually are of no relation.

Yarrow (Venus, Gemini) has been used since ancient times as a "love tonic," which is said to ensure "seven years love for wedded couples." I'm not sure what happens after that! Sometimes classified as a vegetable and sometimes as an herb, it has another well-deserved name: "old man's pepper."

Note: Where appropriate the aphrodisiac qualities of vegetables may be further enhanced by the addition of such herbs as basil, chervil, chives, mint, parsley, sage, tarragon and thyme.

WEEDS AS SOIL INDICATORS
by Deborah Duchon

Most good gardeners know the benefits of having their soil tested from time to time, and most state extension services are happy to oblige with free soil testing. But there are other ways to ascertain conditions besides sending samples off to a laboratory. Existing vegetation, often weeds, are indicators of what condition your soil is in.

Think about it. All kinds of weed seeds fall all over the place all the time. Why do some of them sprout and thrive in certain places and not in others? Why does one little patch of your property always sport chickweed, while another hosts purslane? The answer has to do with growing conditions, and if you know what growing conditions various plants need, then you can tell something about your soil by the vegetation that grows without human interference.

According to Ehrenfried E. Pfeiffer, bio-dynamic farming maven and author of *Weeds and What They Tell* (Bio-Dynamic Farming and Gardening Association, Inc.), there are three major groups and several minor groups of indicators.

Major groups include: acid soil (sorrel, dock, cinquefoil, lady's-thumb, horsetail, hawkweed, knapweed); compacted soil, hardpan, or crusty surface (field mustard, horse nettle, pennycress, morning glory, quack grass, chamomile, pineapple weed); and disturbed or cultivated soil (lamb's-quarters, plantain, chickweed, buttercup, dandelion, nettle, prostrate knotweed, prickly lettuce, amaranth, horehound, mallows, carpetweed).

Minor groups include: sandy soil (goldenrod, aster, yellow toadflax, partridge pea, broom); salty soil (shepherd's-purse, Russian thistle, sea plantain, sea aster, *Artemesia maritima*); alkaline soil (sagebrush, woody aster); limestone soil (pennycress, peppergrass, wormseed, field madder, mountain bluet); poor drainage (smartweed, mild water pepper, hedge bindweed, white avens, swampy horsetail, meadow pink, Canada and narrow-leaved goldenrod, joe-pye weed).

Possibly the most complete source of information on this subject is Robert Kourik's *Designing and Maintaining Your Edible Landscape Naturally* (Metamorphic Press, 1986), one of the few gardening books that expresses an appreciation for wild plants. The following list of *edible* wild plants as soil indicators is extracted from the book, which also includes many non-edible and poisonous species.

Plant Name	Latin Name	Soil Indications
Agrimony	*Agrimonia eupatoria*	Dry
Amaranth	*Amaranthus retroflexus*	Dry; disturbed
Bracken (eastern)	*Pteridium aquifolium*	Low potassium and phosphorous; alkaline
Chickweed	*Stellaria media*	Disturbed; high fertility
Chicory	*Cichorium intybus*	Disturbed; clay; high fertility
Clover	*Trifolium spp.*	Low nitrogen
Coltsfoot	*Tussilago farfara*	Wet; sandy; compacted
Daisy (oxeye)	*Chrysanthemum leucanthemum*	Wet; neglected
Dandelion	*Taraxacum officinale*	Disturbed; clay; acid
Dock/sheep sorrel	*Rumex spp.*	Wet; acid
Goldenrod	*Solidago spp.*	Wet; sandy
Henbit	*Lamium amplexicaule*	Disturbed; low fertility
Horehound	*Marrubium vulgare*	Disturbed
Johnny-jump-up	*Viola spp.*	Acid
Lamb's-quarters	*Chenopodium spp.*	Disturbed; high fertility
Milkweed	*Asclepius syriaca*	Clay
Mustard	*Brassica spp.*	Compacted; acid
Pineapple weed	*Matricaria matricarioides*	Compacted
Plantain	*Plantago spp.*	Wet; disturbed; clay; acid
Queen Anne's lace	*Daucus carota*	Neglected, low fertility
Rose	*Rosa spp.*	Neglected; low nitrogen
Stinging nettle	*Urtica dioica* or *U. urens*	Wet; disturbed; acid
Shepherd's-purse	*Capsella bursa-pastoris*	Sandy; salty
Sow thistle	*Sonchus arvensis*	Clay; acid
Yarrow	*Achillea millefolium*	Low potassium

Kourik cautions that a single plant does not an indicator make. Individuals may grow in atypical situations, and certain species have wide tolerances. Rather, he suggests using plant communities as indicators. By community, he means more than one plant of a single species as well as other indicator species. For instance, one plant that prefers acidic soil might be a marginal indicator, but two or more of different species are more reliable. In the same vein, use only lush, healthy-looking plants as indicators, as stunted, sickly plants are probably not growing in their most favored habitats.

This information is based mostly on Kourik's own observations on the West Coast. It is quite possible that his observations are not 100% correct for all areas of the world. It should be taken only as a guide to a fairly new area of inquiry. You may have made similar observations of your own.

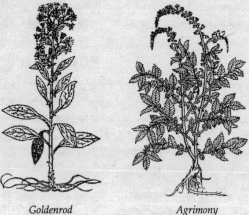

Goldenrod   Agrimony

THE LIVE CHRISTMAS TREE

by Louise Riotte

Like everything else, Christmas trees have advanced in price. For some households it may make sense to buy a small live tree which can either be kept as a house plant, such as a Norfolk Island pine (*Araucaria excelsa*) or a pine or fir of another type which may be placed in the yard after Christmas. According to Rudolph Steiner, pines are ruled by the Moon in Aquarius.

Few candidates for a Christmas tree are lovelier than the Norfolk Island pine with its bright grass-green foliage and and symmetrical branches which are produced in regular whorls of five at short but regular intervals. It is one of the most popular house plants and is the best formal plant for house decoration. Trimmed at Christmas time with tiny blue or red lights it becomes a focal point for the Christmas celebration. Make a bright skirt for the pot and place Christmas packages around the base and the whole room takes on a festive air. Since these pines grow slowly, you can enjoy your investment for a number of years to come—as well as having a pretty year-round house plant.

While the Norfolk Island pine can stand a great deal of neglect, as long as it is in a cool place and the soil about its roots kept moist, it will give its owner much more pleasure, last longer and look better if given proper care.

Potted in the house, it may be expected to grow from three to five feet. It thrives in a compost of two-thirds loam, one-third leaf mold, and a free scattering of sand. The plants do best if repotted annually until they are placed in seven to eight pots. After this, they need not be repotted, but it is beneficial in spring to remove some of the surface soil and replace with fresh compost. A sprinkling of fertilizer every month from March to September will help to keep the plants healthy.

This species is propagated by seeds and, preferably, by cuttings of terminal shoots that develop from specimens that have been cut back. It thrives best in a cool greenhouse or sunroom. Cuttings will sometimes take root if inserted in sandy soil out-of-doors.

The Norfolk Island pine has a relative bearing a rather strange name. The monkey puzzle (*Araucaria araucana*) has intricately ramifying branches covered with stiff, prickle-tipped leaves and is native to southern Chile and Tierra del Fuego; in the United States it is hardy in the far South and on the Pacific Coast. Male and female cones are usually produced on different trees. When mature, the female cones are the size and shape of a coconut.

If you are planning to buy a rooted Christmas tree which later can be planted in your yard there are a number of choices including balsam fir (*Abies balsamea*), Douglas fir (*Pseudotsuga taxifolia*), red cedar (*Juniperus virginiana* or *Thuja plicata*), and many types of pines.

The "ball" is the gardening term for the mass of soil and roots formed by plants grown in pots, and for the mass of soil held by a plant's roots when transplanted out-of-doors. Nurseries supply evergreens with their roots "balled and burlapped," that is, lifted with plenty of soil and wrapped tightly with burlap to keep them intact. The abbreviation "B and B" is sometimes used for this type of plant protection which also helps to keep the roots from drying out. The live Christmas tree you buy to plant outside will quite likely be treated in this manner.

The warm air in the house will dry your tree, so you should delay bringing it indoors until you are ready to trim it. Lights strung on the tree will also have a drying effect, so keep them switched off when the room is not occupied. It is important to keep the soil ball moist. Either place it on a piece of plastic or in a container large enough to accommodate it easily. Place a piece of plastic over it if you plan to put a skirt around the tree. In a cool room it should be possible to let the tree stay up from Christmas until after the New Year's festivities.

If the tree is to be taken down after Christmas Day or a few days after, it is a good idea to have a planting hole prepared for it in advance. If you live in a very cold climate where the ground freezes, you might even dig this hole in the late fall, return the loose earth, and cover the hole with boards.

Having planted your tree, water it to prevent air pockets and drying out. Mulch heavily with whatever materials are at hand: hay, leaves, dried grass clippings, sawdust, pecan hulls, etc. This will help to prevent the tree from heaving out of the ground should alternate freezing and thawing occur. In the spring and following summer, care for your tree just as you would any other evergreen of its type. In the years to come it will always be a pleasant memory of a Christmas past recalled lovingly by family and friends.

Your tree will have a better chance of survival if you plant it in Cancer, Scorpio or Pisces. If this means holding it out of the ground longer you can, in a pinch, use Libra or Taurus.

Note: A balsam will not drop its needles like a spruce. Place the cut end of tree in a holder containing cold water. Add water as needed. Use a floral preservative or glycerine in the water.

THE FLYING FLOWERS
by Louise Riotte

*I do not know whether I was then a man
dreaming I was a butterfly,
or whether I am now a butterfly
dreaming I am a man.*

—Chuang Tse

Humankind has noticed, loved and been impressed by butterflies for a very long time and each spring sees a renewal of wonder at just how they come to be. They seem to simply appear out of nowhere to astonish us with their exquisite and fragile beauty as we watch them flying from flower to flower.

A deeper look soon begins to tell us about their seemingly mysterious origin. Butterfly food, nectar, supplied by flowers often has no relation to plants upon which they prefer to lay their eggs, where their often less attractive young—caterpillars—delight to feed.

One of my readers wrote: "I grow parsley as much for the butterflies as us!" What a lovely attitude to take, for sharing is important and, with the exception of the white cabbage butterfly, butterflies seldom exist in numbers great enough to be detrimental—even the plants their caterpillars feed upon are seldom seriously damaged. By the laws of symbiosis they must retain enough vigor to propagate themselves so they will be there for another generation of caterpillars to munch on.

My reader added, "I have little idea what else they like." That is something I am about to remedy. For those who are interested, it is no big task to set aside a small space in the flower garden where butterflies can lay their eggs on their favorite food.

Butterflies are indeed mysterious—they may take different forms of coloration at different seasons of the year. I have written extensively about butterflies in my book *Sleeping with a Sunflower* (Storey Communications) and mention in particular the tiger swallowtail: "The curious thing is that

a female butterfly may lay a dozen eggs, some of which will develop into the usual yellow form and the rest into the black form, both groups being of the same sex. The black form is so entirely distinct in appearance that the two were originally described as separate species."

Why not begin by explaining just what plants swallowtails (*Papilionidae*) consider their favorite food. According to Clarence M. Weed, D.Sc., writing in the book *Butterflies*, the caterpillars of the black swallowtail are generally found feeding upon carrots, parsnips, parsley and various wild species belonging to this order.

The giant swallowtail is a tropical species, abundant throughout the Southern states, which, during recent years, seems to be gradually extending its northern range. In the orange-growing regions of the Southern states the caterpillars feed upon the leaves of citrus fruits and thus are often called "orange puppies" or "orange dogs."

The blue swallowtail's commonest food is the Dutchman's-pipe or aristolochia, which is frequently planted as an ornamental vine for porches. It also feeds upon wild ginger or asarum.

The beautiful green-clouded swallowtail (*P. troilus*) has tiny caterpillars which feed upon sassafras and spice bushes on which they make themselves protective nests.

The tiger swallowtail (*P. glaucus*), perhaps the most glorious of them all, lays its eggs upon a great variety of trees and shrubs, for the food plants of the larvae are unusually varied and include tulip trees, birches, wild cherries, apples, poplars, ash and several other common trees or shrubs.

The exotic zebra swallowtail (*Iphiclides ajax*) is, according to S.F. Denton, found abundantly in southern Ohio where the females lay their eggs upon the small papaw bushes. The zebra is a southern butterfly found as far west as Texas and the Rocky Mountains and having its northern limits in a zone ranging approximately from Massachusetts to Nebraska. It is especially abundant in the Southern states east of the Mississippi River.

The lovely, fragile "orange tips," somewhat smaller than other whites and yellows, feed progressively on the seasonal developing plants of the mustard family. They feed upon the host plant through the spring, completing their growth before the plant dies and then changing to chrysalids which remain dormant through the summer, fall and winter and come forth as butterflies the following spring. The insect has thus adapted itself in a most remarkable manner to the yearly history of the plant host.

In the "tribe of the yellows," the cloudless sulphur (*Callidrayas ebule*) stands out. It delights in laying its eggs on the leaflets of various species of wild senna. The orange sulphur usually produces two broods a year and its young prefer to live upon leguminous plants, especially alfalfa, buffalo clover, wild senna, and other species of *Trifolium* and *Cassia*.

The fascinating fritillaries show their beautiful colors best in the light of tropical sunshine, yet I find them in my state of Oklahoma and there is also a glorious species of northern spangled fritillaries.

The variegated fritillary (*Euptoieta claudia*) lays its eggs for a summer brood of caterpillars upon the leaves of violets, May apples, portulaca, and stonecrop. They become mature in time to disclose the butterflies of the second brood in August and September.

The great spangled fritillary (*Argynnis cybele*) lays its eggs upon the leaves and stems of wild violets, apparently without much reference to the particular species—sometimes they even drop their eggs loosely upon the violet plant with no attempt to fasten them in place!

The life history of the angle wings is exceedingly interesting. According to *Plants of the Southwest*, butterflies, unlike bees, can see red and butterfly flowers are often brilliantly colored—deep pink, scarlet, bright blue—and are generally very fragrant. Butterfly weed (*Asclepias tuberosa*) is a spectacular vivid orange. Its cousin, the common milkweed (*A. syriaca*), has silvery pink flowers and is the specific host of the monarch butterfly. Other excellent butterfly plants of the West are indigo bush, shrubby cinquefoil and coneflower. The females of the violet-tip angle wing tribe fly for several weeks, sipping nectar from many kinds of flowers. Then they search for the leaves of the elm, hop, nettle, false nettle, and other related plants for a place to drop their eggs.

Red admiral or nettle butterflies actually prefer to deposit their eggs upon the leaves of nettle, only one or a few eggs laid on each leaf. Instinctively this butterfly seems to be aware of the protective qualities of the host plant which furnishes both food and safety for its young.

The painted beauty (*Vanessa huntera*), occurring from Canada to the Southern states and beyond, is an excellent illustration of how butterflies often take advantage of any peculiarity of the food plant which has protective value. The caterpillar feeds upon the leaves of the common everlasting or graphalium. This widely distributed and fairly abundant plant is found along roadsides and in fields and pastures. Notable for its woolly covering on stems, leaves and flowers—this dry, hairy surface being so evident that the flowers will apparently continue to blossom when they have dried, hence its common name, everlasting or, as the French call a similar flower, immortelle.

The mourning cloak (*Nymphalis antiopa*) does not bear a particularly happy name for so beautiful an insect. Somehow we always think of butterflies as inhabitants of warm regions, yet upon entering the woods during a midwinter thaw one is likely to see in an open glade several dark-colored butterflies flitting from tree to tree or resting with expanded wings in the sunniest spots. These butterflies have endured the coldest weather and if they are to survive until another season must continue to endure still more. The caterpillars of mourning cloaks are restricted to comparatively few food plants. In regions where they are not especially abundant, they are likely to be found upon willow, poplar or elm. Because they are most likely to be found where there is a good growth of elm, they have been called spiny elm caterpillars.

No group of American butterflies has attracted as much attention as those known as the sovereigns. This includes the viceroy (*Limenitis archippus*), which prefers to lay its eggs on a willow or poplar. The red-spotted purple (*Basilarchia astyananax*) prefers to breed on the apple, pear, cherry, rose and many other common trees and shrubs, laying its eggs on the extreme tip of the leaves, which helps to preserve them from attack by ants, spiders, ichneumon flies, and other enemies.

The interesting tribe of the emperors includes the goatweed emperor, so called because the females deposit eggs singly upon the leaves of young goatweed plants. The gray and tawny emperor prefer the leaves of hackberry trees.

Probably no butterfly is more in evidence or better beloved than the strikingly beautiful monarch who delights our eyes from June until

October. As previously mentioned, they seek out milkweed plants and lay their eggs upon them.

BUTTERFLIES AND HELIOTROPISM

It has long been known that the green surfaces of plants respond to the stimulus of the sun's rays in a most remarkable manner. This response has commonly been called *heliotropism*. It has been observed that many animals respond in certain definite ways to the stimulus of direct sunshine and the same term has been applied in this case.

One of the earliest observations, that of Clarence M. Weed, was published in *Nature Biographies* (June, 1901). The article discussed the habit of the mourning cloak butterfly: "On a spring-like day in early November I came across one of these butterflies basking in the sunshine upon the ties of a railway track. It rested with its wings wide open. On being disturbed it would fly a short distance and then alight, and I was interested to notice that after alighting it would always turn about until the hind end of its body pointed in the direction of the sun, so that the sun's rays struck its wings and body nearly at right angles. Repeatedly watching this I was struck by its habit of getting into the position in which the most benefit from the sunshine was received, and it is of interest as showing the extreme delicacy of perception toward the warmth of sunshine which these creatures possess."

THE MYSTIC MOON

MOONLORE

by Verna Gates

THE DARK OF THE MOON

Leaving the Earth in darkness, the Moon takes a few days off to go seal hunting. The Moon is actually the very wicked Anninga, who needs a monthly rest from his depravity. It began long ago, when, in a moment of unholy passion, Anninga grabbed his sister, Malina, by the shoulders. In old Greenland, when you grabbed a woman by the shoulders, it signaled your desire for a more intimate embrace. Malina, stunned and sickened at her brother's suggestion of incest, flung herself into the sky where she runs across the heavens as the Sun, pursued by her lusty brother, the Moon.

Tired of the chase, Anninga rests for a few days each month and dines on the fat seals of the North Atlantic, until he's filled out again in his full power as the Full Moon. Now healthy, his romantic urges are so strong, they're felt by the creatures of Earth, inspiring all to love. A more gentle faction argues that Anninga was only teasing, and Malina shouldn't have slapped soot on his face and stormed off to the sky. According to these good people, Anninga just chases her to apologize. (1)

Now, if you lived far to the south, on the island of Bali, you would consider the day of the dark Moon (in the ninth month, of course) as a very good day indeed. For on this day, all the devils plaguing the island are expelled. To achieve this end, the priests set out a prepared feast at the crossroads and blow a horn summoning all devils to eat. Those devils who don't show up voluntarily find themselves forcefully invited by torch-wielding men shouting, "Go away!" Once at the feast, the poor devils can't eat in peace, for the priests curse them until they can stand it no longer and they leave the island. Everyone then takes a three-day vacation, which, I suppose, is free of deviltry. (2)

THE NEW MOON

There are a few things you should always do in the New Moon: cut hair, butcher, and turn coins. If you go back to ancient Rome, you'll find that the Emperor Tiberius would call his barber at no other time than during the new or waxing Moon, for the simple reason that he preferred watching his hair turn gray rather than turn loose. (3)

As for butchering, every good German hausfrau knows that meat slaughtered in the old Moon will shrink to nothing in the frying pan. Of course, if you follow the African tradition of turning a coin at the New Moon, you'll have plenty of prosperity to buy more sausage, should yours shrivel.

For the Aborigines, the New Moon serves as a sign of sensibility returning. During the waning Moon, they watch the Moon woman dance, sing, and drink to excess. The strain of her endless celebrations reduces her full figure to hardly more than skin and bones. When the Moon appears new again, it means she has regained her senses and has decided to take a rest and fatten back up.

THE FULL MOON

For all of the talk of the Moon and madness, the Full Moon is actually considered good luck by many cultures. In the mists of the British Isles, the Druids viewed the Full Moon as the ultimate emblem of good luck. Meanwhile, their neighbors fashioned their Gaelic word for Full Moon from the word for good fortune.

Marrying on the Full Moon gives the couple the best start, so much so that German Jews of the Middle Ages insisted on exchanging vows under a canopy blessed by a fully rounded lunar orb.

The Full Moon is also a great time to rid yourself of pesky ants. The trick is to go out at midnight, on three successive nights, during the peak of the

Moon, and wake the sleeping ants. Using a stone, knock at the entrance of the ant bed, as loudly as you please, and say three times, "Ants pay the rent, ants pay the rent, ants pay the rent." It will take about three days for the ants to realize not only do they have an annoying neighbor, but also they have no money, which will embarrass them enough to find a new abode. (4)

In the far northern realm of the Inuit, some say the Full Moon is the fair side of an injured lady. She is the sister of a magician, who was so powerful he could command the ice to split open and call out the fish; he could lure the seals with his songs until they willingly stepped out of their own skins. Yet, even these great powers could not equal his control over the most mysterious of elements—fire. So mighty was he, he decided to take fire into the sky to warm all the villages. He took his sister with him. At first, the warm, blazing home in the heavens was happy. But as all wise men know, power corrupts. Evil consumed the magician as surely as the fire consumes the log.

Finally, his sister could no longer stand his cruelty, and fought with him. During the battle, he flashed his obedient flames across one side of her face. She fled in horror. Now, the New Moon is considered her burnt side; the Full Moon, her beautiful, unscarred face. The Sun in his shame runs across the sky to avoid seeing his wounded sister. (5)

THE WANING MOON

Is a mouse nibbling away at the Moon? Or a wolf? Or perhaps a Chinese dragon, or maybe the seven demons of the Semites? Or it could be that the crescent Moon is the Egyptian god Osiris, losing a monthly battle with his dismembering enemies? (6)

Whatever causes the Moon's phases, one thing is certain, no self-respecting carpenter would use wood not cut with the waning Moon. In fact, the prudent French Forest Laws prohibited felling timber during a full or waxing Moon. When the Moon shrinks, so does the sap, making cutting easier and drying faster. (7)

THE ECLIPSE

In the past, eclipses have caused great wonderment and also great danger. The Chinese saw it as an omen of bad luck for the Emperor. To save him, they must take immediate action to drive away the Moon-eating dragons with gongs and fire crackers.

Once, two negligent astrologers decided to make a day of revelry instead of tending to the skies. Unfortunately, the Emperor was caught in an eclipse without preparation. The two unlucky astrologers who'd lost their heads in drink, now lost their heads for real. The power of the Moon and of the Emperor was not to be taken lightly. In fact, as recently as the 1800s, the young emperor Tung Chih died of small pox during an eclipse. (8)

The Orinoco tribes avoided eclipse disaster by burying lighted brands deep beneath the earth. These hidden fires stayed burning bright, out of sight, so the Moon couldn't find them and eclipse all light along with her. (9)

THE MAN IN THE MOON

Whose face do we see when we look up at the Moon? It could be the repentant, but still sinful Cain, bringing the Lord an offering of briars, the unwanted weeds of his lush fields. Or it could be Isaac we see, who remains eternally busy gathering the wood for his own sacrifice. Or perhaps, it's the man so wicked with ambition that he worked his fields on Good Friday. Caught red-handed with a pitchfork loaded with thorns, he was whisked away to the Moon. He lives there with his companion, a naughty woman who is being punished for churning butter on the Sabbath.

The Buddhists don't see a man in the Moon—they see a hare. The father of Buddhism, Sakyamuni, spent an early life as a hare who kept company with a fox and an ape. One day they were visited by the god Indra. Dutifully, the ape and fox found food suitable for such an important guest. Unfortunately, the hare could find nothing worthy for Indra to eat. So, a good and noble host, the hare threw himself into the fire, offering his own flesh as food. To reward the hare's great sacrifice, Indra rescued him, offering him a home on the Moon. (10)

The Hottentots tell a different story of the Moon rabbit, one where this animal is hardly a hero. You see, a long time ago, the Moon sent a rabbit to Earth with a message of rebirth. "People," the Moon said, "will be born, grow fat and healthy, dwindle into old and shriveled age, and then come back new again, just like the Moon and its phases."

Alas, the Moon chose a dumb bunny who scrambled the message. He said, "People will only live one life." The Moon now had to keep his messenger's word and bring death to all humanity. He was so mad at the message-botching rabbit that he threw a stick at him, forever splitting the rabbit's upper lip. In revenge, the rabbit raked his claw across the Moon's face before falling to Earth. (11)

HOW THE MOON GOT IN THE SKY

As husband and wife, the Sun and Moon whiled away many happy hours on Earth, laughing and singing, telling stories, and playing with the animals. They also loved to visit their friends. Sun especially enjoyed his deep friendship with Water. Everyday he sat by Water's side as they talked of Heaven and Earth, for both knew them well.

It occurred to Sun one day, that he always went to visit Water, but Water never came to the lovely home he shared with Moon. So one day, Sun and Moon invited Water to come home with them. Water sadly refused, saying that he was too big and there was too much of him for any house to hold.

"How can you say that!" replied Sun and Moon. "Our home is quite large and fine, and just to prove our sincerity, we'll even make it larger!" And so they did. Water agreed to come and visit the very next day.

Water knocked and Moon graciously opened the door. Her smile soon eclipsed. It shocked her to see how much of Water there really was. A whole school of whales played on the front yard. Barnacles clung to the neatly painted fence. Sharks were breaking through the tops of the trees. In Water flowed, rising higher and higher. Sting rays rested on the table tops. Catfish padded through the carpet. Silver dolphins leapt over the sofa.

Moon and Sun were greatly troubled. Yet still they invited Water to keep coming. Surely, they thought, there must be an end to him. The Water kept rising and Sun and Moon retreated first to the upper floor dining area, then to the third floor bedrooms, then finally, to the attic. There they found delicate minnows flashing through the boxes of memories stored there. Finally Sun and Moon were pushed so far into the top of their house, they were crushed up against the roof!

Water said, "Sun and Moon, there's still more of me, should I keep coming?"

Not to offend his friend, Sun said "Yes." But Moon thought better of it and begged Water to return home. And return home Water did. Unfortunately, Sun and Moon could not come down from the ceiling. They were stuck! And they're stuck still, we can see them pressed against the heavens as a result of Water's fateful visit. Since they can no longer play on Earth, they devote their lives to working in the skies, and so benefit the people of the Efik and Ibibio tribes in Africa and people in other villages as well. (12)

NOTES

(1) Paul Katzeff, *Full Moons: Fact and Fantasy about Lunar Influence*. (Secaucus, NJ: Citadel Press, 1981), pp. 4-5.

(2) Sir James Frazer, *The Golden Bough*. (New York, NY: Collier Books, 1922), pp. 645-646.

(3) Katzeff, op. cit., p. 15.

(4) John O. West, *Mexican-American Folklore*. (Little Rock, AR: August House, 1988), p. 144.

(5) Timothy Hartley, *Moon Lore*. (Rutland, VT: Charles E. Tuttle, 1970), pp. 1-2.

(6) Katzeff, op. cit., p. 4.

(7) Alexander Porteous, *Forest Folklore, Mythology and Romance*. (New York, NY: Macmillan Company, 1928), pp. 37-38.

(8) N.B. Dennys, *The Folk-Lore of China*. (New York, NY: Benjamin Blom, Inc., 1972), p.118.

(9) Frazer, op. cit., p. 90.

(10) Dennys, op. cit., p. 118.

(11) Katzeff, op. cit., p. xiv.

(12) Paul Radin, *African Folktales & Sculpture*. (Kingsport, TN: Kingsport Press, 1952), p.41.

HOW TO FIND YOUR MOON SIGN

Every year we give tables for the position of the Moon during that year, but it is more complicated to give tables for the Moon position in any year because of its continuous movement. However, the problem was solved long ago by Grant Lewi in *Astrology for the Millions*, a do-it-yourself manual (available from Llewellyn). Here's Lewi's system:

1. Find your birth year in the Moon Tables.
2. Run down the left-hand column and see if your date is there.
3. If your date is in the left-hand column, run over this line until you come to the column under your birth year. Here you will find a number. This is your base number. Write it down, and go directly to the part of the direction under the heading "What to Do with Your Base Number" on the next page.

4. If your birth date is not in the left-hand column, get a pencil and paper. Your birth date falls between two numbers in the left-hand column. Look at the date closest *after* your birth date, run over this line to your birth year. Write down the number you find there, and label it "top number." Having done this, write directly beneath it on your piece of paper the number printed just above it in the table. Label this "bottom number." Subtract the bottom number from the top number. If the top number is smaller, add 360 to it and then subtract. The result is your difference.

5. Go back to the left-hand column and find the date next *before* your birth date. Determine the number of days between this date and your birth date by subtracting or counting on your fingers. Write this down and label it "intervening days."

6. In the table of difference below, note which group your difference (found at 4 above) falls in.

Difference	Daily Motion
80-87	12 degrees
88-94	13 degrees
95-101	14 degrees
102-106	15 degrees

*Note:*If you were born in a leap year *and* use the difference between February 26th and March 5th, use the following table:

Difference	Daily Motion
94-99	12 degrees
100-108	13 degrees
109-115	14 degrees
115-122	15 degrees

7. Write down the "daily motion" corresponding to your place in the proper table of difference above. Multiply this daily motion by the number labeled "intervening days" (found at 5).

8. Add the result of 7 to your bottom number (under 4). This is your base number. If it is more than 360, subtract 360 from it and call the result your base number.

WHAT TO DO WITH YOUR BASE NUMBER

Turn to the Table of Base Numbers and locate your base number in it. At the top of the column you will find the sign your Moon was in. At the left you will find the degree your Moon occupied at ...

7 AM of your birth date if you were born under Eastern Standard Time.

6 AM of your birth date if you were born under Central Standard Time.

5 AM of your birth date if you were born under Mountain Standard Time.

4 AM of your birth date if you were born under Pacific Standard Time.

If you don't know the hour of your birth, accept this as your Moon's sign and degree.

If you do know the hour of your birth, get the exact degree as follows:

If you were born *after* 7 AM, Eastern Standard Time (6 AM Central Standard Time, etc.), determine the number of hours after the time that you were born. Divide this by two. Add this to your base number, and the result in the table will be the exact degree and sign of the Moon on the year, month, date and hour of your birth.

If you were born *before* 7 AM Eastern Standard Time (6 AM Central Standard Time, etc.), determine the number of hours before the time that you were born. Divide this by two. Subtract this from your base number, and the result in the table will be the exact degree and sign of the Moon on the year, month, date and hour of your birth.

TABLE OF BASE NUMBERS

	Aries (13)	Taurus (14)	Gemini (15)	Cancer (16)	Leo (17)	Virgo (18)	Libra (19)	Scorpio (20)	Sagittarius (21)	Capricorn (22)	Aquarius (23)	Pisces (24)
0 deg.	0	30	60	90	120	150	180	210	240	270	300	330
1 deg.	1	31	61	91	121	151	181	211	241	271	301	331
2 deg.	2	32	62	92	122	152	182	212	242	272	302	332
3 deg.	3	33	63	93	123	153	183	213	243	273	303	333
4 deg.	4	34	64	94	124	154	184	214	244	274	304	334
5 deg.	5	35	65	95	125	155	185	215	245	275	305	335
6 deg.	6	36	66	96	126	156	186	216	246	276	306	336
7 deg.	7	37	67	97	127	157	187	217	247	277	307	337
8 deg.	8	38	68	98	128	158	188	218	248	278	308	338
9 deg.	9	39	69	99	129	159	189	219	249	279	309	339
10 deg.	10	40	70	100	130	160	190	220	250	280	310	340
11 deg.	11	41	71	101	131	161	191	221	251	281	311	341
12 deg.	12	42	72	102	132	162	192	222	252	282	312	342
13 deg.	13	43	73	103	133	163	193	223	253	283	313	343
14 deg.	14	44	74	104	134	164	194	224	254	284	314	344
15 deg.	15	45	75	105	135	165	195	225	255	285	315	345
16 deg.	16	46	76	106	136	166	196	226	256	286	316	346
17 deg.	17	47	77	107	137	167	197	227	257	287	317	347
18 deg.	18	48	78	108	138	168	198	228	258	288	318	248
19 deg.	19	49	79	109	139	169	199	229	259	289	319	349
20 deg.	20	50	80	110	140	170	200	230	260	290	320	350
21 deg.	21	51	81	111	141	171	201	231	261	291	321	351
22 deg.	22	52	82	112	142	172	202	232	262	292	322	352
23 deg.	23	53	83	113	143	173	203	233	263	293	323	353
24 deg.	24	54	84	114	144	174	204	234	264	294	324	354
25 deg.	25	55	85	115	145	175	205	235	265	295	325	355
26 deg.	26	56	86	116	146	176	206	236	266	296	326	356
27 deg.	27	57	87	117	147	177	207	237	267	297	327	357
28 deg.	28	58	88	118	148	178	208	238	268	298	328	358
29 deg.	29	59	89	119	149	179	209	239	269	299	329	359

		1901	1902	1903	1904	1905	1906	1907	1908	1909	1910
Jan.	1	55	188	308	76	227	358	119	246	39	168
Jan.	8	149	272	37	179	319	82	208	350	129	252
Jan.	15	234	2	141	270	43	174	311	81	213	346
Jan.	22	327	101	234	353	138	273	44	164	309	84
Jan.	29	66	196	317	84	238	6	128	255	50	175
Feb.	5	158	280	46	188	328	90	219	359	138	259
Feb.	12	241	12	149	279	51	184	319	90	221	356
Feb.	19	335	111	242	2	146	283	52	173	317	94
Feb.	26	76	204	326	92	248	13	136	264	60	184
Mar.	5	166	288	57	211	336	98	229	21	147	267
Mar.	12	249	22	157	300	60	194	328	110	230	5
Mar.	19	344	121	250	24	154	293	60	195	325	105
Mar.	26	86	212	334	116	258	22	144	288	69	192
Apr.	2	175	296	68	219	345	106	240	29	155	276
Apr.	9	258	31	167	309	69	202	338	118	240	13
Apr.	16	352	132	258	33	163	304	68	204	334	115
Apr.	23	96	220	342	127	267	31	152	299	77	201
Apr.	30	184	304	78	227	354	114	250	38	164	285
May	7	267	40	177	317	78	210	348	126	249	21
May	14	1	142	266	42	172	313	76	212	344	124
May	21	104	229	350	138	275	40	160	310	85	210
May	28	193	313	87	236	2	123	259	47	172	294
Jun.	4	277	48	187	324	88	219	358	134	258	30
Jun.	11	11	151	275	50	182	322	85	220	355	132
Jun.	18	112	238	359	149	283	48	169	320	93	218
Jun.	25	201	322	96	245	11	133	267	57	180	304
Jul.	2	286	57	197	333	97	228	8	142	267	40
Jul.	9	21	160	283	58	193	330	94	228	6	140
Jul.	16	121	247	7	159	291	57	178	330	102	226
Jul.	23	209	332	105	255	18	143	276	66	188	314
Jul.	30	295	66	206	341	105	239	17	151	275	51
Aug.	6	32	168	292	66	204	338	103	237	17	148
Aug.	13	130	255	17	168	301	65	188	339	111	234
Aug.	20	217	341	113	265	27	152	285	76	197	323
Aug.	27	303	77	215	350	113	250	25	160	283	62
Sep.	3	43	176	301	75	215	346	111	246	27	157
Sep.	10	139	263	27	176	310	73	198	347	121	242
Sep.	17	225	350	123	274	35	161	294	85	205	331
Sep.	24	311	88	223	358	122	261	33	169	292	73
Oct.	1	53	185	309	85	224	355	119	256	35	166
Oct.	8	149	271	36	185	320	81	207	356	130	250
Oct.	15	233	359	133	283	44	169	305	93	214	339
Oct.	22	319	99	231	7	130	271	42	177	301	83
Oct.	29	62	194	317	95	233	5	127	266	44	176
Nov.	5	158	279	45	193	329	89	216	5	139	259
Nov.	12	242	6	144	291	53	177	316	101	223	347
Nov.	19	328	109	239	15	140	280	50	185	311	91
Nov.	26	70	203	325	105	241	14	135	276	52	185
Dec.	3	168	288	54	203	338	98	224	15	148	268
Dec.	10	251	14	155	299	61	185	327	109	231	356
Dec.	17	338	118	248	23	150	289	59	193	322	99
Dec.	24	78	213	333	115	249	23	143	286	61	194
Dec.	31	176	296	61	213	346	107	232	26	155	277

		1911	1912	1913	1914	1915	1916	1917	1918	1919	1920
Jan.	1	289	57	211	337	100	228	23	147	270	39
Jan.	8	20	162	299	61	192	332	110	231	5	143
Jan.	15	122	251	23	158	293	61	193	329	103	231
Jan.	22	214	335	120	256	23	145	290	68	193	316
Jan.	29	298	66	221	345	108	237	32	155	278	49
Feb.	5	31	170	308	69	203	340	118	239	16	150
Feb.	12	130	260	32	167	302	70	203	338	113	239
Feb.	19	222	344	128	266	31	154	298	78	201	325
Feb.	26	306	75	231	353	116	248	41	164	286	60
Mar.	5	42	192	317	77	214	2	127	248	26	172
Mar.	12	140	280	41	176	311	89	212	346	123	259
Mar.	19	230	5	136	276	39	176	308	87	209	346
Mar.	26	314	100	239	2	124	273	49	173	294	85
Apr.	2	52	200	326	86	223	10	135	257	35	181
Apr.	9	150	288	51	184	321	97	222	355	133	267
Apr.	16	238	14	146	286	48	184	318	96	218	355
Apr.	23	322	111	247	11	132	284	57	181	303	96
Apr.	30	61	208	334	96	232	19	143	267	43	190
May.	7	160	296	60	192	331	105	231	4	142	275
May.	14	246	22	156	294	56	192	329	104	227	3
May.	21	331	122	255	20	141	294	66	190	312	105
May.	28	69	218	342	106	240	29	151	277	51	200
Jun.	4	170	304	69	202	341	114	240	14	151	284
Jun.	11	255	30	167	302	65	200	340	112	235	11
Jun.	18	340	132	264	28	151	304	74	198	322	114
Jun.	25	78	228	350	115	249	39	159	286	60	209
Jul.	2	179	312	78	212	349	122	248	25	159	293
Jul.	9	264	39	178	310	74	209	350	120	244	20
Jul.	16	349	141	273	36	161	312	84	206	332	123
Jul.	23	87	237	358	125	258	48	168	295	70	218
Jul.	30	187	321	86	223	357	131	256	36	167	302
Aug.	6	272	48	188	319	82	219	360	129	252	31
Aug.	13	359	150	282	44	171	320	93	214	342	131
Aug.	20	96	246	6	133	268	57	177	303	81	226
Aug.	27	195	330	94	234	5	140	265	46	175	310
Sep.	3	281	57	198	328	90	229	9	138	260	41
Sep.	10	9	158	292	52	180	329	102	222	351	140
Sep.	17	107	255	15	141	279	65	186	312	91	234
Sep.	24	203	339	103	244	13	149	274	56	184	319
Oct.	1	288	68	206	337	98	240	17	148	268	52
Oct.	8	18	167	301	61	189	338	111	231	360	150
Oct.	15	118	263	24	149	290	73	195	320	102	242
Oct.	22	212	347	113	254	22	157	284	65	193	326
Oct.	29	296	78	214	346	106	250	25	157	276	61
Nov.	5	26	177	309	70	197	348	119	240	7	161
Nov.	12	129	271	33	158	300	81	203	329	112	250
Nov.	19	221	355	123	262	31	164	295	73	202	334
Nov.	26	305	88	223	355	115	259	34	165	285	70
Dec.	3	34	187	317	79	205	359	127	249	16	171
Dec.	10	138	279	41	168	310	89	211	340	120	259
Dec.	17	230	3	134	270	40	172	305	81	211	343
Dec.	24	313	97	232	3	124	267	44	173	294	78
Dec.	31	42	198	325	87	214	9	135	257	25	181

		1921	1922	1923	1924	1925	1926	1927	1928	1929	1930
Jan.	1	194	317	80	211	5	127	250	23	176	297
Jan.	8	280	41	177	313	90	211	349	123	260	22
Jan.	15	4	141	275	41	175	312	86	211	346	123
Jan.	22	101	239	3	127	272	51	172	297	83	222
Jan.	29	203	325	88	222	13	135	258	34	184	306
Feb.	5	289	49	188	321	99	220	359	131	269	31
Feb.	12	14	149	284	49	185	320	95	219	356	131
Feb.	19	110	249	11	135	281	60	181	305	93	230
Feb.	26	211	334	96	233	21	144	266	45	191	314
Mar.	5	297	58	197	343	107	230	8	153	276	41
Mar.	12	23	157	294	69	194	328	105	238	6	140
Mar.	19	119	258	19	157	292	68	190	327	104	238
Mar.	26	219	343	104	258	29	153	275	70	200	323
Apr.	2	305	68	205	352	115	240	16	163	284	51
Apr.	9	33	166	304	77	204	337	114	247	14	149
Apr.	16	130	266	28	164	303	76	198	335	115	246
Apr.	23	227	351	114	268	38	161	285	79	208	331
Apr.	30	313	78	214	1	123	250	25	172	292	61
May.	7	42	176	313	85	212	348	123	256	23	160
May.	14	141	274	37	173	314	84	207	344	125	254
May.	21	236	359	123	277	47	169	295	88	217	339
May.	28	321	88	222	11	131	259	34	181	301	70
Jun.	4	50	186	321	94	220	358	131	264	31	171
Jun.	11	152	282	45	182	324	93	215	354	135	263
Jun.	18	245	7	134	285	56	177	305	96	226	347
Jun.	25	330	97	232	20	139	268	44	190	310	78
Jul.	2	58	197	329	103	229	9	139	273	40	181
Jul.	9	162	291	54	192	333	101	223	4	144	272
Jul.	16	254	15	144	294	65	185	315	104	236	355
Jul.	23	338	106	242	28	148	276	54	198	319	87
Jul.	30	67	208	337	112	238	20	147	282	49	191
Aug.	6	171	300	62	202	341	110	231	15	152	281
Aug.	13	264	24	153	302	74	194	324	114	244	4
Aug.	20	347	114	253	36	157	285	65	206	328	95
Aug.	27	76	218	346	120	248	29	156	290	59	200
Sep.	3	179	309	70	213	350	119	239	25	161	290
Sep.	10	273	32	162	312	83	203	332	124	252	13
Sep.	17	356	122	264	44	166	293	75	214	337	105
Sep.	24	86	227	354	128	258	38	165	298	70	208
Oct.	1	187	318	78	223	358	128	248	35	169	298
Oct.	8	281	41	170	322	91	212	340	134	260	23
Oct.	15	5	132	274	52	175	303	85	222	345	115
Oct.	22	97	235	3	136	269	46	174	306	81	216
Oct.	29	196	327	87	232	7	137	257	44	179	307
Nov.	5	289	50	178	332	99	221	349	144	268	31
Nov.	12	13	142	283	61	183	313	93	231	353	126
Nov.	19	107	243	12	144	279	54	183	315	91	225
Nov.	26	206	335	96	241	17	145	266	52	189	314
Dec.	3	297	59	187	343	107	230	359	154	276	39
Dec.	10	21	152	291	70	191	324	101	240	1	137
Dec.	17	117	252	21	153	289	63	191	324	99	234
Dec.	24	216	343	105	249	28	152	275	60	199	322
Dec.	31	305	67	197	352	115	237	9	162	285	47

		1931	1932	1933	1934	1935	1936	1937	1938	1939	1940
Jan.	1	60	196	346	107	231	8	156	277	41	181
Jan.	8	162	294	70	193	333	104	240	4	144	275
Jan.	15	257	20	158	294	68	190	329	104	239	360
Jan.	22	342	108	255	32	152	278	67	202	323	88
Jan.	29	68	207	353	116	239	19	163	286	49	191
Feb.	5	171	302	78	203	342	113	248	14	153	284
Feb.	12	267	28	168	302	78	198	339	113	248	8
Feb.	19	351	116	266	40	161	286	78	210	332	96
Feb.	26	77	217	1	124	248	29	171	294	59	200
Mar.	5	179	324	86	213	350	135	256	25	161	306
Mar.	12	276	48	176	311	86	218	347	123	256	29
Mar.	19	360	137	277	48	170	308	89	218	340	119
Mar.	26	86	241	10	132	258	52	180	302	69	223
Apr.	2	187	334	94	223	358	144	264	34	169	315
Apr.	9	285	57	185	321	95	227	355	133	264	38
Apr.	16	9	146	287	56	178	317	99	226	349	128
Apr.	23	96	250	18	140	268	61	189	310	80	231
Apr.	30	196	343	102	232	7	153	273	43	179	323
May.	7	293	66	193	332	103	237	4	144	272	47
May.	14	17	155	297	64	187	327	108	235	357	139
May.	21	107	258	28	148	278	69	198	318	90	239
May.	28	205	351	111	241	17	161	282	51	189	331
Jun.	4	301	75	201	343	111	245	13	154	280	55
Jun.	11	25	165	306	73	195	337	117	244	5	150
Jun.	18	117	267	37	157	288	78	207	327	99	248
Jun.	25	215	360	120	249	28	169	291	60	200	339
Jul.	2	309	84	211	353	119	254	23	164	289	64
Jul.	9	33	176	315	82	203	348	125	253	13	160
Jul.	16	126	276	46	165	297	87	216	336	108	258
Jul.	23	226	8	130	258	38	177	300	69	210	347
Jul.	30	317	92	221	2	128	262	33	173	298	72
Aug.	6	41	187	323	91	211	359	133	261	21	170
Aug.	13	135	285	54	175	305	97	224	346	116	268
Aug.	20	237	16	138	267	49	185	308	78	220	355
Aug.	27	326	100	232	10	136	270	44	181	307	80
Sep.	3	49	197	331	100	220	8	142	270	31	179
Sep.	10	143	295	62	184	314	107	232	355	125	278
Sep.	17	247	24	147	277	58	194	317	89	228	4
Sep.	24	335	108	243	18	145	278	55	189	316	88
Oct.	1	58	206	341	108	229	17	152	278	40	188
Oct.	8	151	306	70	193	322	117	240	4	134	288
Oct.	15	256	32	155	287	66	203	324	100	236	13
Oct.	22	344	116	253	27	154	287	64	198	324	98
Oct.	29	68	214	350	116	239	25	162	286	49	196
Nov.	5	161	316	78	201	332	126	248	12	145	297
Nov.	12	264	41	162	298	74	212	333	111	244	22
Nov.	19	353	125	262	36	162	296	73	207	332	108
Nov.	26	77	222	0	124	248	33	172	294	58	205
Dec.	3	171	325	87	209	343	135	257	19	156	305
Dec.	10	272	50	171	309	82	220	341	120	253	30
Dec.	17	1	135	271	45	170	306	81	217	340	118
Dec.	24	86	231	10	132	256	43	181	302	66	214
Dec.	31	182	333	95	217	354	142	265	27	167	313

		1941	1942	1943	1944	1945	1946	1947	1948	1949	1950
Jan.	1	325	88	211	353	135	258	22	165	305	68
Jan.	8	50	176	315	85	219	348	126	256	29	160
Jan.	15	141	276	50	169	312	87	220	340	123	258
Jan.	22	239	12	133	258	52	182	303	69	224	352
Jan.	29	333	96	221	2	143	266	32	174	314	75
Feb.	5	57	186	323	95	227	358	134	265	37	170
Feb.	12	150	285	58	178	320	96	228	349	131	268
Feb.	19	250	20	142	267	62	190	312	78	234	359
Feb.	26	342	104	231	11	152	274	43	182	323	83
Mar.	5	65	196	331	116	236	8	142	286	46	179
Mar.	12	158	295	66	199	328	107	236	10	139	279
Mar.	19	261	28	150	290	72	198	320	102	243	8
Mar.	26	351	112	242	34	161	281	53	204	332	91
Apr.	2	74	205	340	125	244	16	152	294	55	187
Apr.	9	166	306	74	208	337	117	244	19	148	289
Apr.	16	270	36	158	300	81	206	328	112	252	17
Apr.	23	360	120	252	42	170	290	63	212	340	100
Apr.	30	83	214	350	133	254	25	162	302	64	195
May	7	174	316	82	217	346	127	252	27	158	299
May	14	279	45	166	311	90	215	336	123	260	26
May	21	9	128	261	50	179	299	72	221	349	110
May	28	92	222	1	141	263	33	173	310	73	204
Jun.	4	184	326	91	226	356	137	261	36	168	307
Jun.	11	287	54	174	322	98	224	344	134	268	34
Jun.	18	17	137	270	60	187	308	81	231	357	119
Jun.	25	102	231	11	149	272	42	183	318	82	213
Jul.	2	194	335	99	234	7	145	269	44	179	316
Jul.	9	296	63	183	332	106	233	353	144	277	43
Jul.	16	25	147	279	70	195	318	89	241	5	129
Jul.	23	110	240	21	157	280	52	192	327	91	224
Jul.	30	205	343	108	242	18	153	278	52	190	324
Aug.	6	304	71	192	341	115	241	3	153	286	51
Aug.	13	33	156	287	80	203	327	98	251	13	138
Aug.	20	119	250	30	165	289	63	201	336	99	235
Aug.	27	216	351	117	250	28	162	287	61	200	332
Sep.	3	314	80	201	350	125	249	13	161	296	59
Sep.	10	41	165	296	90	211	336	108	260	21	146
Sep.	17	127	261	39	174	297	74	209	345	107	246
Sep.	24	226	359	126	259	38	170	295	70	209	341
Oct.	1	323	88	211	358	135	257	22	170	306	67
Oct.	8	49	174	306	99	220	344	118	269	30	154
Oct.	15	135	272	47	183	305	84	217	353	116	256
Oct.	22	236	8	134	269	47	180	303	80	217	351
Oct.	29	333	95	220	7	144	265	31	179	315	75
Nov.	5	58	181	317	107	229	352	129	277	39	162
Nov.	12	143	283	55	192	314	94	225	1	125	265
Nov.	19	244	18	141	279	55	189	311	90	225	0
Nov.	26	343	104	229	16	153	274	39	189	323	84
Dec.	3	67	189	328	115	237	360	140	284	47	171
Dec.	10	153	292	64	200	324	103	234	9	136	274
Dec.	17	252	28	149	289	63	199	319	100	234	9
Dec.	24	351	112	237	27	161	282	47	199	331	93
Dec.	31	76	198	338	123	246	9	150	293	55	180

		1951	1952	1953	1954	1955	1956	1957	1958	1959	1960
Jan.	1	194	336	115	238	6	147	285	47	178	317
Jan.	8	297	67	199	331	107	237	9	143	278	47
Jan.	15	30	150	294	70	200	320	104	242	9	131
Jan.	22	114	240	35	161	284	51	207	331	94	223
Jan.	29	204	344	124	245	17	155	294	55	189	325
Feb.	5	305	76	207	341	116	246	18	152	287	56
Feb.	12	38	159	302	80	208	330	112	252	17	140
Feb.	19	122	249	45	169	292	61	216	340	102	233
Feb.	26	215	352	133	253	27	163	303	63	199	333
Mar.	5	314	96	216	350	125	266	27	161	297	75
Mar.	12	46	180	310	91	216	351	121	262	25	161
Mar.	19	130	274	54	178	300	86	224	349	110	259
Mar.	26	225	14	142	262	37	185	312	72	208	356
Apr.	2	324	104	226	358	135	274	37	169	307	83
Apr.	9	54	189	319	100	224	360	131	271	34	170
Apr.	16	138	285	62	187	308	97	232	357	118	269
Apr.	23	235	23	150	271	46	194	320	82	217	5
Apr.	30	334	112	235	6	146	282	46	177	317	91
May	7	62	197	330	109	232	8	142	279	42	177
May	14	146	296	70	196	316	107	240	6	127	279
May	21	243	32	158	280	54	204	328	91	225	15
May	28	344	120	244	15	155	290	55	187	326	100
Jun.	4	71	205	341	117	241	16	153	288	51	186
Jun.	11	155	306	79	204	325	117	249	14	137	288
Jun.	18	252	42	166	290	63	214	336	101	234	25
Jun.	25	354	128	253	26	164	298	63	198	335	109
Jul.	2	80	214	351	125	250	24	164	296	60	195
Jul.	9	164	315	88	212	335	126	259	22	147	297
Jul.	16	260	52	174	299	72	223	344	110	243	34
Jul.	23	3	137	261	37	173	307	71	209	343	118
Jul.	30	89	222	2	134	258	33	174	304	68	205
Aug.	6	174	324	97	220	345	134	268	30	156	305
Aug.	13	270	62	182	308	82	232	353	118	254	42
Aug.	20	11	146	269	48	181	316	79	220	351	126
Aug.	27	97	232	11	143	267	43	183	314	76	215
Sep.	3	184	332	107	228	355	143	278	38	166	314
Sep.	10	280	71	191	316	92	241	2	127	265	50
Sep.	17	19	155	278	58	189	325	88	230	359	135
Sep.	24	105	242	20	152	274	54	191	323	84	225
Oct.	1	193	341	116	237	4	152	287	47	174	324
Oct.	8	291	79	200	324	103	249	11	135	276	58
Oct.	15	27	163	287	68	198	333	98	239	8	143
Oct.	22	113	252	28	162	282	64	199	332	92	235
Oct.	29	201	350	125	245	12	162	295	56	182	334
Nov.	5	302	87	209	333	114	256	19	144	286	66
Nov.	12	36	171	297	76	207	341	109	247	17	150
Nov.	19	121	262	37	171	291	73	208	341	101	244
Nov.	26	209	0	133	254	20	173	303	65	190	345
Dec.	3	312	95	217	342	124	265	27	154	295	75
Dec.	10	45	179	307	84	216	348	119	255	27	158
Dec.	17	129	271	46	180	299	82	218	350	110	252
Dec.	24	217	11	141	263	28	184	311	73	199	355
Dec.	31	321	103	225	352	132	273	35	164	303	84

		1961	1962	1963	1964	1965	1966	1967	1968	1969	1970
Jan.	1	96	217	350	128	266	27	163	298	76	197
Jan.	8	179	315	89	217	350	126	260	27	161	297
Jan.	15	275	54	179	302	86	225	349	112	257	36
Jan.	22	18	141	264	35	189	311	74	207	359	122
Jan.	29	105	225	1	136	275	35	173	306	85	206
Feb.	5	188	323	99	225	360	134	270	35	171	305
Feb.	12	284	64	187	310	95	235	357	121	267	45
Feb.	19	26	150	272	46	197	320	81	218	7	130
Feb.	26	113	234	11	144	283	45	182	315	93	216
Mar.	5	198	331	109	245	9	142	280	54	180	313
Mar.	12	293	73	195	332	105	244	5	142	277	54
Mar.	19	34	159	280	71	205	329	90	243	15	139
Mar.	26	122	243	19	167	291	54	190	338	101	226
Apr.	2	208	340	119	253	18	151	290	63	189	323
Apr.	9	303	82	204	340	116	252	14	150	288	62
Apr.	16	42	167	288	81	213	337	99	253	23	147
Apr.	23	130	253	28	176	299	64	198	347	109	235
Apr.	30	216	349	128	261	27	161	298	71	197	333
May	7	314	90	213	348	127	260	23	158	299	70
May	14	51	176	298	91	222	345	109	262	32	155
May	21	137	263	36	186	307	74	207	357	117	245
May	28	225	359	137	270	35	172	307	80	205	344
Jun.	4	325	98	222	357	137	268	31	168	309	78
Jun.	11	60	184	308	99	231	353	119	270	42	163
Jun.	18	146	272	45	195	315	82	217	6	126	253
Jun.	25	233	10	145	279	43	183	315	89	214	355
Jul.	2	336	106	230	6	147	276	40	178	318	87
Jul.	9	70	191	318	108	241	1	129	279	51	171
Jul.	16	154	281	56	204	324	91	227	14	135	261
Jul.	23	241	21	153	288	52	193	323	98	223	5
Jul.	30	345	115	238	16	156	286	47	188	327	97
Aug.	6	79	200	327	116	250	10	138	288	60	180
Aug.	13	163	289	66	212	333	99	238	22	144	270
Aug.	20	250	32	161	296	61	203	331	106	233	14
Aug.	27	353	124	246	27	164	295	55	199	335	106
Sep.	3	88	208	336	126	259	19	147	297	68	189
Sep.	10	172	297	77	220	342	108	249	30	152	279
Sep.	17	260	41	170	304	72	212	340	114	244	23
Sep.	24	1	134	254	37	172	304	64	208	344	115
Oct.	1	97	217	344	136	267	28	155	308	76	198
Oct.	8	180	306	88	228	351	117	259	38	161	289
Oct.	15	270	50	179	312	82	220	350	122	254	31
Oct.	22	10	143	262	47	182	313	73	217	353	123
Oct.	29	105	226	352	146	275	37	163	318	84	207
Nov.	5	189	315	97	237	359	127	268	47	168	299
Nov.	12	281	58	188	320	93	228	359	130	264	39
Nov.	19	19	151	271	55	191	321	82	225	3	131
Nov.	26	113	235	1	157	282	45	172	328	92	215
Dec.	3	197	326	105	245	7	138	276	55	176	310
Dec.	10	291	66	197	328	102	237	7	139	273	48
Dec.	17	30	159	280	63	202	329	91	234	13	139
Dec.	24	121	243	11	167	291	53	183	337	101	223
Dec.	31	204	336	113	254	14	149	284	64	184	320

		1971	1972	1973	1974	1975	1976	1977	1978	1979	1980
Jan.	1	335	109	246	8	147	279	56	179	318	90
Jan.	8	71	197	332	108	243	6	144	278	54	176
Jan.	15	158	283	69	207	328	93	240	18	139	263
Jan.	22	244	20	169	292	54	192	339	102	224	4
Jan.	29	344	117	255	17	156	288	64	188	327	99
Feb.	5	81	204	342	116	253	14	153	287	63	184
Feb.	12	167	291	79	216	337	101	251	26	147	271
Feb.	19	252	31	177	300	62	203	347	110	233	14
Feb.	26	353	126	263	27	164	297	72	199	334	109
Mar.	5	91	224	351	124	262	34	162	296	72	204
Mar.	12	176	312	90	224	346	122	262	34	156	293
Mar.	19	261	55	185	309	72	226	356	118	243	37
Mar.	26	1	149	270	37	172	320	80	208	343	130
Apr.	2	100	233	360	134	270	43	170	307	80	213
Apr.	9	184	320	101	232	355	131	273	42	164	302
Apr.	16	271	64	194	317	82	235	5	126	254	46
Apr.	23	9	158	278	47	181	329	88	217	352	139
Apr.	30	109	242	8	145	278	52	178	318	88	222
May	7	193	329	111	240	3	141	282	50	173	312
May	14	281	73	203	324	92	243	14	134	264	54
May	21	19	167	287	55	191	337	97	226	3	147
May	28	117	251	16	156	286	61	187	328	96	231
Jun.	4	201	339	120	249	11	151	291	59	180	323
Jun.	11	291	81	213	333	102	252	23	143	273	63
Jun.	18	29	176	296	64	201	346	106	234	13	155
Jun.	25	125	260	25	167	295	69	196	338	105	239
Jul.	2	209	349	129	258	19	162	299	68	188	334
Jul.	9	300	90	222	341	111	261	32	152	282	72
Jul.	16	40	184	305	72	212	354	115	243	24	163
Jul.	23	133	268	35	176	303	78	206	347	114	248
Jul.	30	217	0	137	267	27	172	308	77	197	344
Aug.	6	309	99	230	350	120	271	40	161	290	83
Aug.	13	51	192	314	81	223	2	124	252	34	171
Aug.	20	142	276	45	185	312	86	217	356	123	256
Aug.	27	225	10	146	276	36	182	317	86	206	353
Sep.	3	317	109	238	360	128	281	48	170	299	93
Sep.	10	61	200	322	90	232	10	132	262	43	180
Sep.	17	151	284	56	193	321	94	228	4	132	264
Sep.	24	234	20	155	284	45	191	326	94	215	2
Oct.	1	325	120	246	9	136	291	56	179	308	103
Oct.	8	70	208	330	101	241	19	140	273	51	189
Oct.	15	160	292	66	202	330	102	238	12	140	273
Oct.	22	243	28	165	292	54	199	336	102	225	10
Oct.	29	334	130	254	17	146	301	64	187	318	112
Nov.	5	79	217	338	112	249	27	148	284	59	197
Nov.	12	169	300	76	210	339	111	247	21	148	282
Nov.	19	253	36	175	300	63	207	347	110	234	18
Nov.	26	344	139	262	25	156	310	73	195	329	120
Dec.	3	87	226	346	122	257	36	157	294	67	206
Dec.	10	177	310	84	220	347	121	255	31	156	292
Dec.	17	261	45	185	308	72	216	356	118	242	28
Dec.	24	355	148	271	33	167	318	81	203	340	128
Dec.	31	95	235	355	132	265	44	166	303	76	214

		1981	1982	1983	1984	1985	1986	1987	1988	1989	1990
Jan.	1	226	350	129	260	36	162	300	71	205	333
Jan.	8	315	89	225	346	126	260	36	156	297	72
Jan.	15	53	188	309	73	225	358	119	243	37	168
Jan.	22	149	272	35	176	319	82	206	348	129	252
Jan.	29	234	0	137	270	43	172	308	81	213	343
Feb.	5	324	98	234	354	135	270	44	164	306	82
Feb.	12	64	196	317	81	236	6	128	252	48	175
Feb.	19	157	280	45	185	328	90	217	356	138	260
Feb.	26	242	10	145	279	51	182	316	90	222	353
Mar.	5	332	108	242	15	143	280	52	185	313	93
Mar.	12	74	204	326	104	246	14	136	275	57	184
Mar.	19	166	288	55	208	337	97	227	19	147	268
Mar.	26	250	20	154	300	60	191	326	111	230	1
Apr.	2	340	119	250	24	151	291	60	194	322	103
Apr.	9	84	212	334	114	255	22	144	286	66	192
Apr.	16	175	296	66	216	346	106	237	27	156	276
Apr.	23	259	28	164	309	69	199	336	119	240	9
Apr.	30	349	130	258	33	160	302	68	203	331	113
May	7	93	221	342	124	264	31	152	297	75	201
May	14	184	304	75	225	355	114	246	36	165	285
May	21	268	36	175	317	78	207	347	127	249	18
May	28	358	140	266	41	170	311	76	211	341	122
Jun.	4	102	230	350	135	272	40	160	307	83	210
Jun.	11	193	313	84	234	3	123	255	45	173	294
Jun.	18	277	45	185	325	87	216	357	135	258	27
Jun.	25	8	149	275	49	180	320	85	219	352	130
Jul.	2	110	239	359	146	281	49	169	317	92	219
Jul.	9	201	322	93	244	11	133	263	55	181	304
Jul.	16	286	54	196	333	96	225	7	143	266	37
Jul.	23	19	158	284	57	191	328	94	227	3	138
Jul.	30	119	248	7	155	290	57	178	327	101	227
Aug.	6	210	331	101	254	19	142	272	66	189	313
Aug.	13	294	64	205	341	104	236	16	152	274	48
Aug.	20	30	166	293	66	202	337	103	236	13	147
Aug.	27	128	256	17	164	299	65	187	335	111	235
Sep.	3	218	340	110	264	27	151	281	75	197	321
Sep.	10	302	75	214	350	112	247	24	160	282	59
Sep.	17	40	174	302	74	212	345	112	245	23	156
Sep.	24	138	264	26	172	309	73	197	343	121	243
Oct.	1	226	349	119	274	36	159	292	84	206	329
Oct.	8	310	86	222	359	120	258	32	169	291	70
Oct.	15	50	183	310	84	220	354	120	255	31	165
Oct.	22	148	272	35	181	319	81	206	352	130	251
Oct.	29	234	357	130	282	44	167	303	92	214	337
Nov.	5	318	96	230	8	129	268	40	178	300	79
Nov.	12	58	193	318	93	229	4	128	265	39	175
Nov.	19	158	280	44	190	329	90	214	2	139	260
Nov.	26	243	5	141	290	53	175	314	100	223	345
Dec.	3	327	106	238	16	139	277	49	185	310	88
Dec.	10	66	203	326	103	237	14	136	274	48	185
Dec.	17	167	288	52	200	337	98	222	12	147	269
Dec.	24	252	13	152	298	62	184	324	108	232	355
Dec.	31	337	114	248	24	149	285	59	193	320	96

		1991	1992	1993	1994	1995	1996	1997	1998	1999	2000
Jan.	1	111	242	15	145	281	53	185	317	92	223
Jan.	8	206	326	108	244	16	136	279	56	186	307
Jan.	15	289	54	210	337	99	225	21	147	270	37
Jan.	22	18	158	299	61	190	329	110	231	2	140
Jan.	29	119	252	23	155	290	62	193	326	101	232
Feb.	5	214	335	116	254	24	145	287	66	193	315
Feb.	12	298	63	220	345	108	235	31	155	278	47
Feb.	19	29	166	308	69	201	337	119	239	12	148
Feb.	26	128	260	32	164	299	70	202	335	111	240
Mar.	5	222	356	124	265	32	166	295	76	201	337
Mar.	12	306	87	229	354	116	259	39	164	285	72
Mar.	19	39	189	317	77	211	360	128	248	22	170
Mar.	26	138	280	41	172	310	90	212	343	121	260
Apr.	2	230	5	133	275	40	175	305	86	210	345
Apr.	9	314	98	237	3	123	270	47	173	294	83
Apr.	16	49	198	326	86	220	9	136	257	31	180
Apr.	23	148	288	50	180	320	98	221	351	132	268
Apr.	30	238	13	143	284	48	183	315	95	218	353
May	7	322	109	245	12	132	281	55	182	302	93
May	14	57	207	335	95	228	18	144	267	39	190
May	21	158	296	59	189	330	106	230	1	141	276
May	28	247	21	154	292	57	191	326	103	227	1
Jun.	4	330	119	253	21	141	291	64	190	311	102
Jun.	11	66	217	343	105	236	28	152	276	48	199
Jun.	18	168	304	68	199	340	114	238	11	150	285
Jun.	25	256	29	165	300	66	199	337	111	236	10
Jul.	2	339	129	262	29	150	300	73	198	321	111
Jul.	9	74	227	351	114	245	38	160	285	57	209
Jul.	16	177	313	76	210	348	123	246	22	158	293
Jul.	23	265	38	175	309	75	208	347	120	245	19
Jul.	30	349	137	272	37	160	308	83	206	331	119
Aug.	6	83	237	359	123	255	48	169	293	67	218
Aug.	13	186	322	84	221	356	132	254	33	166	302
Aug.	20	273	47	185	318	83	218	356	129	253	29
Aug.	27	358	146	282	45	169	317	93	214	340	128
Sep.	3	93	246	7	131	265	56	177	301	78	226
Sep.	10	194	331	92	231	4	141	263	43	174	311
Sep.	17	281	56	194	327	91	228	5	138	261	39
Sep.	24	8	154	292	53	178	326	102	223	349	137
Oct.	1	104	254	16	139	276	64	186	310	89	234
Oct.	8	202	339	101	241	13	149	273	53	183	319
Oct.	15	289	66	202	337	99	238	13	148	269	49
Oct.	22	16	164	301	61	187	336	111	231	357	148
Oct.	29	115	262	25	148	287	72	195	318	100	242
Nov.	5	211	347	111	250	22	157	283	61	193	326
Nov.	12	297	76	211	346	107	247	22	157	277	58
Nov.	19	24	174	309	70	194	346	119	240	5	159
Nov.	26	126	270	33	156	297	80	203	328	109	251
Dec.	3	220	355	121	258	31	165	293	69	202	334
Dec.	10	305	85	220	355	115	256	31	165	286	67
Dec.	17	32	185	317	79	203	357	127	249	13	169
Dec.	24	135	278	41	166	306	89	211	338	117	260
Dec.	31	230	3	131	266	41	173	303	78	211	343

YOUR PERSONAL MOON SIGN
by Gavin Kent McClung

The Moon is the point of life potential through which we contact the universe at the "gut level" of experience. Here is where we unthinkingly absorb nourishment from outside ourselves and where we instinctively give sustenance to others. The Moon represents life at the wavelength of feeling and mothering. Both men and women must fulfill this role or operate at this frequency from time to time.

ARIES MOON

Anyone who knows an Aries Moon also knows the boost of feelings associated with a person of high emotional aspiration. This active, often impetuous force is powered by a keen imagination and a compass-like search for the "true north" of inward, person-to-person situations. This may result in a shy appearing or jumpy person, always ready to be off and away from close confrontations.

Here, the first impulse that occurs is likely to be adopted. There is clearly something chancy, something risky about this person's approach. Sparks may sometimes fly, if one is not so quick to start up as an Aries Moon. They may know they are right, whether they know what they are right about or not. Once the relative steadiness of maturity has arrived, the Aries Moon can be a supportive dynamo for the less adventurous.

Severance from anything that is perpetually binding is likely to tempt them rather sooner than later. The emotional level is transient, yet ever ready to extend the hand of reconciliation. The Aries Moon automatically reassigns him or herself to new tasks and challenges, and it is wise not to interfere with this constant process of renewal.

TAURUS MOON

A personal goal for this person is to establish practical results, concrete expression wherever this is appropriate in connection with his or her feelings and emotions, and sometimes where it may *not* be so appropriate. Pie in the sky is not enough to provide satisfaction here. For Taurus Moon, the pie should be on the table, on a plate, and in ample supply. The search for true value in life may be this person's best contribution to society. They can forcibly supply the rest of us with the drive to integrate the idea of "pie in the sky" with the reality of "plate on the table."

Taurus Moon will generally tend to see things in summation, to demand that one's position in life be made manifest in reality. The orientation to material values is primary. The source of all this inward solidity is probably the deep-rooted and persistent imagination of this person, which does not allow them to accept substitutes in life, but drives ever onward to obtain "the real thing."

GEMINI MOON

This Moon sign is perpetually drawn toward life itself, living it, feeling it, breathing it in. This, in turn, results in the effect of breathing life into life itself. Quickness and versatility are exceptional here, though others may sometimes construe these traits as being deceptive. But this perception may simply reflect two persons operating at two different speeds. Gemini adapts very fast, and relatively unjudgmentally, to whatever he or she faces.

There is a mental approach to the feeling level here, but these feelings are the same as everyone else's, and Gemini Moon is quite aware of their presence within. But he or she does not feel bound to dwell on things too long. The result can be a tendency to work things over a little at a time—for a long, long time. It would be a little contradictory for this Moon sign not to be a little contradictory.

With Gemini Moon, a basic assumption is that everything in life is imminent, is about to happen. This sense of urgency presses them into a constant search for the true body of experience, and they manage to acquire much knowledge as they go along through life.

CANCER MOON

Contacting a Cancer Moon will nearly always result in an unusual expansion of what was meant earlier by "gut level" experience in life, for Cancer is itself ruled by the Moon. Everything lunar functions at high pitch in this sign. Moods are enlarged dramatically; sensitivity and changeability may be exaggerated in some way.

This person "lives to feel." The need to nurture others is great. If you need a bowl of chicken soup, the Cancer Moon will usually provide at least a gallon of it. The problem is generally one of keeping things in perspective. For Cancer Moon, it may take some hard work.

There is the sense of "summation" with a Cancer Moon, but powered here by a real feeling for the group need, which they will home in on quite naturally and almost always try to satisfy. They strive to offer every encouragement for development to others in their sphere of activity. Generosity as such is almost an obligation and sometimes he or she will nearly demand to help you, as if it were their inborn right. The effects of constructive flux or change for the better that a Cancer Moon produces can benefit all who chance to fall beneath their goodwill beams.

LEO MOON

This person has a positive feel for leadership and a sense of preeminence in their emotions as well, which they and others must take into account. The air of assurance is always present to some degree, regarding the relative importance of his or her personal position in a given situation.

Where give and take are involved, there is a notable freedom of giving and the taking is "understood" since Leo feels that what is his is *his*, no questions asked. There is a great air of vitality and fire and also some stubbornness about changing one's way or altering one's position. Yet Leo Moon tends to sense the overall purpose in emotional situations and often takes the lead in resolving them.

Leo Moon communicates a kind of sufficiency to others that is often unmistakable, as if karma or inevitable forces had put this person into the place he or she occupies. Sometimes the appearance of overconfidence is a relatively transparent cover for the need of respect from others that may lie deep within the psyche. Leo Moon demands its due in deference from others, and pays for this in kindness and concern for their ultimate welfare.

VIRGO MOON

Assimilation to the world as it is, the accommodation of reality "the way things are" is a power that activates this person. Virgo Moon will bend and give, in all the right places, to handle whatever comes his or her way, but this is not to suggest that they themselves are able to "feel" adaptively, better than most. In fact, they are often so well organized that small discrepancies are easily detected, and seem more aggravating to them.

The same mental component that allows Gemini to feel intensely present in the moment is applied by Virgo in terms of mastering technique and routine. Virgo Moon wants to be ready for all eventualities, and may be overly analytical about how to meet them, over planning for the future. This may drive those around them crazy, but it certainly is a force for order in general. Organization as an actual feeling is paramount.

This Moon sign is well equipped to make intuitive choices, and the craftsmanship with which they pursue life is often a source of amazement for others. For Virgo Moon, prudence is prudent.

LIBRA MOON

This person has emotional identification with the concept of equality or equivalence, as such. They are forever testing the winds of every situation to see what is needed to bring things into alignment.

They have the acquisitiveness of Taurus, but this force runs more toward aesthetic harmonies than toward materialistic realizations. There is a positive repulsion for things that are out of tune, and the only area where Libra Moon can go overboard is in the rejection of extremism itself. Their sensitive openness to others must not be infringed upon, or they may "turn off" completely.

A sort of dialectic process is forever operative within the breast of the Libra Moon, and thus their alert attendance upon the value of "rightness" in life. They have a special appreciation for poignancy of emotion, and feel a real sense of presence in the life that expresses these in a measured way. The Libra Moon sense of relaxed poise is based on a true fidelity to past experience, which always sees them prepared for newer ventures.

SCORPIO MOON

These people know the value of true creativity in making active application of some of life's stronger impulses. This comes from a determination and control that is always oriented toward bringing unused or neglected facets of life into fuller expression. Others may be surprised, or even "turned off" by the results, but they will seldom fail to be attracted in one way or another.

Scorpio Moon has the ability to take the initiative in direct and sometimes unsettling ways. There is notable power to focus single-mindedly even obsessively on specific goals. It may be difficult for other people to relate to this kind of intensity.

As a product of their drive toward emotional maturity, this Moon sign often appears to be overindulging, when from a certain point of view they are actually "testing the limits," and busily separating the "wheat from the chaff" of experience. Few know sooner than this person when a situation has lost its merit, or has become outmoded. Scorpio Moon can provide the transmutation of experience through a great power to lift even if the lifting involves a sudden "drop."

SAGITTARIUS MOON

Sagittarius Moon has a broad spectrum of contact with its surroundings, and prefers not to be held to any specific point for very long. There may be a tendency here to take an overview approach emotionally, or to view present resources as the means to possibly very distant ends.

A level of enthusiasm is present here that carries over into warm and spontaneous feelings. The imagination is open to stimulation, and there is often a sense of great buoyancy. This can sometimes produce a certain fitfulness that must be recognized as being more natural for this person than for most others. One must not expect to pin down a Sagittarius Moon very easily.

The relativity of standpoint is important to a Sagittarius Moon. That is, this person will strive to find out where another person is "coming from" in order to fix or to understand their own position better. There is very little desire, however, to "corral" another person emotionally. The inner liberty of Sagittarius is itself sufficient motivation to allow full freedom for others, and this person expects to receive an equal measure of the leeway he or she gives in return. The secret of the Sagittarius Moon is its fluidity.

CAPRICORN MOON

An essential function of this placement is discrimination, and not necessarily in the negative sense of putting down a thing. Here also is the power to know imaginatively and instinctively what is discriminating in the sense of being distinctive or "high class." As long as this does not become an obsession, the Capricorn Moon can become the very model of emotional class and style.

There is a high sensitiveness to the correct way of providing structure to life, of getting things in proper order, making them work right. Filling in all the blanks in life is important to a Capricorn Moon, and they may be rather quick to point out where others have failed to do so. As long as they apply the hard rules of life to themselves, then their sense of authority in guiding others is not without constructive foundation.

This Moon sign has a great drive to express completion in life, and may suffer a secret fear of the inadequacy of all of us in the face of extremely high ideals or standards in life. Truly adult and responsible guidance of life's course is a major orientation here. If this person consciously or unconsciously calls our own attention to some deficiency in ourselves, perhaps we should heed the implicit advice that is being offered.

AQUARIUS MOON

The "friendship" potential of this Moon sign will seldom fail to manifest itself. There is a constant opening up and reaching out, which often will provide an inventive twist to his or her relationships. But to maintain a steady course, Aquarius Moon will usually remain somewhat objective.

Sensitiveness to the right of independence in others is usually high in this person's awareness. This is a practice that most of us try to follow, but none with more sincerity than an Aquarius Moon. There may be ingenious or unconventional results, or unusual associations that are often viewed as being ahead of their time somehow. Substantial ability to make feelings have real effects in the world will be seen here.

Aquarius Moon will tend to penetrate to the heart of any emotional dilemma rather quickly, and often this person is a fine reader of character. There is a particular felicity of detachment here, which yet will successfully avoid becoming separated from others. This is because this combination is almost an embodiment of the term "humanitarian," in the best and truest sense of that word.

PISCES MOON

This combination has exceptionally sympathetic openness to whatever is taking place in one's surroundings. A constant, subtle "all-surrounding" impulse is at work. Sometimes the Pisces Moon feels so many things at once that there is a muddle in trying to identify them all. There may be a kind of passivity that is based on gentleness or kindliness. But passivity is still passivity.

This Moon sign has an inward leading that requires constant clarification of one's obligations or responsibilities to oneself and to other persons. This means guarding against any unusual lapse into simply letting important things take care of themselves. The beauty of life is highly appreciated, and steps to make oneself part of the action will be taken by the Pisces Moon.

What really drives the Pisces Moon onward is the sense of incompleteness it seems to see in all directions in life. It is a privilege for this individual to sustain others who may themselves have lapsed into vacillation. The constructive sacrifice that does not infringe upon one's own integrity attracts this person. Simple argument will seldom force them out of their position, partly because this position is seldom very clearly known itself.

LUNAR CYCLES

• Your **lunar high** occurs when the Moon is in the same sign as your natal Sun. If you are a Sagittarius, for example, your lunar high will occur when the Moon is in Sagittarius. The result would be a time of inspiration, when new ventures could be successfully implemented. It is a day when you are most emotionally like your Sun sign. It is a day when your thinking is most sound.

• Your **lunar low** occurs when the Moon is in the sign opposite your natal Sun. If you are a Taurus, your lunar low would occur when the Moon is in Scorpio. Since you are least sure of your decisions on this day, try to postopone major decisions. You will run into opposition in whatever you may start. This is, however, a good day to exchange ideas since you are much more aware of other people. You may feel restless and will want to keep busy. Plan constructive (but not demanding) projects.

• If you know the sign and degree of the Moon at the time of your birth, you can determine your **lunar birthday**—when the transiting Moon is conjunct (in the same sign as your natal Moon). If your natal Moon is in Gemini, your lunar birthday is when the Moon is in Gemini. This is a time when you respond rather than initiate. You might be absorbed in feelings and sensations. You will often want to be in the company of women on this day.

• If you know the positions of your natal planets, you can plot the Moon's passage over these points.

Mercury: A good day for ideas and communications.

Venus: Go out and have a good time.

Mars: Work hard. You may be irritating or irritated.

Jupiter: Don't overindulge. You feel optimistic and self-confident.

Saturn: Look into yourself. You are realistic and feeling serious today.

Uranus: Surprises and excitement. A good day to explore and experiment.

Neptune: You are very emotional. You may forget things and feel lost.

Pluto: You want to be alone.

WORLD EVENTS

INTERNATIONAL PREDICTIONS
by Noel Tyl

SPECIAL MEASUREMENTS

Transiting Mars and Saturn make a critical conjunction at 5 Pisces 19 on March 14, 1994 at 5:01 AM, GMT. This powerful conjunction, which occurs approximately every two years, is reinforced by the Full Moon eclipse on May 25 at 3 Gemini-Sagittarius 43 at 3:39 AM, GMT. Both of these phenomena make a square aspect with the United States' Ascendant, signifying again a strong developmental tension toward a new national image (SA Sun conjunct the Moon at the Midheaven).

The very telling Mars-Saturn transit, which always traces the lines of unrest and upset in the world, has with its occurrence a special quality: it is *peregrine*. This astrological term comes from the Latin word meaning "foreign." When a planet makes no conventional (Ptolemaic) aspect with any other planet in the horoscope and is not in a sign of essential dignity, it is said to be peregrine, and the observed effects are that the planet "runs away" with the horoscope. In the case of this conjunction, both Mars and Saturn are peregrine and the hot-and-cold nature of the conjunction, the aggressive-in-spite-of-controls thrust will dominate. Their symbolization is "foreign" to the horoscope at hand.

THE PLUTONIC POWER THREAD

The planet Pluto—stark power, crucially defined perspective—weaves its way around the Sun and within the life maps of our leaders and their countries. From now to the end of 1995 (more on this specific issue in next year's *Moon Sign Book*), transiting Pluto at the very end of Scorpio continues to symbolize a revolutionary spirit of change, the focus of force, and the screaming efforts for so much of the world to renew life perspective. The Uranus-Neptune conjunction has helped punctuate this grand Plutonic background (as we discussed last year) and our planet has witnessed extraordinary upheaval of the oppressed, wanting to change out-dated structures, confronting force with force, establishing perspectives for the new millennium.

THE UNITED STATES

Many of my predictions have indeed come to pass. But a big one, the election of Bill Clinton as president, was missed. At the time I was preparing these predictions, Bush was secure. Hardly anyone knew who this Clinton was. Clinton was not in our national consciousness. In relation to the United States' horoscope, I still maintain that the wrong man was elected.

Clinton will be a weak president. His horoscope (August 19, 1946 at 8:51 AM in Hope, Arkansas) simply has no bite to it. He is charismatic, almost to the point of dandyism, and is fired with enormous self-confidence, education, and loads of communication skills. But, his inauguration address notwithstanding, he is unable to effect change. When others deputized to do the job make their recommendations, he will delay. Privately, he is "puffy," moody, and pompous about his personal views, but, all in all, he has great difficulty making decisions. Behind the rhetoric and gloss, there is little innovation and power.

It is absolutely no secret that Clinton's wife is his greatest asset; Hillary Clinton dominates Bill Clinton's horoscope. She is his claim to fame.

In April and May of 1993, Bill Clinton surely had some logs fall across his track: he will have had to find better ways of doing things; his political honeymoon will have ended abruptly. But he will have recovered strongly in the last weeks of July through staff changes and political maneuvering.

Hillary will have come to the rescue and probably received even more power and public outreach responsibility (Clinton's Solar Arc Moon conjunct his Midheaven and trine his Ascendant, with transiting Mars square his Uranus). At the same time, he will have reacted impulsively, pushing to use the country's force, within what is an ongoing caretaker relationship between the United States and the rest of the world.

The United States' horoscope (July 4, 1776 at 2:13 AM in Philadelphia, Pennsylvania) is under very interesting pressure for a change of national image. I think the outlines of this new national image will be defined around September 1993 and then go through critical growing pains in March and April 1994 and then again in November.

Clinton will continue struggling, and times will have been very difficult for him in September especially. In Ocotober and November, the probability is extremely high that Clinton will have flexed our national foreign-affairs muscle and used force in intervention abroad. Clinton will appear to have great emotional conviction, but the United States will still be confused about its role in the new world order.

1994 will begin with international criticism of the United States for its intervention in Yugoslavia. We will have to learn how to manage rather than deploy our power as the world's only supernation. I think we will be learning that we cannot police the world with armed force.

Our standard of living suffers greatly. This is

a major issue for the United States and for Bill Clinton in the spring of 1994 and throughout most of 1995. In November 1994, the United States surely will flex its muscles once more and the whole issue will arise again. There will be a very vocal public outcry dividing those who favor the "give 'em hell" posture from those who favor "let them take care of themselves" position. As our new national image stabilizes, there will be an intense spring and autumn; an image of "force or no force" will signify the United States' outreach to the world.

Clinton will be a changed (and perhaps beaten) man throughout all of this enormous responsibility. Benchmark times for his maturation within the heady allure of power tactics are certainly April-June and September-November 1994.

The Plutonic power thread is also present within the personal horoscope of President Clinton, especially during the period of June-September 1994. The pressure on Clinton is enormous. The structure that is missing in his administration at its beginning must somehow be created by those around him, including the Republicans and especially by the intercession of his wife. He stands for change, but he is unable to take control and make it happen. In actuality, the astrology of our president suggests all too strongly only the cosmetic maintenance of the status quo, *not* the establishment of the new image the country is calling for so strongly.

RUSSIA

The predictions made so successfully for the USSR and its leader Gorbachev in 1991 were possible due to an extraordinarily reliable chart for the former Soviet Union, the chart for the revolution (November 8, 1917 at 2:12 AM EET in Leningrad [formerly Petrograd]). The exact time had been frozen on a clock face, perhaps by a stray bullet, when Bolshevik Red Guards under the direction of Lenin had arrested the Provisional Government. The fall of the Soviet Union was keyed by the Solar Arc of Pluto square the Midheaven of that chart.

But that chart is not valid any more with the changes in that enormous nation. Until a regeneration chart becomes clear within the corroboration of historical events linked to timings that have been suggested and, indeed, may yet be coming, as politics still jostle national identity, the chart of leader Boris Yeltsin must be used for the thrust of the many countries to become one country. Yeltsin's horoscope (February 1, 1931, 3:32 AM R3T, [-4:00H] in Sverdlovsk, USSR) is apparently also well-timed. Yeltsin's political tensions with the old communist guard were predicted in last year's publication, with the promise that he would prevail in the spring of 1993. Indeed he did. The tensions began with the powerful transit of Uranus opposed his natal Pluto in February (a tremendous clash between demand and power) and was resolved in a public referendum, clearly in Yeltsin's favor, in late April 1993, with SA Node semi-square Mars and transiting Jupiter exactly conjunct his 4 Libra 10 Midheaven (and other measurements). This Jupiter was extremely powerful for Yeltsin, establishing a station upon the Midheaven just as the referendum was completed.

When we look ahead for Yeltsin, we see more of the same: enormous energy and enormous good luck. The man's horoscope is so filled with tension and drive that it is singularly remarkable. His meeting with President Clinton was like a jet plane meeting a Piper Cub! I cannot help thinking that Yeltsin behaved properly and was grateful for the aid he solicited and received, but, in private, scoffed at the unseasoned and not-so-deep American president.

Yeltsin lives on adrenaline, on Mars. Transiting Mars aspects make personal headlines for him whenever they occur. Yeltsin will have risen to secure popularity and a more peaceful country image at the end of 1993 (progressed Moon trine Jupiter; SA Venus sesquiquadrate Jupiter, Venus ruling the Midheaven). Then transiting Jupiter takes over in square to Yeltsin's Sun in January, a nice start for the year.

Jupiter squares his Sun again in April 1994 and still again in September 1994. I think Russia will continue to grow in stability throughout 1993 and 1994. Only toward the end of 1994, in early November, perhaps, will we see Yeltsin a bit confused in international negotiations that may well have to do with global or space communications and/or oil commerce. Overall, the picture through

Yeltsin's horoscope appears very good. Though the growing pains are loud, a new Russia will be born from Yeltsin's efforts.

Ousted leader Mikhail Gorbachev will be heard from again, in a sad, desperation-out-of-frustration way, especially in December 1993 and January 1994. The issues—impulsive, out-spoken rebellion against what he sees as erroneous principles in his country's government—will bring him into the headlines repeatedly in May and October (if his efforts are not silenced).

ISRAEL

The predictions regarding Israel (May 14, 1994 at 4:00 PM EET in Tel Aviv) made in 1991 came to pass. A new government was elected in 1992, as Pluto opposed the national Sun, and the land-for-peace negotiations with the Palestinians resumed in February 1993 and probably will have been completed successfully for both parties in September 1993. Behind the scenes, Israel is sorely hurting for money. Enormous debt pressures prevail at home. Munitions, money, and mercy are all mixed up in the Israel outreach to the world. All the bluffing and hidden agendas should clear out by the end of 1993 and Israel will begin to make some deals.

Yet, 1994 steers Israel to a very important change: one of astrology's strongest and most reliable measurements, transiting Uranus conjunct the fourth cusp (i.e. opposed the Midheaven), takes place in Israel's national chart early in March, at the end of June, and late in December 1994. The three "hits" tell us that Israel will be working out a "new start" somehow, a *revolutionary* stance with regard to its world position. The probability of force, armed skirmishes, is very strong in the spring and at the end of 1994. This new stance will take all year to develop. It is motivated by the need for money, bargained for by the trade-off of land for peace and commerce—all designed to improve its international trade position. The new party in power will hear some not inconsiderable static from the hard-liners now out of power, but after almost a year of haggling, Israel will mark its history with as much stabilization as it has ever had—after the next series of concessions, negotiations, and aggressive tactics, culminating in November and December 1994. A quiet period of integration with the rest of the world will then follow for a bit.

Transiting Pluto is now approaching opposition with the national Mars in the spring of 1994 and at the end of the year. These are key times for changes in Israel, and there will be force, struggle, and extraordinary ruthlessness, probably cloaked by the accord of a Palestinian settlement. The force will be part of the martyrdom politics favored by Israel (i.e. we have made peace with the Palestinians, now help us financially in our impoverished state and let us get away with murder in our other squabbles).

IRAQ

In my predictions presented in last year's *Moon Sign Book*, I suggested cryptically that "the United States will be duped abroad somehow, very dramatically, probably coming to light in early June 1993. The deception will be from Iraq." On May 8, 1993, just as these predictions for 1994 were going to press, headlines everywhere read, "U.S. Links Iraq to Plot to Assassinate Bush in Kuwait." In preparing that prediction fourteen months earlier, I could find no more appropriate word for Iraq's insidious use of force emerging in secrecy than "duped." Iraq is still a presence to be feared.

With every predictive thrust into its future, we come closer and closer to confirming the reliability of the Iraq national horoscope (August 23, 1921 at precisely 6:00 AM in Baghdad) and the conjectural horoscope for Saddam Hussein (April 28, 1937 at 8:18 AM in Tikrit, Iraq). The transiting Mars-Saturn conjunction discussed earlier in this article occurs in conjunction with the seventh cusp of the Iraq chart. The chart for the moment of this powerful conjunction, viewed from Baghdad, has the Uranus-Neptune conjunction directly overhead. All this means more forceful, hidden, collusive, and insidious aggression from Iraq.

The key times will be late in March 1994, with Saddam himself very much in the news, and at the end of May, triggered by the lunar eclipse. This is the period that begins a grand arcing effort for Iraq to become a world power, controlling the Middle

East. Transiting Pluto begins its application to square with the national Mercury and Sun, ruling the nation's Ascendant and Midheaven, and twelfth house, respectively. This means the peacocks are coming home to roost in the time period which begins the summer of 1994 and continues all through 1995.

GERMANY

Germany will begin to make headlines strongly in the spring, signalling the build-up to the federal elections at the end of 1994. Chancellor Helmut Kohl (April 3, 1930 at 6:30 AM in Ludwigshafen, Germany) will be under extreme pressure, beginning in November-December 1993; his voice will be dulled and labeled ineffective by the aggressive bloc of German voters. Between June and December 1994, Kohl will wage a losing battle. It would not be surprising if he withdrew from the election process by October 20, 1994.

ITALY

Interestingly, in Rome—where the May 25 eclipse is precisely rising—there is the potential for similar civil unrest. The focus there could very well be finance, bank fraud, or government collusion. The particularly apt time for this to come to light is within the first ten days of July.

YUGOSLAVIA

The problems in Serbia are obviously Plutonic as well. Transiting Pluto will continue its onslaught to square with Serbia's Uranus all through 1994. At the same time, transiting Pluto will square its own natal position. This is about as rough as it gets, and 1994 will be worse for Yugoslavia.

SOUTH AFRICA

Populist uprisings in South Africa will continue, especially forceful in Capetown. Beyond civil rights, there probably will be the introduction of money, wage, and taxation issues. Watch carefully in late March-early April.

We see the Plutonic power thread in South Africa, with transiting Pluto square to the Ascendant of the Union of South Africa. These apparently unending struggles so far to the south will continue through 1995.

PERU, URUGUAY AND ARGENTINA

The eclipse of the Sun on May 10 at 5:07 PM, GMT occurs directly overhead at 77 West 03 and 12 South 03, bringing Lima, Peru into the news. There, we can expect to see activity to change the government in power. The unrest is most focused during the periods June 18-20 and November 10-13, 1994 and is probably vitalized within the voice of labor.

The tensions in Peru can easily share news with unrest in Uruguay and Argentina. (Montevideo and Buenos Aires, the capital cities, are very closely related to the occurrence of the Full Moon eclipse May 25.)

NORWAY

Gentle Norway is not exempt from world tensions. King Harald V (February 21, 1937 at 12:45 PM CET in Skaugum, Norway) is a most retiring individual with an extremely powerful, high-presence wife. His seventh cusp—his presentation of self to the world, his wife—is being highly stressed throughout all of 1993 by the conjunction of transiting Uranus and Neptune. His country is having extreme financial problems and is facing the extraordinary financial drain of hosting the coming Winter Olympics.

Transiting Pluto opposes Norway's national Midheaven—the Norwegian independence chart (June 7, 1905 at 11:00 AM CET in Oslo). I feel this portends more than world publicity for this small nation. A major change is in store for the royal family, precipitated by Harald's private life and by the economic woes, all brought to the surface by exposure through the Olympics.

THE VATICAN

In late 1993 and throughout 1994, the force of Pluto focuses very strongly on the Vatican and on Pope John Paul II.

The chart for Vatican independence (June 7, 1929 at 11:00 AM in Rome, Italy) is very reliable. The tests of astrological measurements for the demise and installation of five popes since 1939 show remarkable congruence between measurements and occurrences, especially clearly in the complex time period in 1978 when Pope Paul VI died (August 6), Pope John Paul I took office (August 26) and himself died 33 days later (September 28), with Pope John Paul II, the present pope, taking office on October 16, 1978.

Ancient predictions about the papacy are alarming in the light of the present decline of Catholicism throughout the world and the general chaos between East and West, which indeed had papal religious origins issuing from the third century. Specifically, Malachy O'Morgair (canonized as St. Malachy), born in the eleventh century, made an astoundingly accurate prediction of the sequence of popes from his time to the end of the twentieth century, describing the popes' names or origins in telling Latin epithets. These prophecies for the most part have come true. Two more popes are to follow Pope John Paul II. Obviously, world perspectives for Catholicism are changing within the new political world order.

The present pope (born May 18, 1920, probably near 1:00 PM in Wadowice, Poland) has his Sun and Moon almost exactly conjunct the Midheaven of the Vatican chart; and his Saturn is exactly conjunct the Vatican Ascendant.

Both the Vatican and Pope John Paul II are under extreme signals for change. The tension is for change of world status, public perspective and, indeed, leadership. They began in April 1993, December 1993, and will probably peak in March 1994. Should the changes be delayed by understandings beyond our astrology, another critical time will be in late October 1994.

Grand changes in the Vatican over the past 54 years have always included strong measurements involving Mars, the Ascendant, and/or the Midheaven in the Vatican chart. In three of the five major shifts in the papacy since 1939, Solar Arc measurements have involved the Midheaven, Saturn, and Pluto. Early in 1994, the basic astrological picture for change is suggested by transiting Saturn square and transiting Pluto opposed the pope's Sun; transiting Pluto opposed the Vatican Midheaven, transiting Jupiter square the Vatican Mars, and, above all, Solar Arc Saturn square to the Vatican Midheaven.

The first non-Italian pope elected since Adrian VI of Utrecht in 1522, Pope John Paul II's work to internationalize the papacy and support the voice of oppressed peoples everywhere focused strongly first in his native Poland. His inspiration reinforced the heroic "Solidarity" movement there and greatly stimulated the major changes still underway throughout the Near and Middle East. We could say that this pontiff's work has been completed. New perspectives beckon.

AROUND THE WORLD

We can anticipate governmental disruptions in New Zealand, upsets in Czechoslovakia, and the beginnings of rebellion in Nigeria. The hot times in all these locations are in May 1994. (Interestingly, the cause of religion will somehow inflame and/or rationalize these upsets.)

In Japan there will be national business tension around foreign debt balance. The squeeze is on as its mercantile power grows and living space diminishes.

Perhaps with our own new national image in the re-making, the United States will indeed look more to the homefront, as the economy improves, as Israel fights its way to stabilization, as the Middle East itself focuses almost entirely on Iraq, as we overlook the bubbles of anxiety in South America, let Germany straighten out its leadership problems, commiserate with a still-stalled Yugoslavia (in our embarrassment from intervening), as we buttress the new Russia with finance and know-how, and see the world inexorably working itself out of chaos into a new order.

WEATHER PREDICTIONS
by Nancy Soller

1994 should be an interesting year for weather watchers because the Uranus-Neptune conjunction, which brought dry weather to many parts of the country, is separating and therefore losing much of its power. Normal weather conditions will slowly return. The Northeast will see normal weather conditions, although spring will be dry in this part of the country. This will have nothing to do with the Uranus-Neptune conjunction. Pluto will be prominent on spring ingress charts set for New England locations. The separating Uranus-Neptune conjunction will be found on charts set for the Western Plains and the Rockies in the winter and spring and on charts set for the Rockies in the summer. These areas should be dry during those seasons.

    The 1993-94 winter will see wet, chill weather in the Northeast and south along the Atlantic

Seaboard. There will be dry weather in the Rockies and dry weather, related to a Mars ingress location, on the West Coast. Chill and windy weather will be found on the Alaskan Panhandle and mild weather is predicted in many locations in this state.

Spring will bring dry weather to the Northeast and much of the Atlantic Seaboard, seasonable weather to the Midwest and Eastern Plains and dry weather to the Western Plains and Rockies. Seasonable weather is predicted for the West Coast and all of Alaska except the Panhandle.

In the summer the southern portions of the Atlantic Seaboard will be hot and dry and this weather will also be found in the Midwest. Dry weather here this season will have no relation to the Uranus-Neptune conjunction. Mars and Pluto are prominent on summer ingress charts set for these areas.

Also in the summer, most of the Plains will be wet and the West Coast dry, windy and cool. Much of Alaska will be wet and chill.

Fall will be wet and chill in the Far Plains, but many locations in the Rockies will be dry and warmer than usual. The West Coast likely will be wet and much of Central Alaska will be warm and dry because the Uranus-Neptune conjunction (opposing Mars) sits on the midheaven of fall charts set for locations here. Weather in other parts of the country should be seasonable.

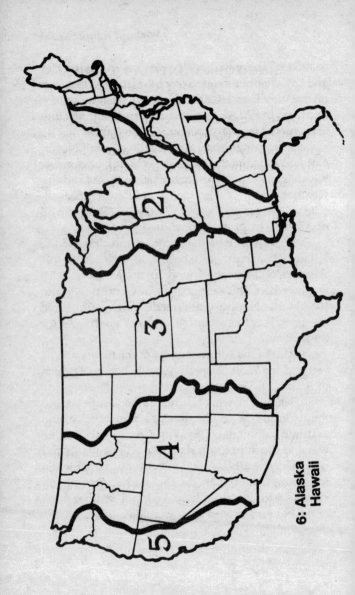

6: Alaska
Hawaii

USING YOUR MONTHLY WEATHER PREDICTIONS

In using the weather predictions that follow remember that precipitation can come on the day given, the day before or the day after. Winds usually come on the day given. Precipitation and wind dates affect an area when the planets indicating precipitation and/or wind are prominent on a chart set for that area for the time the weather-changing aspect is perfect. Seasonal predictions are based on the planets prominent at a given location at the time of the seasonal ingress.

•NOVEMBER 1993•

Zone 1: Dry weather is forecast for this zone. Temperatures will be a little more mild than usual. Watch for precipitation the first two days of the month and again around the 7th and 8th. The 19th, 20th, 24th and 28th are likely to result in snow north and rain south. The dry weather should continue through most of December.

Zone 2: Dry weather and seasonable temperatures are forecast. The month should open with precipitation. Rain is predicted for the 8th with more rain or snow coming on the 19th, 24th and 28th. Much of this precipitation will be scant or short-lived. Dry weather this month is likely to continue through most of the month of December.

Zone 3: Relatively dry weather with seasonable temperatures is forecast for this zone. The month is likely to open with precipitation and more is due the 7th and 9th. Snow north and rain south is predicted for the 11th, 15th, 19th, 24th, 27th, 28th and 29th, but not in large amounts. The dry weather should continue through December.

Zone 4: Eastern portions or this zone will be dry, but wet weather is predicted for central and western portions. Temperatures at many locations here will be a little below normal. Precipitation is likely on the 3rd, 7th and 9th; also on the 11th, 15th, 19th and 24th. The last week of the month should see about three days of snow. November weather patterns will continue through December.

Zone 5: Both precipitation and temperatures are likely to be normal this month. Watch for precipitation on the 7th, 11th, 14th-16th, 28th and 29th. Other dates could result in precipitation originating over the Pacific, reaching land. This should be a good month weather-wise and it should be followed by more of the same weather in December.

Zone 6: Dry weather is forecast for most of Alaska this month. Temperatures will be markedly above normal in the central part of the state. Western Alaska will have the most seasonable weather. Dates most likely to result in snow include the 1st, 2nd, 7th, 8th, 11th, 15th, 19th, 20th, 24th and 27th-29th. Hawaii will have a pleasant, normal month.

Dates to Watch

Watch for winds November *1st*, 2nd, *6th*, *7th*, *11th*, *13th-15th*, *17th*, *23rd*, 24th, *27th*, *29th* and *30th*.

Watch for rain November 2nd, 3rd, 4th, 7th, 8th, 9th, 11th and 13th-15th.

Watch for snow November 16th, 20th, 21st, 24th and 27th-29th.

•DECEMBER 1993•

Zone 1: Dry weather with seasonable temperatures is predicted. The Northeast will see the biggest deficits in precipitation. Snow is most likely on the 5th, *10th*, 12th-15th, 17th, 20th and 23rd. Rain south is likely on many of these days. A clear Christmas is forecast. The coming year will bring more moisture to areas now very dry.

Zone 2: Seasonable temperatures and relatively normal precipitation patterns are predicted for this zone. Snow north and rain south will be most likely on the 5th, *10th*, 12th, 13th and 15th; watch also the 17th, 20th and 23rd. Snow falling on the 23rd may stick, creating a white Christmas at some locations. A seasonable month weather-wise will set the pattern for the rest of the winter.

Zone 3: Normal temperatures and precipitation patterns are forecast for this zone; any weather irregularities will probably constitute a slight tendency to dryness. Snow north and rain south will most likely come on the 3rd, 5th, *10th*, 12th, 17th, 20th, 23rd and 29th. Winds, ranging from brisk to destructive, will be a possibility the 3rd, 5th, mid-month, the 19th and 22nd.

Zone 4: Relatively normal weather is forecast east, but much or the rest of this zone will have extremely wet weather this month. Areas in this zone and to the west should have a white Christmas. Additional snow dates include the 3rd, 13th, 14th, 23rd and 29th. In addition, the *10th* and 17th could result in snow east. Wet weather this month will be followed by very dry weather in January.

Zone 5: Normal precipitation and temperature patterns are predicted for this zone, but to the north British Columbia will have a very dry month. Christmas Day should see a snowstorm in much of Washington and Oregon. Watch for snow also on the 3rd, 12th-15th, 23rd and 29th. Good weather this month will be followed by chill, dry and windy weather in January.

Zone 6: The Alaskan Panhandle will have mild temperatures more mild than normal and less precipitation than is usual this month. Central Alaska will be cold, dry and windy. A pleasant month is forecast for Hawaii. Watch for snow in Alaska on the 5th, *10th*, 12th, 13th and 15th; also on the 17th, 20th and 23rd. Snow on the 23rd will make Christmas white.

Dates to Watch

Watch for winds December *3rd-5th*, *12th*, 13th, *15th*, 17th, *19th*, *22nd*, 23rd, 24th, *25th* and 27th.

Watch for snow December 3rd, 6th, *10th*, 12th, 13th, 15th, 17th, 20th, 23rd, 24th, 25th and 29th.

•JANUARY 1994•

Zone 1: Chill weather is predicted. There should be more precipitation this month than there has been in a one-month period for a long time. Very chill weather should open the month. Watch for precipitation on the 6th, 8th, 12th, 13th, 19th, 22nd (north), 27th, 28th and 31st. Watch for temperature dips January 8th, 14th and 17th.

Zone 2: Temperatures in this zone should be a little higher than usual and there will be clear, blue skies on days when there is no precipitation. Watch for snow north and/or rain south January 4th, 6th, 8th, 9th, 12th, 19th, 27th and 31st. Watch for temperature dips January 3rd, 9th, 14th and 17th. Snowfall, when it comes, will be generous.

Zone 3: Lack of precipitation should characterize the weather here this month with the possible exception of areas near the Mississippi. Temperatures will be normal for the season, but there will be several days of sharp temperature drops. Best chances for precipitation will come on the 2nd, 3rd, 13th, 17th, 19th, 27th and 31st. Snowfall, when it comes, will be sparse.

Zone 4: Dry weather is predicted for this zone in January. Temperatures will be seasonable. The extreme western portions of this zone could see much wind. Precipitation most likely will occur on January 3rd, 9th, 11th (west), 13th, 16th, 27th and 31st. Dry weather this month will likely continue through the rest of the winter. Temperature dips are due the 1st, 9th, 13th and 16th.

Zone 5: Dry weather and temperatures above normal are predicted for this zone in January. Dry, mild weather this month could continue through the winter. Look for precipitation January 19th and 30th. Bad weather, originating over the ocean, could reach land on other dates, but most of this should be deflected north or south. There will be few sharp temperature dips.

Zone 6: Beautiful, clear skies and temperatures a little above normal are predicted for Alaska in January. The exception will be the Panhandle where generous precipitation is predicted and where temperatures will be chill. Hawaii will have a normal, pleasant month. Precipitation most likely will be on the 1st-3rd, 6th, 8th, 12th, 13th, 19th, 27th and 31st.

Dates to Watch

Watch for winds January *1st-3rd, 6th, 8th-10th, 12th-16th,* 17th, *18th, 22nd, 28th, 30th* and *31st.*

Watch for snow January 2nd, 3rd, 5th, 6th, 8th, 11th-13th, 15th-17th, 19th, 21st, 27th, 28th, 30th and 31st.

•FEBRUARY 1994•

Zone 1: Northern portions of this zone will be chill with much precipitation. Areas farther south will have clear skies and temperatures milder than usual. Precipitation should open the month with the most occurring on the 13th, 16th, 17th and 21st.

Also watch for generous precipitation on the 26th. Wet weather this month should continue through most of March.

Zone 2: Mild temperatures and many clear days are predicted for this zone in February. The month should open with precipitation with more coming on the 3rd, 10th, 13th, 16th and 17th. Snowfall is due north on the 21st and 26th. Weather patterns in effect in this zone should continue through most of March. Warmer weather should cause early blooming.

Zone 3: Extremely dry weather is predicted for this zone. Temperatures should be seasonable. Best chances for precipitation will come on the 3rd, 7th, 10th, 13th and also on the 17th, 18th and 24th. Snowfall north and rain south, when they come, will be scant. The dry weather in this zone this month should continue through most of March.

Zone 4: Dry weather is forecast for this zone in February. Temperatures west will be above normal. Chances for precipitation are most likely February 3rd and 24th. If there is other precipitation it will be very scant and sporadic. Dry weather this month will continue through March and the entire spring season. Normal weather patterns may be delayed indefinitely.

Zone 5: Dry weather is predicted for this zone in February. Temperatures will be above normal. Watch for possible precipitation February 3rd, 10th, 18th, 22nd and 25th. These rain and snow dates are likely to result in sporadic, light precipitation. Stormy weather, originating over the ocean, could reach land on other dates, but most will be deflected north or south.

Zone 6: Mild, relatively sunny weather is predicted this month for Alaska, with the exception of the Panhandle, which should be dry, windy and cold. Hawaii should have a mild, pleasant month. Watch for possible precipitation in Alaska February 1st, 3rd, 7th, 13th, 16th, 17th, 20th and 26th. Alaskan temperatures in the central part of the state will be much higher than usual.

Dates to Watch

Watch for winds February *1st, 10th, 15th, 16th, 19th, 20th, 22nd-24th* and *26th-28th.*

Watch for snow February 1st, 3rd, 7th, 10th, 14th, 16th-19th, 21st, 22nd, 24th, 26th and 27th.

•MARCH 1994•

Zone 1: A chill, wet month is predicted for northern portions of this zone; southern areas will have seasonable temperatures and normal precipitation. Watch for precipitation March 4th 13th, 24th, 27th and 29th. April will bring a tendency to dry weather throughout this zone which should continue through the spring. Water conservation, when possible, is advisable.

Zone 2: Seasonable temperatures and normal precipitation are predicted for this zone in March. Pleasant, normal weather this month should continue throughout the spring. Watch for precipitation March 4th, 13th, 14th, 24th, 27th and 29th. A storm originating west of the Mississippi will open the month. Strong, destructive winds or a tornado are due March 6th.

Zone 3: Dry weather with seasonable temperatures is forecast for this month. Western portions of this zone may suffer dry weather that forecasts dry weather for several months ahead. The best chances for precipitation will come on the 1st, 4th, 6th, 14th, 20th, 24th, 27th and 29th. March 6th could see strong, destructive winds or a tornado.

Zone 4: Very dry weather is forecast for this zone in March. Temperatures should be seasonable. Very dry weather this month would be a harbinger of dry weather that should continue through the spring. Best dates for precipitation include the 1st, 2nd, 4th, 6th, 20th and 27th (east). Strong, destructive winds are likely several times during the month.

Zone 5: Very dry weather with temperatures markedly above normal is forecast for this zone this month. More normal temperatures and more normal precipitation should return at the end of the month or soon after. Best dates for rain or snow include the 6th, 20th and 27th. There will be winds, but temperatures will be mild and the winds will not be especially cold.

Zone 6: Cold, windy weather is forecast for the Alaskan Panhandle, but other parts of the state should have a rather mild month. Watch for precipitation March 2nd, 4th, 13th, 14th, 24th, 27th and 29th. Winds could come on many dates on the Panhandle. The end of the month could bring warmer weather to the Panhandle and heavy rain north. Hawaii will have a normal, pleasant month.

Dates to Watch

Watch for winds March *1st*, 4th, *5th*, *6th*, 7th, *12th*, *14th*, *16th*, 18th, *24th*, 25th, *29th* and *30th*.

Watch for rain March 20th, 24th, 25th, 27th and 29th.

Watch for snow March 1st, 4th, 7th, 12th, 13th and 14th.

•APRIL 1994•

Zone 1: Dry weather is predicted for this zone in April. Temperatures will be above normal. The farther north a location is in this zone the more likely it is to be very dry. The best chances for rain will occur on the 2nd, 5th, 7th (south), 13th, 23rd, 28th and 30th. Rain on the 30th is likely to affect only the southern portions of this zone.

Zone 2: Mild, pleasant weather is predicted for this zone in April. As in areas to the east, there will be many dry days. The best chances for rain will come on the 2nd, 5th, 7th, 8th, 13th, 23rd, 28th and 30th. Mild, pleasant weather this month forecasts a generally mild, pleasant spring. Strong winds, however, are a possibility on some days and tornado activity should not be ruled out.

Zone 3: Mild, pleasant weather is predicted for areas in this zone which are near the Mississippi and most of the rest of this zone will have a normal month. About one hundred degrees west, however, extremely dry weather is predicted. There will be very little rainfall here. Dates when precipitation is possible include April 5th, 7th, 8th, 13th, 23rd and 30th. Tornadoes are also possible.

Zone 4: Very dry weather is predicted for the Rockies. Only the extreme western portions of this area will see moisture. Dry weather this month will affect most of this area throughout the entire spring season. Light rain is predicted in some areas on the 7th, 8th, 22nd, 23rd and 30th. Temperatures in most portions of this zone will be seasonable.

Zone 5: Seasonable temperatures and normal rainfall are predicted for this zone in April. Watch for rain on the 8th, 18th, 20th, 25th and 30th. Other dates may bring moisture from storms originating over the Pacific. Nice weather this month should continue through the rest of the spring. Several of the rain dates could also result in strong winds.

Zone 6: Dry weather with temperatures well above normal are predicted for the Alaskan Panhandle. A portion of the central part of the state will see chill, wet weather; to the west it will be chill, but not especially wet. Best dates for precipitation include the 2nd, 5th, 7th, 13th, 20th, 25th, 28th and 30th. Hawaii will have a pleasant month with normal temperatures and precipitation.

Dates to Watch

Watch for winds April *4th*, 5th-7th, *8th*, 9th, 11th, 16th, *22nd-24th* and *30th*.

Watch for rain April 3rd, 5th, 6th, 8th, 11th, 13th, 19th, 20th, 22nd-25th, 28th and 30th.

•MAY 1994•

Zone 1: Dry, hot weather is predicted for northern areas in this zone this month; southern areas will have a little more moisture and seasonable temperatures. Hot, dry weather north should continue through the entire spring season; hot, dry weather south and west should continue through the summer. The best chances for rain come on the 6th, 15th, 17th (south), 24th and 26th.

Zone 2: Slightly dry weather and mild temperatures are predicted for this zone in May. Easternmost portions of this zone should see an extremely dry, hot summer as well. Areas near the Mississippi and a little to the east may eventually see generous precipitation. Dates which should result in rainfall include the 6th, 17th, 26th and 30th. A tornado is possible May 8th.

Zone 3: Most areas in this zone will see normal to slightly dry weather. Temperatures will be seasonable. Areas in the far west, however, will be extremely hot and dry. This month and June will be the last months with drought in the far western plains; summer will bring precipitation west. The best chances for rain in May come on the 4th, 6th, 14th, 17th, 18th and 30th.

Zone 4: Very hot and dry weather is forecast for May. Western portions of this zone, however, will have near-normal precipitation and near-normal temperatures. Watch for rainfall May 4th, 6th, 14th, 16th, 18th, 26th and 30th. Summer will bring increased moisture to eastern portions of this zone, but to the west it will be dry, cool and windy.

Zone 5: Seasonable temperatures and near-normal precipitation are predicted for this zone in May. Watch for rainfall on the 2nd, 4th and 6th; also on the 14th, 16th, 18th, 26th and 30th. Normal weather patterns in May and June will be followed by a summer with below-normal temperatures, little precipitation and much wind. Conservation of water is recommended.

Zone 6: A warm, dry May is predicted for the Alaskan Panhandle; central parts of the state will see a chill, wet month. Western portions of Alaska will be chill and dry. Watch for precipitation May 2nd, 4th, 6th and 15th; also on the 17th, 24th, 26th and 30th. Hawaii will have a pleasant, normal month with a seasonable summer following.

Dates to Watch

Watch for winds May 6th, *8th*, *15th*, *17th* and *18th*.

Watch for rain May 2nd, 4th, 6th, 14th-16th, 18th, 26th and 30th.

•JUNE 1994•

Zone 1: Dry, hot weather is predicted for northern portions of this zone; to the south both temperatures and precipitation patterns will be seasonable. Watch for rainfall June 1st, 6th, 9th and 10th. More rain is due June 19th. In the north rain-fall will likely be short-lived and scant. At the end of the month the hot, dry weather will shift south.

Zone 2: Seasonable temperatures and precipitation patterns are predicted for this zone for most of the month. At the very end of the month central portions of this zone will begin to see very hot, dry weather. Eastern portions of this zone will see rainfall June 1st. Other dates likely to result in rain include the 6th, 9th, 10th, 11th and 19th.

Zone 3: Seasonable temperatures and normal precipitation are predicted for most of this zone in June. The exception is the most western portions of this zone which will see some extremely dry weather. The last week of the month may see rainfall in central portions of this zone. Dates likely to result in rain include the 9th, 10th, 11th, 16th, 19th, 23rd and 24th.

Zone 4: Very dry weather is predicted for this zone in June. Temperatures will not vary much from normal the first part of the month, but the end of the month will be dry, chill and windy. The best chances for precipitation will come on the 9th, 10th and 11th; also on the 16th, 19th, 23rd and 24th. Dry, chill and windy weather at the end of the month will set the weather patterns for the summer.

Zone 5: A pleasant, seasonable month is forecast. The exception may be the last week of the month which could bring a temperature dip and wind. A slight chill then will be followed by a sum-

mer with cool temperatures. The best chances for
rainfall come on the 2nd, 11th, 16th, 19th and 23rd,
but other dates are not excluded.

Zone 6: A hot, dry month is predicted for the
Alaskan Panhandle; central parts of the state are
likely to see more precipitation. The last week of
the month should be pleasant throughout the state
with a pleasant summer following. Watch for precipitation June 1st, 2nd, 6th, 9th-11th, 16th, 19th,
23rd and 24th. A normal, pleasant month is predicted for Hawaii.

Dates to Watch

Watch for winds June *1st, 6th*, 9th, *10th, 11th,
23rd, 24th*, 25th, *26th, 27th* and *28th*.

Watch for rain June 1st, 2nd, 6th, 9th, 11th,
16th, 17th, 23rd, 24th, 27th and 28th.

•JULY 1994•

Zone 1: Seasonable temperatures and a tendency to
dryness are forecast for most areas, but southern
portions will have very hot and dry weather. The
best chances for precipitation come on the 7th, 11th,
14th, 16th (north), 20th, 21st (north), 23rd, 28th and
30th. Weather patterns in effect this month should
continue through most of the summer.

Zone 2: Very hot, dry weather is forecast for
this zone in July. This will be true for both northern
and southern portions. Dry weather this month is
likely to precede hot, dry weather throughout the

entire summer. Best chances for rainfall come on the 7th, 11th, 14th and 20th; also on the 23rd, 28th and 30th. Rainfall, when it comes, should be light.

Zone 3: Wet weather is predicted for July. Temperatures should be seasonable. Watch for rain on the 7th, 11th, 15th, 28th and 30th. Rainfall is likely to be generous; other dates may also result in wet weather as well. Generous rainfall in July forecasts wet weather for the entire summer season. Temperatures should continue to be moderate.

Zone 4: Seasonable temperatures and normal precipitation are predicted for this zone. July 4th could see some rain, as could July 7th, 11th, 15th and 30th. A pleasant month with moderate temperatures will be followed by more pleasant, moderate weather throughout the rest or the summer season. Fall, however, should be very wet and chill.

Zone 5: Cool, dry and windy is the forecast for this zone in July. The weather north will be much more chill than weather south, but most areas in this zone will have lower temperatures and more wind than normal. Dates when precipitation is most likely include July 4th, 7th, 11th, 15th, 20th, 23rd and 30th.

Zone 6: A pleasant month with beautiful, blue skies and seasonable temperatures is predicted for most of Alaska. Precipitation is most likely on the 4th, 7th, 11th, 14th-16th, 20th, 21st, 23rd and 28th-30th. Hawaii will have a pleasant, normal month. Good weather this month will be followed by similar weather throughout the summer.

Dates to Watch

Watch for winds July *7th*, 11th, *15th*, *17th*, *18th*, *20th*, *23rd*, 28th, *29th* and *31st*.

Watch for rain July 4th, 7th, 11th, 14th-16th, 20th-23rd and 28th-30th.

•AUGUST 1994•

Zone 1: Blue skies and seasonable temperatures are forecast for northern portions of this zone in August. To the south it will be extremely hot and dry. There will be little rainfall anywhere in this zone the first two weeks of this month; only the 2nd is likely to result in rain. Rainfall is likely, however, the 18th, 22nd, 27th (north) and 28th-30th.

Zone 2: Extremely hot, dry weather is forecast in August. The first two weeks of the month are likely to see no rain, except on the 2nd. The last two weeks of the month should see some precipitation, but it will be short-lived and scant. Best dates for rain include the 18th, 22nd and 27th-30th. Hot, dry weather should continue through the summer.

Zone 3: Dry weather may be found this month in areas closest to the Mississippi, but most areas in this zone will see generous amounts of rainfall in August. This is especially true of the last two weeks of the month; the first two weeks of the month will not be especially wet. Watch for rain August 1st, 2nd, 21st, 27th, 28th and 29th.

Zone 4: Areas to the east may be wet, but most areas in the Rockies will be extremely dry.

Temperatures could be slightly above normal. The entire month will be dry, but there will be a slight chance of precipitation the 1st and 2nd. Other dates which could result in moisture include the 14th, 21st, 28th and 29th. September will also be dry.

Zone 5: Areas in this zone will be dry this month. Temperatures will be below normal and winds may be a prominent feature. Rainfall is possible on the 1st and 2nd; also on the 14th, 21st, 28th and 29th. Dry weather this month should continue through September. Fall should bring more normal precipitation patterns to this zone.

Zone 6: Seasonable amounts of precipitation and normal temperatures are forecast for almost all of Alaska this month. Skies will be blue and beautiful for most of the month. Watch for precipitation on the 2nd, 14th, 18th, 21st, 22nd and 27th-30th. A normal summer will be followed by a dry autumn. A nice, seasonable month is forecast for Hawaii.

Dates to Watch

Watch for winds August 1st, 3rd, *6th*, *13th*, *15th*, *17th*, 18th, 22nd, *23rd*, 29th and *30th*.

Watch for rain August 1st, 2nd, 14th, 18th, 21st, 23rd, 27th, *28th*, 29th and 30th.

•SEPTEMBER 1994•

Zone 1: Pleasant, slightly dry weather north and very hot and dry weather south are the predictions for this zone in September. The month will open with rainfall and more rain is predicted for the 13th, 17th, 20th and 30th. Also, the 12th could bring rain to some parts of this zone. Pleasant weather north this month will precede an autumn of beautiful weather.

Zone 2: Very hot, dry weather is predicted for most of this zone in September, but some areas near the Mississippi may see generous rainfall. The best chances for rain should come on the 1st, 12th, 13th, 17th, 20th and 30th. At the very end of the month temperatures should become more seasonable and a pleasant, beautiful fall is predicted.

Zone 3: Very wet weather is forecast for this zone in September. Temperatures should be seasonable. Watch for rainfall on the 1st, 12th, 13th, 17th (east), 18th, 26th (west) and 30th. However, precipitation is not limited to these dates. The last week of the month may see beautiful weather east, but the west will see a chill, wet fall.

Zone 4: Pleasant weather with normal temperatures and normal precipitation is forecast for this zone for most of September. The last week of the month should see the beginning of warm, abnormally dry weather that will continue through the fall. Watch for rainfall on the 12th, 13th (east), 18th, 20th, 26th and 27th. Other dates could also result in rain.

Zone 5: Cool, dry weather is predicted for this zone for most of September, but the last week of the month may see an increase in rainfall. The best chances for rain will come on the 12th, 18th, 20th, 26th and 27th. Wet weather at the end of the month could set the pattern for a wet fall. Temperatures should be seasonable. There may be additional rain coming from over the ocean.

   Zone 6: Beautiful weather is forecast for most of this month in Alaska, but the end of the month will be wet on the Panhandle and dry in central parts of the state. Dry weather in Central Alaska will continue throughout the fall. Watch for rain on the 1st, 6th, 12th, 13th, 17th-20th and 26th-30th. Hawaii will have a beautiful, normal month.

Dates to Watch
   Watch for winds September 1st, 5th, *12th*, 15th, *18th-21st*, 27th and *30th*.
   Watch for rain September 1st, 6th, 12th, 13th, 17th, 18th, 20th, 26th and 28th-30th.

•OCTOBER 1994•

Zone 1: Dry weather and temperatures a little below normal are predicted for this zone in October. Dry weather will be especially noticed north with weather to the south a little wetter. Rainfall will be most likely October 13th, 14th, 21st, 22nd and 27th-29th. Other dates could result in rain south. Watch the 9th, 11th and 19th of October.

   Zone 2: Slightly dry weather with temperatures a little above normal is predicted for this zone in October. Rainfall, when it comes, is likely to be short-lived and scant. The best chances for rain will occur on the 9th, 11th, 13th, 14th and 21st; also on the 22nd and 27th-29th. Areas near the Mississippi will have many days of beautiful, blue skies.

Zone 3: Eastern portions of this zone will have beautiful weather in October, but western portions of this zone will be wet and chill. Rainfall is most likely on the 9th, 11th, 13th, 19th, 21st and 22nd; also on the 27th-29th. Rainfall east is likely to be short-lived and scant. October weather patterns should continue through the fall.

Zone 4: The very eastern portions of the Rockies may be wet in October, but other areas in this zone will be very dry with temperatures markedly above normal. This includes most of the Rockies and also some desert areas in the Southwest. The best chances for rain will come on the 9th, 11th, 13th and 19th; also on the 27th (east), 28th and 29th.

Zone 5: Heavy precipitation north in this zone is possible in October; southern areas will have a more normal precipitation pattern. Rainfall is most likely this month on the 9th, 11th, 19th, 21st and 27th-29th. Other dates may result in rain originating over the ocean. Precipitation patterns north should continue throughout the fall.

Zone 6: The Alaskan Panhandle will be wet, but central parts of the state will be dry in October. Dry areas are likely to have above-normal temperatures. Hawaii will have a pleasant, normal month. The best chances for precipitation in Alaska include the 13th, 14th, 21st, 22nd and 27th-29th. Precipitation patterns set now should continue all fall.

Dates to Watch

Watch for winds October *9th*, 10th, *13th*, *16th*, *21st*, *22nd*, *25th*, 28th and 29th.

Watch for rain October 9th, 10th, 11th, 13th-15th, 19th, 22nd and 27th-*30th*.

•NOVEMBER 1994•

Zone 1: Seasonable temperatures are forecast for this zone. The Northeast will be dry. Most areas south should have normal precipitation. The Everglades, however, could be very dry. Dates most likely to result in precipitation include the 8th, 9th and 10th; also the 13th and 28th. Weather patterns in effect now should continue through December.

Zone 2: Slightly dry weather is forecast for most areas in this zone in November. Temperatures should be seasonable. Rainfall is very likely on the 8th, 9th and 10th; the 13th and 28th are also likely to result in rain. Weather patterns set this month are likely to continue through the rest of the year. Areas near the Mississippi will see an unusual amount of blue skies.

Zone 3: Slightly dry weather is forecast for most areas near the Mississippi. Skies will be unusually blue for the season. Areas to the west, however, will be chill and damp. Precipitation will be likely in some areas on the 2nd; precipitation will also be likely on the 8th-10th, 13th, 18th and 24th. Snow is likely November 27th and 28th.

Zone 4: Eastern portions of this zone may be chill and damp, but most areas here will be dry with temperatures above normal. Dates most likely to result in precipitation include the 2nd, 8th, 9th, 10th and 13th; also the 18th, 24th, 27th and 28th. Weather patterns in effect in this zone this month should continue through most of December.

Zone 5: Seasonable temperatures and generous amounts of precipitation are forecast for this zone in November. Watch for rainfall on the 2nd and more precipitation on the 9th, 10th, 13th and 14th. Snow is possible the 18th, 24th and 26th. Weather patterns in effect this month should continue through December. Desert areas will remain dry south.

Zone 6: The Alaskan Panhandle will be wet this month, but central parts of the state will be very dry. Western Alaska will have seasonable weather and Hawaii will have a normal, pleasant month. Watch for precipitation November 2nd; also on the 8th-10th, 13th, 14th and 18th. The 24th, 26th, 27th and 28th should be wet also.

Dates to Watch

Watch for winds November *4th*, 7th, 12th, *13th*, 14th, *18th*, *20th*, 24th and 27th-29th.

Watch for rain November 2nd, 8th, 10th, 11th, 13th and 14th.

Watch for snow November 18th, 19th and 26th-28th.

•DECEMBER 1994•

Zone 1: Normal temperatures and normal precipitation patterns are forecast for this zone in December. The Northeast will probably be a bit drier than the rest of the zone. Watch for precipitation December 3rd, 8th, 9th, 23rd and 30th. Snow on the 23rd north should stick to the ground through Christmas. There may be snow north on the 30th, making New Year's Day white.

Zone 2: Seasonable precipitation and seasonable temperatures are forecast for this zone in December. Skies may be unseasonably blue west. Watch for snow north on the 3rd, 8th and 9th; areas south could see rain on these dates. The 23rd and 30th likely will see some precipitation in many locations in this zone. Snow on the 23rd may stick causing a white Christmas.

Zone 3: Normal temperatures and precipitation patterns are forecast for this zone east. Areas west and near the Rockies are likely to be wet and chill. Watch for precipitation west on the 2nd and snow in widespread areas in this zone on the 3rd, 8th and 9th. Precipitation in many areas on the 23rd and 30th may make the holidays white.

Zone 4: Areas in the Eastern Rockies will be wet and chill, but central and western portions of this zone will be dry with temperatures markedly above normal. Watch for a generous snowfall on the 2nd and 25th. Eastern sections of this zone may see other snow dates, but the rest of the zone will be relatively snow-free.

Zone 5: Temperatures will be seasonable this month with many areas in this zone seeing generous amounts of precipitation. Snowfall will usher in the month north and there should be generous amounts of snowfall Christmas Day. Other dates may also see some precipitation, especially precipitation originating over the Pacific. December will probably be the last very wet month north.

Zone 6: Parts of the Alaskan Panhandle will be wet, but most areas in Alaska will be very dry this month. Central parts of the state will be warmer than is normal for this time of year. Watch for snowfall on the 2nd (south), 3rd, 8th, 9th, 17th, 23rd and 25th (south); also the 29th and 30th. Hawaii will have a pleasant month, but it may be warmer than usual.

Dates to Watch

Watch for winds December *1st-4th*, 6th, 7th, 14th, *20th*, *23rd* and *24th*.

Watch for snow December 3rd, 4th, 8th, 9th, 18th, 23rd, 25th, 29th and 30th.

Research charts for this article were set by Evelyn Herbertz.

EARTHQUAKE PREDICTIONS
by Nancy Soller

Most big earthquakes occur when planets strike or form hard angles to earthquake-sensitive degrees of the zodiac. It has long been known that eclipse-points constitute earthquake-sensitive degrees, but to this we now add solstice and equinox points and the planetary nodes.

When a big, destructive earthquake occurs usually there are several different kinds of earthquake-sensitive points involved. An example would be the October 17, 1989 San Francisco earthquake. At the time of the earthquake three different planets were forming hard angles with three different recent eclipse points; the earth, at twenty-three degrees of Aries, was just past the solstice/equinox hard angle of twenty-two and a half degrees of Aries while in heliocentric hard angle to Saturn's nodes. Jupiter, at ten degrees of Cancer, was aspecting an October 3, 1986 eclipse point (one of the eclipse points mentioned above) while crossing its own node.

Hard angles involved in earthquake prediction are generally geocentric (earth-centered) and are sometimes heliocentric (sun-centered) and usually involve zero, ninety or one-hundred eighty degree angles involving a planet and a sensitive point. Earthquakes involving solstice and equinox points are triggered at forty-five and twenty-two and a half degrees as well.

Heliocentric hard angles of planets to recent eclipse points also coincide with quakes, but it appears that only heliocentric hard angles of the earth with recent eclipse points act consistently as triggers.

When a big earthquake occurs at a time when a planet is forming a geocentric hard angle to a recent eclipse point other forms of heavenly stress are also in effect. These could be a planet forming a geocentric hard angle to a solstice or equinox point, a planet forming either a geocentric or heliocentric hard angle to a planetary node or multiple planets forming multiple hard angles to recent eclipse points. Hard angles of Mars to Neptune also coincide with this type of quake and a planet in conjunction with the sun at the time of an eclipse can trigger a quake on the same day.

Quakes related to the sensitive solstice and equinox points usually also coincide with other forms of stress. The sensitive points involved in this kind of quake include zero degrees of the cardinal signs, fifteen degrees of the fixed signs, twenty-two and a half degrees of the cardinal signs and seven and a half degrees of the mutable signs.

The planetary nodes involved in earthquake prediction include: eighteen degrees of Taurus, Mercury; sixteen degrees of Gemini, Venus; nineteen degrees of Taurus, Mars; ten degrees of Cancer, Jupiter, twenty-three degrees of Cancer, Saturn; fourteen degrees of Gemini, Uranus; eleven degrees of Leo, Neptune; and twenty degrees of Cancer, Pluto.

Predicting where an earthquake will strike is even harder than predicting when it will strike. One study shows that the San Francisco Bay area had a large number of quakes occurring when the planets Venus, Mars and Saturn were in Taurus, Leo and Scorpio. However, the October 17, 1989 quake in that area did not find any of these planets in any of those signs. A lot more research has to be done before we can predict accurately where an earthquake will strike.

Dates when two or more earthquake-sensitive degrees are being conjuncted and/or squared and/or opposed by orbiting planets include:

January: 1st, 7th, 11th, 14th, 16th, 26th, 27th, 31st
February: 1st, 18th, 25th
March: 7th, 8th, 11th, 29th, 30th
April: 1st, 14th, 19th, 27th, 29th
May: 2nd, 10th, 11th, 18th, 21st, 23rd, 29th
June: 1st, 8th, 21st, 24th
July: 4th, 12th, 13th, 16th, 18th

August: 3rd, 4th, 11th, 17th, 31st
September: 21st, 30th
October: 3rd, 4th, 23rd
November: 4th, 11th
December: 1st, 8th, 9th, 25th, 29th

A BIG QUAKE?

May 10, 1994 is the date of a solar eclipse that is likely to coincide with a big earthquake. The annular eclipse, at nineteen degrees, forty-eight minutes of Taurus, will be visible over most of the United States at a few minutes past noon (Eastern Standard Time).

Pluto will be in wide conjunction with the eclipse point at the time of the eclipse; Mars will square the July 11, 1991 eclipse point of eighteen degrees, fifty-nine minutes of Cancer the day before; Uranus will be crossing Saturn's heliocentric planetary node near the earthquake-sensitive degree of twenty-two and a half degrees of Capricorn; and, probably most importantly, the earth will be on Mar's heliocentric planetary node.

An interesting speculation is whether an earthquake following this eclipse on the same day would be the earthquake prophesied by Nostradamus (Century IX, verses 82 and 83) for May 10 when the sun is at twenty degrees of Taurus. Nostradamus prophesied the destruction of a great city by earthquake and water under this position of the sun and appears to mention an eclipse. (Century X,

verse 67 of Nostradamus' quatrains would probably not refer to an earthquake on this date because
it posits many planets in Taurus as well.)

Where would a quake strike? The ancients
believed that when a planet was conjunct the sun at
the time of an eclipse, a quake was likely on the
same day and in the same general part of the
world. If this were true, it would appear to put the
Western Hemisphere at risk, but would not rule
out a large, destructive earthquake at some other
part of the globe.

BIBLIOGRAPHY

Goodavage, Joseph E. *The Complete Prophecies of Nostradamus.* Translated, edited, and interpreted by Henry C. Roberts. Oyster Bay, NY: Nostradamus Company, 1982.

_____ . *Our Threatened Planet.* New York, NY: Pocket Books, 1978.

Michelsen, Neil F. *The American Ephemeris: 1991-2000.* San Diego, CA: ACS Publications, 1980.

_____ . *The American Ephemeris for the 20th Century.* San Diego, CA: ACS Publications, 1980.

_____ . *The American Heliocentric Ephemeris: 1901-2000.* San Diego, CA: ACS Publications, 1982.

Rosenberg, Diana K. "Stalking the Wild Earthquake," *The Astrology of the Macrocosm.* St. Paul, MN: Llewellyn Publications, 1990.

ECONOMIC FORECAST
by Pat Esclavon Hardy

Welcome to 1994 as an array of planetary energies will dazzle us for another year—always changing, always in motion. Cycles will begin and trends reverse right on cue with the energies of the planets. Stocks, bonds, treasuries, commodities and global markets are all affected by these planetary energies. So in becoming aware of these energies, I would like to recommend strongly that you combine this astrological information with your favorite technical tools.

The major influence of 1994 is still the Uranus/Neptune conjunction, as this is a 171-year cycle and just doesn't go away overnight! We still expect that the blending of these two transcendent energies will provide us with enough market fluctuations to bank on. So all that you have heard about Uranus/Neptune will continue to apply to

1994 as we are just in the infancy of trends that correlate with this significant 171-year cycle that allows us to break away from systems and structures which no longer apply to us personally. Human dignity and spiritual awareness are factors that are incorporated into our daily lives on some level via news or friends or just recognizing them in your personal life—in your family "system."

Another important trend is the Saturn square Pluto aspect that certainly has helped us clean up our acts recently. Saturn gets down to the bare facts and how we are transforming our structured energies, then we start to incorporate our "new systems and structures" to update all that we do on a spiritual, physical and governmental level. The economy is changing for the better and this will be seen as we move into the year.

One of the most favored aspects of the year is Jupiter trine Saturn. The year closes with Jupiter conjunct Pluto, a 12-year cycle that last occurred in 1982 (which, by the way, was the beginning of the Bull Market in the '80s). Expanding on our new systems and structures, re-evaluating and applying, this trend is associated with a better economy! And just in the nick of time, because Pluto will be changing signs (Scorpio to Sagittarius). The level of optimism will increase on many levels and the term "global" will mean more than it did.

The long-term Economic Contraction Cycle (started in 1986-87 and intensified with all the major Capricorn planets in the early '90s) is gradually being modified and a "transition period" of a few years is now in play toward an Economic Expansion Cycle due by 1996-97. This is the year that really makes a difference in how we re-build on the existing foundation/structures that have been scaled down, eliminated and changed. Re-building (Jupiter conjunct Pluto) is a priority now. The excitement is watching it occur and having the opportunities to participate.

•JANUARY•

The new year opens with Moon in Leo and the north node in Sagittarius (fire signs), indicating a driven momentum toward action. What you *do* makes a difference. Political idealism may be seen.

Saturn square Pluto for the last time on the 2nd could bring long term issues to a close within the next 30 days in reference to oil and mining. International laws may be put into effect concerning the oil-transportation industry (Mercury conjunct Mars). This could create significant price fluctuations in which a ripple effect through this industry forces the public to re-evaluate oil as the primary source of fuel, at least in this country. Keep an eye on wheat and oat prices, too.

A New Moon on the 11th conjunct Neptune, Uranus, Mars and Venus shows emphasis on healthcare, medical and human compassion issues. Look for stocks related to these fields making considerable moves. In the financial markets, silver, gold, copper, currencies, bonds and T-bills are highlighted. For the commodity-thinking individual, focus may be on coffee, orange juice and sugar.

Farm holding reports and planting estimates on soybeans may be a little off, starting a price rise.

Between the 16th and 18th, Mars conjunct Neptune and Uranus is setting off volatility in the stock and financial markets. Expect the unexpected on this one, as we are dealing with some rather constricting energies this month. Hostility with foreign countries may once again be seen. The United Nations may be a focus in the news as it tries to restore a sense of balance between countries.

Saturn moves into Pisces, so more emphasis is put on Neptune in Capricorn (a mutual reception), giving more power to the planet quality of both Saturn and Neptune. Weather-wise, this could mean rain, rain and more rain for a majority of the U.S. Naturally in Northern climates, this would equate significant snowfall. As this melts, focus will be on the agricultural sector: cattle, corn, barley, rye and grains in general. Saturn will be in Pisces until April 1996 which should bring more attention to commodities. Many farmers will be dealing with crop issues that will allow them to hedge their crop losses with commodities futures.

•FEBRUARY•

A New Moon on the 10th with Venus square Pluto indicates that soybeans could be due for a correction after a minor run recently. Pork bellies, cattle, meats, metals, T-bonds and currencies could go through a significant correction this month.

Mercury will turn stationary retrograde on the 11th near the New Moon and will last through

March 5th. Letters, mail, telephone services, office machines, computers, automobiles and coworker communication may run into delays, misunderstandings or break down completely. Mercury retrograde periods are also opportunistic in that they allow us to catch up or go back over things. Followup on those "irons in the fire" with phone calls, visits and the personal touch. It's a time to get re-organized and clean out those drawers, closets and files. It's not a time to initiate, but a time to re-evaluate and re-prioritize. This is not a favorable time to sign any important documents.

Transportation stocks should be in a correction or decline phase between the 1st and the 19th due to Mercury retrograde connecting with Saturn. The Mercury retrograde Sun conjunction should put some emphasis on wheat prices.

A very positive business aspect of Venus trine Jupiter on the 24th should allow you to pull in that deal or firm up an offer made some time ago. This is a very good time to pay attention to relationships and partnerships—business and/or personal.

The Full Moon on the 26th opposes Saturn just entering Pisces. The Dow-Jones industrials should show some deterioration around this Full Moon period with focus on healthcare, medical and drug related stocks. As we move into the latter part of the month, Jupiter will turn stationary retrograde on the 28th. This is another signature to deplete stock issues in general.

Commodoties-wise, grains may garner attention. Silver, gold and other metals may show some stirring, especially as we move into March with Pluto at station. Just before this Full Moon period would be the time to check the options or futures prices of metals to position yourself, as metals markets should become very active. This is a reversal time and technical analysis will tell you the trend. Some commodities respond with greater speed, others can take up to several days to reverse trend.

•MARCH•

We start the month off with Pluto turning stationary retrograde, which will last through August 5, 1994. This is excellent for metals activity. Use technical analysis to help correlate dates with the current trend at the time. Significant trend changes should occur. Also keep an eye on the Federal Reserve and other government departments as policy adjustments may focus on trying to keep the economy on a "stable" path.

The stock market should have a decline as we move into the 5th. Watch the dollar and other currencies, too. Mars square Pluto with Mercury stationary direct will provide some headlines. Interest rates may be on the front page. (If the stock market has been moving down into this trend, then this should be a reversal for the averages.) Trends begin to improve through the 14th.

The New Moon on the 12th sextile Neptune focuses on oil and gas issues, either by commodity pricing or actual government pricing to the consumer. Some real opportunities could surface within the healthcare industry.

The Sun trine Pluto on the 18th may be where one can take profits on the metals which were activated at the end of February. Check the technicals to confirm this, as there may be a reversal date here. This is also the week where pork bellies, feeder cattle and some of the metals wind up their last trading days.

March 20th is when a new year begins astronomically—the Spring Equinox, the beginning of the earth year. Markets in general go through fluctuations and reversals around this important time frame—coming into the Easter/Passover holidays.

The Moon conjunct Jupiter trine Mercury on the 29th with the Full Moon on the 27th should provide some positive news. This is a favorable time for the markets in general. This is a very nice business trend emphasizing communications and travel, good for negotiations and setting a plan in motion for a positive end result.

•APRIL•

Mercury conjunct Mars on the 4th could bring news on national defense issues and another reversal date for wheat and oats. Soybeans should be gaining in price now. The manufacturing sector should anticipate better than expected news. The automobile industry may be gaining some momentum and it's starting to show.

The New Moon on the 11th with Mars trine Pluto should give renewed energy toward getting those last minute tax forms completed. Gas and oil prices may change their trend for a few months and metals may look better now. Political news may indicate some type of reform. This is a good opportunity to do a re-evaluation of your goals and strategies for the year. Are you on course? What changes would you like to make to better attain your goals for the rest of the year?

Mars will once again be at 0 degrees of Aries on the 15th (tax day). This is a 2-year cycle and occurred back on May 5, 1992. Mars changes from south declination to north and is on the equator which could bring unstable weather or a mild possibility of an earth disturbance. Check grains and soybeans as this could be a reversal indicator—or at least one that supports other reversal dates within 10 days (before or after) of this date. Other previous dates for this planetary phenomenon are May 31, 1990; July 13, 1988; January 8, 1987; and February 2, 1985. You can check your technical charts and get an idea how your specific stock or commodity correlated.

Neptune stationary retrograde on the 25th and Uranus stationary retrograde on the 30th should provide us with some interesting insights about our "systems." From our personal systems (habits and patterns), to communications systems and highway systems. Focus may be on our infrastructure, an evaluation process on what our needs are for repairing our highways, bridges, etc.

A very positive trend on the 28th of Jupiter trine Saturn is part of a 12-year cycle that correlates with business in general. This aspect will occur once again at the end of August which could emphasize issues and circumstances that began at this time. There should be an increase in business activity now. Those who have birthdays March 1st-4th, July 1st-4th or November 1st-4th could take advantage of the general business trends which are more in their favor at this time. The economy could be showing some signs of improvement and therefore the stock market should be climbing. Commodities, especially soybeans, grains, metals and financials, could be doing well.

•MAY•

Mercury is trine Neptune and Uranus between the 6th and 8th. Airline and technology stocks may show improvement. The way these sectors are changing their base system and approach to the public/consumer will bring welcome relief. The media could uncover something beneficial, possibly in the medical/healthcare fields. Earthquake and earth disturbance studies may have a significant breakthrough—more knowledge in this field may provide better warnings.

We are coming into eclipse periods starting with a solar eclipse on the 10th in Taurus and a lunar eclipse on the 25th in early Sagittarius. Eclipse periods are good benchmarks in time to take a look at the significant trend changes in the marketplace. Soybean prices could climb further than expected this season. The New York Stock Exchange, a Taurus institution which celebrates its birthday on May 17th, could be affected by this solar eclipse. Expect news about the NYSE around this time period. Possible changes have to be made concerning investing with this institution.

Since the U.S. has Sagittarius rising in one of its most popular charts, that of the President, it would probably be safe to say that the U.S. is changing its image in some way. With Bill Clinton , a Leo, favorably active, he could show us some new steps on the global dance floor—a new perspective in the way our neighbors may perceive us.

Last month's Jupiter trine Saturn should spark our business sectors favorably. A shift may be seen in the increase of exporting U.S. goods and a decrease in importing from other countries. If you are a business owner, you may want to check out your participation and capitalize on this trend. Shipments, especially in technology, may be increasing to European and Russian areas.

There are several challenging trends associated with the eclipse period, especially around the 14th-16th when Mars, Venus and Mercury will be in stress aspect to one another correlating with some tops in markets—reversal periods occur *now*. Since these trends come in between the eclipse period, buying and selling in volume should increase. It's also time to go short on some commodities such as soybeans, wheat, oats, corn and other grains—check the technicals and if they are showing a potential trend reversal near this time frame, then you know you can act on it.

Venus trine Jupiter on the 26th and Venus trine Saturn on the 31st should provide some very good news for banks and other financial institutions. Changes in the way the financial system is operating may start to show some positive signs. Just remember this is only temporary. Progress can be made at this time for the economy. Focus may be on government issues and policies. Soybeans and foreign currencies indicate a decline (the dollar is getting stronger!). Cattle trends could be changing.

•JUNE•

Mars opposes Jupiter on the 1st and could focus on what was accomplished the past 6-8 weeks, especially in the economy and general business sector. Now challenges are presented and more efforts will have to be applied in order to proceed with our economic goals. Stock market fluctuations may be seen on the big board as well as a reversal date for wheat, currencies and metals.

The New Moon on the 9th starts a lunar cycle without intense eclipse energy. This may be a good time to purchase some S & P or OEX stock options to sell around the Full Moon. Of course, check the technicals to support your decision (puts or calls).

Venus opposes Uranus and trines Pluto on the 11th, giving us mixed signals as to where the markets are headed. But we could see some excitement on the downside and then reverse quickly—a whipsaw market period. Venus oppose Uranus research indicates that this aspect is the single most accurate short-term (3-10 days) trading mechanism for an abrupt trend reversal.

June 17th is the last trading day for CME S & P 500, index options and NYSE composite (NYFE).

Market manipulation takes place and you will need to watch premiums on those options/futures. This called the "witching hour" due to the wild activity that takes place within a few days of this date.

Mercury is stationary retrograde in the sign of Cancer on the 12th through July 6th. This is a good time to evaluate personal and domestic needs. Go back over anything that needs your attention now. Remember that Mercury retrograde means to go back over or re-do. This could be a better than usual retrograde period in that there are some real benefits to this energy. Import/export areas may be more active than usual. Women may be in the news with a particular focus on Hillary Clinton.

Summer Solstice occurs with a Full Moon and Saturn stationary retrograde on the 23rd, with Mercury trine Jupiter and Mars trine Neptune indicating some favorable market weather. Oil, gas and chemical stocks are favored. Keep an eye on a reversal period in the bond markets. The healthcare industry could be in the news with some advances. The focus may also be on the budget deficit.

The Sun conjuncts Mercury on the 25th, indicating wheat, oats and soybean activity. Business and the economy in general are busier than usual. You may feel like you need longer days to accomplish what is going on now.

Mars trine Uranus on the 27th is very favorable for the technology sector. Some new breakthroughs may start to become mainstream. Stock market activity increases as we come into the holidays and close the first half of the year.

•JULY•

Jupiter is stationary direct on the 2nd, while Mercury is stationary direct on the 6th with Venus square Pluto on the 7th and the New Moon on the 8th. Soybeans and cattle are active, although stocks and indexes may start to decline.

Mars squares Saturn on the 20th with Venus opposing Saturn and the Full Moon conjunct Uranus around the 22nd. What energy! This is a period where major turns are highly anticipated. Focus may be on cattle, stock and financial markets (technology and currencies). If you use Fibonacci retracements and projections as part of your technical analysis, you should see some reversal periods this week. There are just too many indicators so close together and that means trend changes for most markets. Markets may be bottoming out, poised for long-term highs in the DJIA. Significant trends are changing; do your homework now!

Mercury opposes Neptune while Venus trines Neptune around the 30th. This could focus attention on the oil and gas sectors. Some news about pricing could stir up an acceleration of a trend already in progress. Medical and pharmaceutical companies could have news of a breakthrough which could run prices either up or down. Currencies are back in the news. You may need more information or clarity as to what is occurring in the European currency markets. This trend is calling for some stabilization in the marketplace.

The music and entertainment industries may be redefined. There may be positive indications as to where these industries are going. A music or entertainment celebrity may be prominent in some other area and make a humane impact now. A possible merger in Hollywood has rumors blazing.

•AUGUST•

Pluto stationary direct on the 5th and the New Moon in Leo on the 7th bring focus on metals this month. Look for a possible decline in gold, silver, palladium and platinum. The stock and bond markets usually reflect some minor trend changes with Pluto's station. Interest rates may rise during this lunar phase. The pace of things in general will become faster as we move into the 13th. There may be some excitement in the air—the economy should be showing some very positive signals!

The Sun conjunct Mercury inconjunct Neptune on the 13th stimulates the pace of business and communications, but there may be something out of focus or some unclear details that could trip up the anticipated end result. Chemical and pharmaceutical stocks may be a heavy issue this week. Keep an eye on the soybeans as we come into the last trading day on the nearest contract.

The Full Moon on the 21st in Aquarius takes us into a very positive business trend on the 28th with Jupiter trine Saturn (see April 1994), as some business started at that time possibly could be reaching another stage now. Mercury trine Uranus and Neptune puts emphasis on the space, technology and communications industries. A possible development in telecommunications could be presented. This would be a breakthrough or a time when a company would introduce a new product or invention. Stocks and indexes should be pretty active on the upside this week as we come into a holiday. The music and entertainment industries may have some announcements.

Mars trine Saturn on the 30th would be excellent for the business person to focus on a project that would give them creditability in their field of work. Agricultural commodities such as cattle, pork bellies, barley, rye and other grains should have some nice tops this month.

•SEPTEMBER•

Early this month Mars trine Jupiter and Mercury sextile Pluto should activate the stock markets rather nicely as we could hear some enlightening news from the federal reserve. Focus may also be on the international affairs of our government. Stocks that could do well are publishing, media and the entertainment industry. Wheat, oats and soybeans should be in a seasonal correction.

The New Moon on the 5th sextile Mars could be a good time to do a short trade on indexes and sell around the Full Moon where the markets could take a tumble at that time. Those with strong hearts may want to short the indexes (S & P 500 and OEX). Considering they both have their last trading day the third Thursday in September, this could be a pretty active index period.

Mars opposes Neptune with Mercury setting up a T-cross, signaling some intense energy from the 18th through the 26th. The Full Moon appears on the 19th and Mars opposes Uranus with Mercury on the 21st—some planetary clusters to circle on your calendar. Look for some intense market weather (real weather, too) to bring the markets *down*! Autumnal Equinox also occurs on the 23rd, supporting stock market turbulence.

Foundations of the healthcare industry and insurance companies may be shaken this month by these trends. A small jolt in a particular area of the business sector could create an amazing domino effect that takes sudden and unexpected turns. Earth disturbances, such as quakes, tidal waves, hurricanes and tornadoes may be part of the weather pattern at this time.

Mars trine Pluto on the 27th is very favorable for metals and bonds. This is an opportunity to make portfolio adjustments. Venus conjunct Jupiter on the 29th is a great time to relax and enjoy the company of someone who matters to you. Socialize now to further business interests or just enjoy friends. This is great energy for that special intimate relationship, too.

•OCTOBER•

Uranus and Neptune turn stationary direct on the 2nd causing fluctuations in the marketplace. Spotlighted stocks are those involving technology, the computer industry, communications, media, chemicals, pharmaceuticals, healthcare and insurance.

The New Moon occurs on the 5th with Mercury stationary retrograde on the 9th trine Saturn

(Mercury will remain retrograde through October 30th). Cattle, pork bellies and poultry could see considerable price fluctuations.

Venus stationary retrograde on the 13th square Mars would not be a good time for delicate negotiations. Avoid trying to come to a conclusion on any issue at this time. If you are really trying to make this deal work out, avoid doing it from now through the end of the month, when this square is activated once again. Too many complications or issues may be involved and the picture is not clear. Friday the 15th Mars inconjunct Saturn and Venus conjunct Jupiter throws some business plans off course. Currencies may show some improvement.

The Full Moon on the 19th with Sun conjunct Mercury on the 21st may draw one's attention to the commodities once again in the trading pits of wheat, oats and soybeans. Look for a reversal in trends, probably confirming the seasonal decline into the winter months.

Jupiter sextile Neptune on the 28th and then Uranus on November 7th is a wonderful period for the markets and also for making headway in the Neptune/Uranus issues of human dignity and opportunities to re-build systems on some level. Stock market emphasis should be on technology, the computer industry, pharmaceuticals, medical companies, healthcare, oil and gas.

Venus square Mars on the 29th with Sun trine Saturn and Mercury turning stationary direct on the 30th should bring some issues to a head from the middle of the month. The pace of business in general picks up momentum. Portfolio adjustments may also be taking place as we move closer to the end of the year.

•NOVEMBER•

There will be a solar eclipse on the 3rd and a lunar eclipse on the 18th. Eclipses are usually associated with considerable trend changes in the marketplace. I would tend to think we are closing some major "down" trends. This could be a period where there is a major correction and cleaning out of the markets on some level, preparing to move to higher ground in the near term. *This could be the eclipse period that is associated with pinpointing major trend changes on all levels of the markets. Check the technicals and do your homework!*

The Sun conjunct Venus on the 2nd and the New Moon on the 3rd produce a great trend for the retail industry. One should get some good shopping done during this period as you are more likely to find what you want and stumble upon what you didn't know you wanted. The focus now may be on copper and wheat commodities.

Jupiter sextile Uranus on the 7th (see October 28th) is very favorable for the economy.

Saturn is stationary direct on the 9th with Venus trine. Basically there are very positive trends from now through the eclipsed Full Moon on the 18th conjunct Pluto. Bonds and interest rates may be in the news; currencies and a stronger dollar on the Comex. This window of opportunity for business in general is to capitalize on preparing the new phases. Projects and negotiations that are initiated around the next New Moon should have a positive outcome. This aspect is part of a bigger picture (Jupiter conjunct Pluto in December). Get your priorities in order as the pace of excitement in the economy is coming and you will want to be part of it.

Mercury conjunct Venus and the Sun aspecting Neptune on the 13th should provide us with some creative fantasies. Ideals are aroused and focus is on partnerships and relationships. Business relationships should be favorable. Negotiations and planning are important now so pay attention. Things may go smoother than anticipated.

The Sun conjunct Jupiter could correlate with a significant top or bottom in the Dow-Jones industrials. Last month's energy on the 28th may still be riding crests or troughs in the marketplace. This is a minor trend that supports a larger trend next month (Jupiter/Pluto), so you may see some favorable changes going on in economic arenas.

Venus stationary direct on the 23rd may focus our attention on currencies and bond markets. The government may present a plan for 1995 that will make us think.

•DECEMBER•

Jupiter conjunct Pluto on the 2nd with the New Moon is a strong influence for re-evaluation. This is a 12-year cycle that last occurred in 1982. This can be just what the doctor ordered to regain a healthier economy as we move into 1995. This is a long-term trend that will do better with more favorable trends in the near future. We are getting close to Pluto changing signs (January 1995) which in itself is a major trend reversal—and I might mention, is very optimistic. So with these positive indicators now coming on the horizon for 1995, we can begin to plan a brighter future knowing the economic indicators are gaining in our favor.

Mercury square Saturn on the 4th with Venus trine Saturn on the 8th could signal reversal dates for the stock and commodity markets. Jupiter will enter its natural sign of Sagittarius on the 9th, supporting the positive and optimistic anticipation of long term Pluto entering Sagittarius within a few weeks. Jupiter stays in a sign for about a year, while Pluto will stay in Sagittarius until 2009 (approximately 14 years).

The Sun conjunct Mercury on the 14th supports a busier than usual time window. It may seem as though there is not enough time in the day due to the acceleration of business now. A lot of positive energy is going in many different directions. The Full Moon on the 18th heightens the feeling. Index trading closes on the third Thursday, so there may be some strong activity in last minute trading and positioning. Portfolio adjusting would also occur as we finish the year.

Mercury trine Mars on the 20th, near the Winter Solstice, and the Sun trine Mars on the 24th brings great energy to the spirit of the winter holidays, and we can look forward to 1995!

PERSONAL
HOROSCOPES

by Anne Lyddane

Your ascendant is the following if your time of birth was:

If your Sun sign is:	6 to 8 AM	8 to 10 AM	10 AM to NOON	NOON to 2 PM	2 to 4 PM	4 to 6 PM
Aries	Taurus	Gemini	Cancer	Leo	Virgo	Libra
Taurus	Gemini	Cancer	Leo	Virgo	Libra	Scorpio
Gemini	Cancer	Leo	Virgo	Libra	Scorpio	Sagittarius
Cancer	Leo	Virgo	Libra	Scorpio	Sagittarius	Capricorn
Leo	Virgo	Libra	Scorpio	Sagittarius	Capricorn	Aquarius
Virgo	Libra	Scorpio	Sagittarius	Capricorn	Aquarius	Pisces
Libra	Scorpio	Sagittarius	Capricorn	Aquarius	Pisces	Aries
Scorpio	Sagittarius	Capricorn	Aquarius	Pisces	Aries	Taurus
Sagittarius	Capricorn	Aquarius	Pisces	Aries	Taurus	Gemini
Capricorn	Aquarius	Pisces	Aries	Taurus	Gemini	Cancer
Aquarius	Pisces	Aries	Taurus	Gemini	Cancer	Leo
Pisces	Aries	Taurus	Gemini	Cancer	Leo	Virgo

If your Sun sign is:	6 to 8 PM	8 to 10 PM	10 PM to MIDNIGHT	MIDNIGHT to 2 AM	2 to 4 AM	4 to 6 AM
Aries	Scorpio	Sagittarius	Capricorn	Aquarius	Pisces	Aries
Taurus	Sagittarius	Capricorn	Aquarius	Pisces	Aries	Taurus
Gemini	Capricorn	Aquarius	Pisces	Aries	Taurus	Gemini
Cancer	Aquarius	Pisces	Aries	Taurus	Gemini	Cancer
Leo	Pisces	Aries	Taurus	Gemini	Cancer	Leo
Virgo	Aries	Taurus	Gemini	Cancer	Leo	Virgo
Libra	Taurus	Gemini	Cancer	Leo	Virgo	Libra
Scorpio	Gemini	Cancer	Leo	Virgo	Libra	Scorpio
Sagittarius	Cancer	Leo	Virgo	Libra	Scorpio	Sagittarius
Capricorn	Leo	Virgo	Libra	Scorpio	Sagittarius	Capricorn
Aquarius	Virgo	Libra	Scorpio	Sagittarius	Capricorn	Aquarius
Pisces	Libra	Scorpio	Sagittarius	Capricorn	Aquarius	Pisces

1. Find your Sun sign (left column);
2. Determine correct approximate time of birth column;
3. Line up your Sun sign with birth time to find ascendant.

Sign	Glyph	Dates	Ruler	Element	Quality	Nature
Aries	♈	Mar 21–Apr 20	Mars	Fire	Cardinal	Barren
Taurus	♉	Apr 20–May 21	Venus	Earth	Fixed	Semi-Fruitful
Gemini	♊	May 21–June 21	Mercury	Air	Mutable	Barren
Cancer	♋	June 21–July 23	Moon	Water	Cardinal	Fruitful
Leo	♌	July 23–Aug 23	Sun	Fire	Fixed	Barren
Virgo	♍	Aug 23–Sept 22	Mercury	Earth	Mutable	Barren
Libra	♎	Sept 22–Oct 23	Venus	Air	Cardinal	Semi-Fruitful
Scorpio	♏	Oct 23–Nov 22	Pluto	Water	Fixed	Fruitful
Sagittarius	♐	Nov 22–Dec 22	Jupiter	Fire	Mutable	Barren
Capricorn	♑	Dec 22–Jan 20	Saturn	Earth	Cardinal	Semi-Fruitful
Aquarius	♒	Jan 20–Feb 18	Uranus	Air	Fixed	Barren
Pisces	♓	Feb 18–Mar 21	Neptune	Water	Mutable	Fruitful

ARIES
MARCH 21 TO APRIL 20

•JANUARY•

There is a strong accent on your career and public image. You focus on ambitions. Use persistence and practicality and go slowly, building a firm foundation. You may meet someone with similar desires in the love arena. Work only with realities and factual data for ultimate success. A mysterious, hidden legacy is a possibility.

•FEBRUARY•

Spend some time in solitude contemplating the past. Friends and groups with progressive ideas beckon. You need to appraise your inner desires with honesty. This can be a time for endings, consummations or graduations from past outlooks, habits and responses. Listen to your intuitive voice.

•MARCH•

Don't be overly optimistic with legacies or mutual funds. Jupiter went retrograde in late February, indicating the need for caution. Pluto goes retrograde on March 1st, and Mercury also turns retrograde, focusing on communications, travel and transportation. This is not a good time for signing important documents. A new love is a potential.

•APRIL•

Neptune joins Jupiter, Venus and Pluto in retrogression. You should spend some time alone to become acquainted with your inner self. The past is in the spotlight. Love and finances are abundant and well-grounded. Use caution in career matters. A new beginning appeals to you. Communicate with clarity and precision.

•MAY•

Uranus turns retrograde on the 1st, affecting your career and public image. You may feel pulled by practicality, yet still want originality. Flirtations are available with someone witty and charming but fickle. Focus is on communications and short trips. You use your charisma and executive abilities profitably. The money picture continues to be stable.

•JUNE•

Saturn goes retrograde on the 23rd, affecting family, the past, work done in solitude and self-restrictions. Avoid hanging on to what is no longer rewarding. A compassionate love union around home base is evident. Mercury is retrograde after the 13th, so keep the lines of communication open. Check out financial opportunities carefully. Avoid stubbornness and remain practical.

•JULY•

Objectively take stock of career desires, finances and family responsibilities. Jupiter becomes direct on the 2nd, lightening up the legacy/mutual funds region. Now can be a profitable time for decisions. Home base offers comfort and security. You may feel emotionally rewarded in the work sector. Someone intelligent and practical offers a mutually satisfying relationship potential.

•AUGUST•

Pluto turns direct on the 6th and mutual funds and an inheritance are highlighted. Integrating conscious data with subconscious may be productive. A harmonious marriage/love union is available. Children, creativity and public recognition take the limelight. This could be a good time for a relaxing vacation, especially on, near or around water.

•SEPTEMBER•

Your tenacity and patience could be rewarded with a productive position and/or financial expansion. A possible relationship hidden from public view is indicated. Avoid manipulation or jealousy. Your communications are based on a desire for balance, often cloaked in charm. Counseling, arbitration and cooperation are key words, especially in connection with marriage or business partnerships.

•OCTOBER•

Neptune and Uranus turn direct on the 2nd, relieving the pressure on career affairs. Venus goes retrograde on the 13th and Mercury on the 9th, affecting legacies and mutual funds. With Jupiter and Pluto direct, self-discipline with Venus and Mercury is important. You may find outlets through acting, writing, teaching or lecturing. You desire recognition, especially from lovers and children.

•NOVEMBER•

Saturn and Venus go direct, relieving the heaviness regarding family, the past and self-restrictions. Your intense reactions connected with legacies and mutual funds should be clarified. Put all of your cards on the table—emotionally, mentally, creatively, sexually, expansively and subconsciously. Concentrate and positively direct these energies.

•DECEMBER•

You may find pleasure through foreign travel, progressive education, publishing or occult studies. After the 19th, your career goals receive recognition and financial reward. Romance continues to be intense. As you review this year, you must conclude its learning opportunities and envision the new year with exhilaration and joy.

TAURUS
APRIL 20 TO MAY 21

•JANUARY•

Opportunities are available in business, foreign travel, education, the law and publishing. Do some painstaking research before making choices. Romance calls for some testing before fulfillment. You may meet someone from another country or background. Marriage or business partnerships need honest inner probing.

•FEBRUARY•

Use avant-garde techniques to express your skills. Mercury goes retrograde on the 11th, so avoid signing important papers or making legal commitments. Romance may be encountered among friends or groups with interests similar to yours. At the end of the month Jupiter turns retrograde, indicating the need for mutual respect in marriage or business relationships.

•MARCH•

Pluto goes retrograde in your region of marriage or business relationships on the 1st, bringing what needs attention to the surface. Discard old patterns and beliefs. You may be interested in psychic studies, the arts, literature or acting. Others with authority or experience prove helpful. An exciting love potential, perhaps from the past, appears.

•APRIL•

You are productive, especially as you work alone in quiet surroundings. In romance, someone you met last month may now be a permanent partner. Emotional stability is important to you. Neptune turns retrograde on the 25th, slowing down foreign travel, studies, legal affairs and publishing matters. Exercise sufficiently and don't over-indulge. Combine social activities with outdoor physical fun.

•MAY•

Uranus becomes retrograde on the 1st. Your creativity may be strongly accented. Your financial and value system sectors need fine tuning. You may find it difficult to make decisions. The same goes for romance. Dualities and changes keep you riding up and down. Check all communications carefully. Pay attention to the fine print.

•JUNE•

Pluto, Saturn, Jupiter, Uranus and Mars are all in retrogression. Take care in travel, transportation, cars, the mail, what you say and what you sign. You could meet someone romantic around relatives or in your own environment. A new opportunity may be grounded, sold or produced. Work accomplished previously surfaces for recognition. Your money picture continues to be dualistic.

•JULY•

Don't create confrontations in marriage or business relationships, foreign travel, education, the law, organizations, relatives and communications. A vacation could be enjoyable. Jupiter becomes direct on the 2nd, lessening some strains in the marriage and business partnership area. Lovers and children's interests need attention, but not criticism. Finances are ready to take off.

•AUGUST•

Pluto turns direct on the 6th, releasing tensions around marriage and business. Social activities on a grand scale are indicated. Romance may be found at work with someone pleasant and charismatic. You may decide to purchase a larger home or enlarge your present one. Caution is suggested with regard to education, foreign travel and legal matters. Exercise and enjoy outdoor activities.

•SEPTEMBER•

Lovers and children take the limelight and you may expect them to toe the line. Avoid nit picking. Employment indicates a balance between communications and cooperation. Love unions may be on your mind, but avoid impulsive behavior. Don't get caught up in jealousy or power plays. You may be asked to represent your environment and neighbors in a service-oriented project.

•OCTOBER•

Neptune and Uranus turn direct on the 2nd. Trips to other lands and opportunities for training are offered. Legal and publishing matters are settled. Venus becomes retrograde on the 13th and Mercury on the 9th, affecting marriage, love unions and/or business partnerships. Your mentality and emotions come in for scrutiny. Investigate your true values. Emphasis in on your home base.

•NOVEMBER•

Saturn goes direct on the 9th and Venus on the 24th. Saturn indicates effectively working with those in distress. This is a good time for studying psychic matters. With Venus, Mercury and Jupiter, accenting marriage or business relationships, try to release stubborn attitudes. Combine some of these energies with your empathy toward groups. This removes tensions and offers rewards.

•DECEMBER•

Legacies, mutual funds and the regeneration of energies are highlighted. Communicate with honest directness. Toward the end of the month, foreign travel could be interesting, combining business, education/training with pleasure. There is a strong wind of change, challenge and fun, with the new year in the wings. Letting go of the past aids in programming yourself for exciting vistas.

GEMINI
MAY 21 TO JUNE 22

•JANUARY•

Inheritances, mutual funds and regeneration of energies are accented. Practical methods can be helpful. Be cautious in romance. There is a seesawing effect associated with foreign travel, publishing, the law, special education and psychic research. Expansion and progressive action are indicated, as are attention to data and proof.

•FEBRUARY•

Mercury turns retrograde on the 11th, affecting your career and public image. Postpone travel, communications or signing documents. Jupiter goes retrograde on the 28th, urging patience in your work sector. Romance appears sweet, empathetic and may concern your career. Your ambitions may be focused on other countries or people from different backgrounds.

•MARCH•

Pluto joins Jupiter in its retrogression, affecting employment matters. Dreams, times of meditation and inner probing can be methods of discovering important data. Discard what is no longer viable. Take responsibility for what you desire. An exciting love, met through friends or a group, is a potential. Career matters are still on hold.

•APRIL•

Neptune turns retrograde, accenting legacies and mutual funds. Neptune can be indecisive, so deal with what is real. You may be given recognition with friends or groups. Romance has a mysterious ambiance, a hidden, personal touch. Work done in solitude may prove creative. Your career suggests persistence and taking the long-range viewpoint.

•MAY•

Uranus becomes retrograde on the 1st. This may suggest a scattered feeling. Enjoy outdoor exercise and a sensible diet. Avoid confusing emotions with facts. Love is flirtatious. You feel dualistic, indecisive and when confrontations appear you tend to be "out the door." Communications and travel could be interesting. Projecting a different image is a potential.

•JUNE•

Mercury begins a retrogression on the 13th, highlighting changes, transportation and communications. This is not a positive time for speculation. Avoid taking trips or signing papers. Saturn becomes retrograde on the 23rd, slowing down your career sector. Think before you speak or write. Love and finances appear fluid and well-grounded. Continued work done alone may be profitable.

•JULY•

Jupiter turns direct on the 2nd, releasing tensions surrounding your work. Goals can be expansive, and the "bad luck" reaction is lessened. This is a month of heavy retrogressions, with Pluto, Neptune, Saturn and Uranus all in that position. Romance may appear at home. There are mutual feelings for stability and an enduring relationship. Avoid being too critical with others or yourself.

•AUGUST•

Pluto turns direct on the 6th, along with Jupiter, releasing tensions in your employment sector. Communications, relatives and your environment are active and your leadership may be engaged in these areas. Love affairs and children can be charming and pleasant. You may be busy keeping everyone balanced and fulfilled. Finances, investments and values blend action with intuition.

•SEPTEMBER•

Some of past ambitions regarding your work situation come to the forefront for reward. You tend to find emotional fulfillment, as well as a potential love outlet, through employment environments. Avoid appearing jealous and don't make power plays with a romantic relationship. Keeping the peace and seeing all sides can be helpful. Use balance and justice for yourself as well as others.

•OCTOBER•

Neptune and Uranus turn direct on the 2nd, releasing pressures around inheritances and mutual funds. Unexplored concepts surface. Your dreams are available for practical implementation. Venus goes retrograde on the 13th, suggesting that your love affairs need investigation. Mercury becomes retrograde on the 9th, indicating the importance of communicative analysis.

•NOVEMBER•

Saturn becomes direct on the 9th. What you have learned in the past about persistence and practicality can be directed effectively toward goals. Venus becomes direct on the 24th, joining Mercury in the work sector. Emotions and intellect feel free. You could find enjoyment through acting. Your energies are strongly charismatic during this period.

•DECEMBER•

Attention is on love unions and/or business relationships. Partners who are your "opposite twin" in temperament can be fun. A sudden, exciting love union could merge into a longer commitment. You could take trips to countries which offer pleasure and adventure. Later in the month, mutual funds and legacies surface for workable decisions. 1994 has been a strong learning opportunity.

CANCER
JUNE 22 TO JULY 23

•JANUARY•

Pluto spotlights your area associated with children, love affairs and personal creativity. Take time for honest appraisals of your values. Marriage and love unions are strongly highlighted, with Mars, Venus, the Sun, Mercury, Neptune and Uranus all in this sector. This can be a building influence in romance, action, personality, intellect and visions.

•FEBRUARY•

Mercury goes retrograde on the 11th, slowing down transportation and communications. Take astral and educational trips or study psychic matters. Romance is a potential with someone from another culture. Jupiter moves retrograde on the 28th, affecting children and lovers. Avoid impulsive behavior. A sudden legacy may arrive.

•MARCH•

Pluto joins Jupiter in retrogression on the 1st, accenting lovers and children's interests. Release what is no longer viable. Originality and independence in career matters offer rewards. Love may enter your career site, as someone with executive skills and charisma appears on the scene. Take care around special training, foreign travel, the law, publishing and psychic investigation.

•APRIL•

Neptune becomes retrograde on the 25th, giving love unions intrigue. Work without illusions. Friends and organizations offer fun and romance. Dancing, lectures, food and drink, the theater, healing and physical activities open up. Your career appears strong. Use enthusiasm to show off your skills effectively. Keep communication clear.

•MAY•

Uranus turns retrograde on the 1st, affecting love unions and/or business relationships. Check out impulsive opportunities. Work for balance in energy, time and emotions. The past, family traditions, self-restrictions and institutions pose a triple threat. Love appears to have a secretive sense, while dualities occur in your emotions and outer personality. Try not to scatter your time or abilities.

•JUNE•

Pluto, Saturn, Jupiter and Mercury are all retrograde. Lovers and children continue their need for balance. Inner questioning can be helpful. Foreign travel, legal and publishing matters slow down. Your creativity can be activated through planning a new self-image. A tender romance with someone devoted, loving and empathetic is a potential. Social fun occurs with friends and groups.

•JULY•

Jupiter turns direct on the 2nd, taking the heat off your region of lovers and children. There should be rewards for your patience. Project that new you which you were envisioning. A love interest with someone practical, intellectual and communicative appears. You could meet him/her through relatives or neighbors. Try writing, teaching, lecturing, arts and crafts, research and healing.

•AUGUST•

Pluto turns direct on the 6th, joining Jupiter in the lifting of retrogression periods in love unions. Now you can work with facts and honest values. Finances, assets, investments and value systems are accented. Avoid impulsive spending or confusing emotions with money. Take the long-range viewpoint. Romance can be right at your door.

•SEPTEMBER•

Emphasis is on lovers and children. Avoid possessiveness, jealousy and manipulative behavior. Make sure there is justice for all concerned. Your home base is spotlighted, with an accent on playing the host. You may also do some creative work at home. Fashion design, counseling, painting, sculpting or writing can be effective. Relatives and neighbors are helpful and stable.

•OCTOBER•

Neptune and Uranus turn direct on the 2nd, lessening tensions around love unions and business relationships. Venus turns retrograde on the 13th and Mercury on the 9th, intensely affecting lovers and children. Put all the cards on the table. Mutual respect is a must. Your financial picture appears active. Think big, but use common sense.

•NOVEMBER•

Saturn becomes direct on the 9th, lightening the region of foreign travel, the law, publishing, education and psychic research. Cause and effect are evident. This could be an appropriate period for travel by water to other countries. Venus becomes direct on the 24th, releasing the heaviness around children and lovers. Attention to reality is important, so be watchful. Money continues its up-turn.

•DECEMBER•

Your employment region becomes active. Opportunities, travel and rewards appear. You may decide to change your residence or work situation. Be clear about your demands. Use humor and charm, but be practical. Romance can be emotionally exhilarating. After the middle of the month, love unions call for responsible decisions. Mulling over your achievement, you end the year with a smile.

LEO
JULY 23 TO AUGUST 23

•JANUARY•

Home base comes in for attention. Pluto and
Jupiter indicate the need for investigation and balance. Pluto works with releasing whatever is no
longer viable. Jupiter works with actualities, rather
than speculation. Your employment area is also
intensely aspected. Be practical and persistent. The
same applies to romance.

•FEBRUARY•

Mercury turns retrograde on the 11th, suggesting
confusion with legacies and mutual funds. Don't
combine money with emotions. Keep communications clear. Jupiter goes retrograde on the 28th. Do
some self-investigation of your values. Romance is
a potential with an old love. Use caution and avoid
impulsive behavior around the region of love
unions and/or business partnerships.

•MARCH•

Pluto will be retrograde on the 1st, clouding home
base matters. Now is the time for some digging
beneath and behind conscious surfaces. A stimulating and dramatic romance appears, perhaps with
someone from another land or background.
Employment continues its course toward enduring
results. You could take a trip to a foreign country.

•APRIL•

Neptune, in your area of work, moves retrograde on the 25th. Avoid dealing in illusion. Be creative and organize. If possible, wait to implement ideas until Neptune turns direct in October. Your career environment may add a touch of romance. Your love of the limelight may be rewarding. The potential still exists for a trip to other lands.

•MAY•

Uranus joins Neptune in its retrogression on the 1st, focusing on the work region. Remain clear about your goals. Friends and organizations can be fun. Communications, travel and challenges are evident. Teaching, acting, lecturing, writing, publishing, public relations and sales can be successful and interesting. Love continues around your career sector. Maintain clarity regarding mutual funds.

•JUNE•

Mercury turns retrograde on the 13th, accenting the past, family traditions, solitary creativity and institutions. Postpone travel, communications and new ventures. Romance may be mysterious. Saturn goes retrograde on the 23rd, affecting legacies and mutual funds. Home base continues to need your attention. Organizations associated with communications, travel and the public are highlighted.

•JULY•

With Pluto, Neptune, Uranus and Saturn all retrograde this month, you will be glad to know that Mercury becomes direct on the 7th and Jupiter on the 2nd. Work done in solitude may now be made public. Tensions around home base are lessened. Expand your horizons. Romance and money have a balanced outlook. Love and finances are secure. There may be opportunity for public recognition.

•AUGUST•

Pluto becomes direct on the 6th, lifting strains around the home. Mutual respect can be important. A loving relationship with someone pleasant and cooperative can be available through relatives or neighbors. A new image is in store for you. Your mentality is forceful and active. Avoid appearing arrogant or domineering. Be caring.

•SEPTEMBER•

Decisions need to be made concerning home base. Passions and demands can run high, but facts need to be addressed. Love and romance are potentials, but mutual gains are necessary. Finances can become stable. Relatives, your environment and communications can be harmonious. Counseling, arbitration and healing are all highlighted. Entertainment appears cultural and balanced.

•OCTOBER•

Neptune and Uranus go direct on the 2nd, releasing their holding positions in your work sector. You may implement plans effectively. Opportunities open for that new you. Mercury becomes retrograde on the 9th and Venus on the 13th, affecting home base. Decisions surface for attention. Avoid manipulation or jealousy. Use humor and wit to counteract intensities and communicate clearly.

•NOVEMBER•

Saturn becomes direct on the 9th, releasing pressure around legacies and mutual funds. Venus also turns direct on the 24th, so that home base may be more meaningful and valued. You may be doing much hosting, hopefully celebrating happy conclusions to past challenges. There is also a potential for enlarging the home or purchasing a more comfortable residence.

•DECEMBER•

There is emphasis on children and love affairs. Stimulation and progressive opportunities are available. Direct communications are accented, using humor and fun. Your money picture is stable if you are practical. Work only with provable information. Active and intense romance is accented around your home. Your work region becomes an opportune area for rewards and satisfaction.

VIRGO
AUGUST 23 TO SEPTEMBER 23

•JANUARY•

Focus is upon the concerns of lovers and children. There is a dual vibration present. What is new and unexplored opposes illusion, drama and intuition. Work with data and creativity. Romance is affected by these elements. Your work region calls for inventiveness. Take time for some thought regarding relatives, environment and communications.

•FEBRUARY•

Mercury turns retrograde on the 11th, affecting love unions. Confusion in communications may be evident. Jupiter moves into retrogression on the 28th, so slow down and face facts regarding relatives, environment and communications. Don't be overly optimistic. An exciting opportunity in your work sector offers independence.

•MARCH•

Pluto becomes retrograde on the 1st, joining Jupiter, and focuses on working with what has been hidden. Communications, relatives and environment appear for investigation. Emphasis is on love unions. Be practical, but caring. Romance is exciting and may be connected with a legacy or mutual funds. There is an active money or inheritance potential.

•APRIL•

On the 25th, Neptune becomes retrograde in the region of relatives, environment and communications. Avoid illusion and procrastination. Turn your energies into creative efforts and listen to your intuition. Opportunities are evident with legacies and/or mutual funds. Love may be encountered in another land or with someone of a different background. Travel combines business with pleasure.

•MAY•

Uranus accompanies Neptune into retrogression on the 1st. Lovers and children may appear charming but irresponsible, progressive yet stubborn. Use your sense of humor and creative productivity. Your career is being accented. Travel, communications, sales and public relations are emphasized. You may have more than one opportunity. Romance focuses on your career region.

•JUNE•

Saturn turns retrograde on the 23rd, accenting love unions and/or business partnerships. Don't confuse emotional desires with facts. Mercury goes retrograde on the 13th. Communicate clearly and avoid travel and signing important documents. A compassionate love is a potential. Organizations connected with healing and counseling offer you emotional rewards. Your career is exciting.

•JULY•

With Pluto, Neptune, Saturn and Uranus retrograde, it is good that Mercury goes direct on the 7th and Jupiter on the 2nd. Mercury indicates releasing tensions around groups. Jupiter discards irritations and confusions concerning relatives, environment and communications. Someone practical and persistent desires a stable, enduring relationship with you. Investigate this.

•AUGUST

Pluto finally moves direct on the 6th, along with Jupiter, discarding major confusions and tensions around relatives, environment and communications. Combine subconscious data with conscious actions. Romance has an air of mystery. Authority, power and accomplishment accompany this potential partner. Finances appear balanced. This could be a positive time to purchase a gift for yourself.

•SEPTEMBER•

There is much activity around your area of finances, assets, investments and value systems. Keep your checkbook and investment picture on the up and up. You may take a step toward a new image. Make sure any change is based on facts. Romance can be met through relatives or neighbors. Avoid becoming possessive or jealous. Organize and research to envision that new image.

•OCTOBER•

Neptune and Uranus go direct on the 2nd, relieving tensions around children and lovers. Continue to use persistence and a practical outlook. Mercury turns retrograde on the 9th and Venus on the 13th, accenting relatives, environment and communications. Separate feelings and decisions. Finances and values continue their potential for balance.

•NOVEMBER•

Saturn becomes direct on the 9th, affecting love unions. Both partners feel relief and romance is ardent. Factual data and practicality should bring success. Venus turns direct on the 24th, taking the pressure off communications, relatives and environment. You may be offered recognition or a position of authority. Focus your ambitions and express your desires with clarity.

•DECEMBER•

You may want to take a trip to a fascinating country, enlarge your current residence or purchase a trailer, boat or RV. If you cannot get away, enlarge your horizons with studies, reading and social activities. Love continues to be exciting and even exotic. Don't keep the other on a leash, however. Your new image can be projected successfully. As the new year opens, you feel warm and secure.

LIBRA
SEPTEMBER 23 TO OCTOBER 23

•JANUARY•

Your home base affairs indicate that it is time to make a stable and secure residence. You have an emotional, mental, action-based and personality-related accenting. When you decide upon a home base, many doors or paths will open up for you. Romance is evident, along with creativity and originality. Use patience and persistence.

•FEBRUARY•

Mercury turns retrograde on the 11th, spotlighting lovers and children's interests. Be cautious in making choices. This vibration suggests indecision and irresponsibility. Jupiter becomes retrograde on the 28th, accenting money and values. Avoid speculating without research. Emotional rewards can come through healing, counseling, the arts, acting and psychic studies. Romance may be found at work.

•MARCH•

Pluto goes retrograde on the 1st, emphasizing finances and values. Make honest appraisals. Your employment region is important. Divide emotions from actualities. Listen to your intuition and avoid becoming dependent on facts. Someone ambitious, vigorous and active offers enlivening, new love concepts. An impulsive relationship is a potential.

•APRIL•

Neptune goes retrograde on the 25th. Wait and gather proof before making choices regarding home base matters. Illusion could be a barrier. There is emphasis on impulsive love unions. If already in a relationship, exciting vistas may open. A legacy from someone dear to you is a potential. Mutual funds take on practical form. Work moves along similar lines as last month.

•MAY•

Uranus joins Neptune in retrogression on the 25th, affecting home base. Check out all opportunities. Uranus indicates charm, irresponsibility, progression and unrealism. You may find romance with someone from another country. You may find a visit, probably by air, interesting. Communications, travel, sales, public relations, acting, the media, writing, teaching and lecturing are in the limelight.

•JUNE•

Saturn turns retrograde on the 23rd, affecting your work sector. This is not a positive time to rock any boats. Listen to your intuition. Your career holds a retrograde Mercury from the 13th on. Avoid confusing feelings with intellect. This is not a productive time for travel or making changes in career. Romance around your work site is an emotionally rewarding potential. Mutual funds appear stable.

•JULY•

Jupiter turns direct on the 2nd, releasing financial tensions. Mercury becomes direct on the 7th. Irritations and delays retreat from your career sector. Use empathy toward others. Romance appears idealistic, hidden and self-restrictive. This month may appear slow, but there is a strong underpinning of potential growth in many areas of your life.

•AUGUST•

Pluto moves direct on the 6th, removing tensions from your money situation. What was hidden or ignored may surface for new goals. A well-balanced love relationship is a potential with someone who is different from past romantic attachments. Friends and organizations offer you positions of leadership and authority. The theatrical field, politics, the law or government offer possibilities.

•SEPTEMBER•

A balanced outlook, working with vision and practicality are evident. Work done in solitude can be productive, especially creativity combined with precision and research. Love appears intense. You may need to check responses such as jealousy and possessiveness. Finances and values come in for rewards. Avoid emotional spending and be cautious when investing.

•OCTOBER•

Neptune and Uranus go direct on the 2nd, lessening tensions around home base. Friends and organizations offer you outlets for leadership and public recognition. Potentials in a theatrical field can be exciting. Venus turns retrograde on the 13th and Mercury on the 9th, affecting finances and values. Don't give love away impulsively. Pay attention to actions. A new beginning may be possible.

•NOVEMBER•

Saturn turns direct on the 9th, relieving work pressures. Venus becomes direct on the 24th, affecting love and money. Research and be cautious. Don't confuse emotions with finances. Your situation with friends and groups continues to offer you active, gregarious and pleasurable opportunities. Politics, entertainment, the law, government and social charisma are accented.

•DECEMBER•

Your region of relatives, environment and communications are strongly aspected. Travel, writing, acting, teaching, counseling and publishing come into the spotlight. Romance is warm and active and finances appear generous. Creativity combined with practicality suggests profit. As this year closes and you look back at your accomplishments, there is an apparent feeling of security and stability.

SCORPIO
OCTOBER 23 TO NOVEMBER 23

•JANUARY•

Relatives, communications and environment are accented. Much of your time and energy is spent attempting to be constructive. You need to feel secure. Romance is available through relatives or neighbors. You need time for testing. There is a strong thrust toward creating a new image. Avoid appearing aggressive or domineering.

•FEBRUARY•

Mercury turns retrograde on the 11th, focusing on home base. It may be difficult to pin down people or situations. Get sufficient outdoor exercise and an intelligent diet. Avoid manipulation. Jupiter becomes retrograde on the 28th, accenting new beginnings. Be patient and avoid impulse. Romance appears sweet and tender.

•MARCH•

Pluto turns retrograde on the 1st, suggesting a new image. You may need to dig into your subconscious and make an appraisal of your values. Jupiter indicates caution. Your work sector has an original and ambitious thrust. You may receive a position of leadership or be offered more profitable employment. Romance may be encountered at the work site with someone equally ambitious.

•APRIL•

Neptune becomes retrograde on the 25th, affecting relatives, environment and communications. Avoid signing important papers. You need to feel secure and find an enduring relationship with someone warm and supportive. Your employment picture continues to look up. Opportunities where you can use your originality and executive talents are indicated. Express yourself with precision.

•MAY•

Uranus joins Neptune in retrogression on the 1st, so tensions and stress may be encountered with communications and relatives. Use your sharp intellect to cut away the illusiveness. Love appears dualistic and somewhat flirtatious. You may find it difficult to settle upon just one companion. Legacies and mutual funds have ups and downs. Communicate with clarity and work for definite goals.

•JUNE•

Saturn turns retrograde on the 23rd, affecting lovers and children. You may feel restricted, although this is a learning opportunity. Mercury turns retrograde on the 13th, highlighting foreign lands, publishing, occult studies and education. This is not a good time for travel. Separate emotions from actions. A committed relationship may be met with someone from another culture.

•JULY•

Jupiter turns direct on the 2nd, lessening tensions regarding new beginnings. Mercury also becomes direct on the 7th. This may be a good time to visit foreign lands, deal actively with publishing, the law, training and occult interests. Romance can be available through friends or groups with someone intellectual and objective. This relationship may take some time.

•AUGUST•

Pluto moves direct on the 6th, lightening up new beginnings. Career affairs come in for the spotlight, with power and ambition in the saddle. Use charm and leadership to succeed. Romance has a feeling of mystery, a hidden and delightful ambiance. Someone who has a softening effect upon you helps create a harmonious relationship potential. Travel by water is available.

•SEPTEMBER•

Accompanying that new beginning mentioned previously is romance. Respect each other and avoid power plays or jealousy. The arts can be profitable. Friends and groups offer pleasure combined with learning opportunities. Research, healing, counseling and working with precision and discretion offer success. You could be requested to use your analytical skills with organizations or groups.

•OCTOBER•

Neptune and Uranus turn direct on the 2nd, lessening friction around relatives, environment and communications. Combine creativity with practical concepts. Mercury goes retrograde on the 9th and Venus on the 13th, slowing down new beginnings. Try to maintain a sense of balance. Avoid signing important papers and keep emotions on a tight leash. You find rewards in working alone.

•NOVEMBER•

Saturn becomes direct on the 9th, affecting children and love affairs. You may feel responsibilities lightened. What you have done returns with mathematical exactitude. Venus turns direct on the 24th and you are able to think, feel, expand and act in positive ways. Career matters continue their up-swing toward leadership, power, authority and public recognition. You are definitely "on stage."

•DECEMBER•

Finances, assets and value systems are accented. You discover new methods for success. Travel, communications and changes are important. Use caution, however, and check out all opportunities. Avoid impulsive behavior. Romance accelerates and concentrates on a new era in relationships. Precision, discretion and investigation can be successful when working with groups and organizations.

SAGITTARIUS
NOVEMBER 23 TO DECEMBER 22

•JANUARY•

Money and values are accented. Get your finances in order. Avoid impulsive spending or investment. Analyze and test before coming to conclusions. This is also true of your romantic situation. Be understanding with relatives and neighbors and communicate with clarity. Work done in solitude and occult studies can be enjoyable.

•FEBRUARY•

Mars turns retrograde on the 11th, highlighting your home base. Avoid confrontations and tension. Use your sense of humor. Check the facts before taking action. Jupiter moves to retrogression on the 28th, affecting the past, family traditions and self-restrictions. Use patience and don't appear rebellious. Romance surrounds home base.

•MARCH•

Pluto turns retrograde on the 1st, joining Jupiter in your region of the past, family traditions, institutions and self-restrictions. Watch for important data through dreams and meditation. Discard past customs, outlooks and people that are no longer viable. A love relationship with someone ambitious and vital is a potential. Children may make you proud. Stay serene and cooperative.

•APRIL•

On the 25th, Neptune becomes retrograde, accenting finances and values. Don't believe in monetary promises. Investigate before taking action. Use this influence for creative productivity. Romance may be encountered at the work site with someone pleasant and stable. Love affairs and children play a big part in your life. Originality and independence are key words.

•MAY•

Uranus joins Neptune in retrogression on the 1st, focusing on your money region. This month could see a love union if you can overcome dualities. You are a natural flirt and find it difficult to settle down. Your work sector indicates that persistence is rewarded. Someone elderly or in a position of authority is calling for assistance at home base. Compassion can be helpful, but avoid dependency.

•JUNE•

Saturn becomes retrograde on the 23rd, accenting home base. This part of your life has long-range importance. Mercury turns retrograde on the 13th, highlighting legacies and mutual funds. Think through what you speak or write. Trips are not suggested, nor are major changes. An inheritance could be delayed. Don't confuse feelings with money in connection with mutual funds.

•JULY•

Jupiter will be direct on the 2nd, releasing tensions around the past, family traditions, institutions and self-restrictions. Make progressive actions. Mercury turns direct on the 7th, lessening confusions around legacies and mutual funds. You may receive an inheritance. Romance appears at work with someone reserved, intellectual, investigative and elegant. Be practical with finances.

•AUGUST•

Pluto joins Jupiter in becoming direct on the 6th. An energetic transformation is a potential. Take a trip to another land, begin special training, publish or work with psychic data. Your charisma is high and ambition sparkles effectively. Romance with an attractive and charming person occurs through friends or groups. You may receive a legacy.

•SEPTEMBER•

Your career and public image suggest attention to detail and routine. However, using persistence and patience you may show off successfully. This can be a balancing act. Love has a hidden quality. Communications and your natural salesmanship brings recognition among friends and groups. Combine social activities with educational, progressive outlets. Work done alone is productive.

•OCTOBER•

Uranus and Neptune go direct on the 2nd, releasing financial tensions. Creative yet practical actions can be successful. Mercury turns retrograde on the 9th and Venus on the 13th, affecting the past, family and institutions. Your intellect plus emotions need discipline and direction. Don't get swept away. Much ambition and strong energy in this area need integration and balance.

•NOVEMBER•

Emphasis is on the past, family traditions, self-restrictions and institutions. Venus turns direct on the 24th, so your emotions are under better control. Do some deep inner searching and trust your self-integrity. Saturn becomes direct on the 9th, lightening up matters around home base. This has been a long learning stretch but now offers rewards. Overseas travel can be profitable.

•DECEMBER•

Progressive, independent and optimistic actions appear as fun plus achievement. You should know just who you are and project it colorfully. Love continues its mysterious ambiance. There appear no definite decisions. The career sector still needs duty, service and precision to achieve recognition. As 1994 draws to a close, you have one foot out the door toward the new year.

CAPRICORN
DECEMBER 22 TO JANUARY 21

•JANUARY•

Your self-image is highlighted. Persistence and practicality help you achieve this particular goal. Your emotions, vitality, intellect, plus personality and the assistance of Uranus and Neptune are all collected in this region. Build a constructive new pattern. This is also true of romance. Be cautious and then go for it. Watch your budget carefully.

•FEBRUARY•

Mercury moves retrograde on the 11th, affecting your relatives, environment and communications. Be direct in speaking and writing and avoid signing documents or taking trips. Don't take on too many responsibilities. Jupiter becomes retrograde on the 28th, affecting friends and organizations. Avoid impulsive actions and investigate before making commitments.

•MARCH•

Pluto turns retrograde on the 1st, joining Jupiter in the region of friends and organizations. Review past habits and concepts. A new residence or an addition is possible. Romance is right at your front door with someone vital and ambitious. Avoid confusions or delays with messages or travel plans. Don't confront relatives or neighbors now.

•APRIL•

Neptune will be retrograde on the 25th, focusing on new beginnings. Don't get caught up in illusion. Be careful about addictive behavior. You may start your own business or profession at home. Love appears more secure. Children can be fun, caring and responsible. Anger and restlessness go the distance this month. Don't make power plays at home. Mutual respect and space are necessary.

•MAY•

On the 1st, Uranus turns retrograde, joining Neptune in the area of new beginnings. You may need more relaxation and sleep than usual. Don't permit seesawing vibrations to steer you off course. Your employment sector is accented. Multiple job opportunities may appear. Travel, communications and changes are highlighted. Romance is flirtatious.

•JUNE•

Saturn moves into retrogression on the 23rd, spotlighting relatives, environment and communications. The principle of cause and effect is important. Mercury turns retrograde on the 13th, affecting love unions. Avoiding necessary confrontations for mutual goals is not successful. Venus accompanies this vibration, indicating the need for sensitivity and intuition. Work for long-range results.

•JULY•

Jupiter becomes direct on the 2nd, accenting friends, groups and organizations. Activate plans for expansion. Mercury becomes direct on the 7th, lessening tensions around marriage and love unions. Romance may be encountered through someone from another country or background. A visit to another land may combine business with romantic pleasure. Keep balance at work.

•AUGUST•

Pluto becomes direct on the 6th, accompanying Jupiter in the release of tensions in the area of friends and groups. A generous legacy as well as abundant mutual funds are available. Romantic attachment with someone charming, attractive and compatible is available at the career site. Your career is a combination of work and pleasurable rewards. Love unions appear vital and caring.

•SEPTEMBER•

Foreign countries, people with different backgrounds, the law, publishing, occult studies and education are highlighted. Practical plans can be implemented. Career affairs continue to be balanced. Love discovered through friends or groups can be passionate, with a touch of exotic mystery. You may use your precision and critical talents successfully through trips, training or research.

•OCTOBER•

Uranus and Neptune turn direct on the 2nd, lightening up your self-image sector. Venus turns retrograde on the 13th and Mercury on the 9th, accenting friends, groups and organizations, and your emotions and intellect. Avoid anger and appearing too authoritative. Don't deal in power plays. This area of your life appears active. Be a leader, but a generous one.

•NOVEMBER•

Saturn becomes direct on the 19th, releasing friction around relatives, environment and communications. You receive the results of the causes you projected previously. Venus becomes direct on the 24th, so emotions and romance are on an even keel. Your ambitions are high and you want to be at the top. Mutual funds and a legacy may appear. This could also be recognition of your talents.

•DECEMBER•

The past, family traditions, institutions, work done in solitude and self-restrictions are highlighted. There is an active ambiance revving up your energies. You may feel more enthusiastic than usual. Freedom and independence are important to you. Delegate responsibility if necessary—"too many cooks spoil the broth." An ardent romance is evident through friends and groups.

AQUARIUS
JANUARY 21 TO FEBRUARY 19

•JANUARY•

The past, family traditions, institutions and self-restrictions are emphasized. Probe the meaning of learning experiences you have encountered. Romance, action, your mentality, communication, your outer personality and the work of Uranus and Neptune come within this region. Your career situation is also in the spotlight.

•FEBRUARY•

Mercury turns retrograde on the 11th, affecting new beginnings. Communications and travel need caution. Avoid signing documents and keep communications direct. Jupiter moves retrograde on the 28th, accenting your career. Don't act impulsively or attempt to implement big plans. Romance can be tender. Don't confuse financial matters with emotions. Try not to lend or borrow.

•MARCH•

Pluto moves retrograde on the 1st, indicating a good time to evaluate your true desires. Keep to your budget. Don't make impulsive investments or financial decisions. Romance with someone vital and ambitious may be discovered through family or neighbors. You may be asked to take on a position of leadership in your community.

•APRIL•

On the 25th, Neptune turns retrograde, accenting the past, institutions, family and self-restrictions. Neptune tends to fog basic realities. Avoid dependency, addictive behavior and illusion. Use this planet creatively, for sensitive, psychic studies as well. Romance is right at your door. Relatives, neighbors and communications offer recognition and approval. You may reach the top of the ladder.

•MAY•

Uranus turns retrograde on the 1st, affecting the past, family, institutions and self-restrictions. There may confusion and delays. You may need more rest than usual, with Uranus governing a highly-keyed nervous system. Avoid projecting inventive ideas until Uranus is direct. Love is flirtatious and indecisive, but fun. Children tend to be adaptable, flexible and witty.

•JUNE•

Mercury goes retrograde on the 13th, highlighting employment. Keep communications aboveboard. Avoid traveling or making changes. Romance may be met at work with someone who is empathetic and comforting. Saturn turns retrograde on the 23rd, affecting finances. Caution and practicality are suggested. Avoid confrontations at home base. Use your energies creatively.

•JULY•

Jupiter turns direct on the 2nd, lessening tensions around your career. Consider bigger opportunities in this region. Mercury becomes direct on the 7th, lightening up your employment sector. You may communicate with success, travel and make changes based on facts. Listen to your intuition and be sensitive to work opportunities. Romance is reserved and analytical.

•AUGUST•

Pluto turns direct on the 6th, releasing irritations and delays around your career. Direct energies toward more progressive goals. This month could also suggest a summer wedding or love union with someone ambitious, forceful and charismatic. Work for mutual respect and space. Your work situation has a service-oriented influence. Healing, counseling and nurturing are accented.

•SEPTEMBER•

You may receive a deserved legacy and work for mutual goals with available funds. A trip, by air, to another country is evident. You could combine business with pleasure connected with the law, publishing, government, politics or education. Romance discovered at the career site appears vibrant. Avoid jealousy and power plays. You may receive recognition for your successful career effort.

•OCTOBER•

Uranus and Neptune become direct on the 2nd, releasing their hold on the past, family, institutions and self-restrictions. There appears an active thrust toward a love union with someone in authority. This could be an impulsive liaison. Mercury goes retrograde on the 9th, affecting career. Venus moves into retrogression on the 13th. Watch your emotions and intellect.

•NOVEMBER•

Saturn turns direct on the 9th, releasing tensions around your money picture. Responsibilities are lessened. Dealing only with facts can offer successful results. Venus becomes direct on the 24th, removing friction at your career site. Past anger, jealousy and manipulations dissipate. Express yourself with seriousness. Show your executive and leadership qualities.

•DECEMBER•

Emphasis is on friends, groups and organizations. Educational, theatrical, political and public-oriented fields are open. Optimistic people appeal to you and offer broader outlets for your talents. You may take an interesting trip to some place totally new to you. Perhaps attending lectures, classes and seminars offer "travel" opportunities. Romance continues to be vigorous in your career area.

PISCES
FEBRUARY 19 TO MARCH 21

•JANUARY•

Take stock in friends, organizations and groups. Work with routine and details. You may be offered situations where you can give assistance. Romance could be met among these groups. Love has a reserved, almost cautious ambiance. Be persistent and keep communications concise. Balance your time and energy with fun.

•FEBRUARY•

Mercury goes retrograde on the 11th, affecting self-image. Do some investigation and decision-making. Work only with proof. Jupiter turns retrograde on the 28th affecting foreign travel, publishing, training, the law and psychic investigation. Avoid beginning any of these paths without planning. A tender romance is a potential.

•MARCH•

Pluto moves into retrogression on the 1st, accenting travel to foreign lands, the law, publishing, education and occult studies. Discard no longer viable outlooks. Pluto surfaces with important matters calling for transformation. Your money picture suggests progression in assets, investments and values. You want your own business. Romance is idealistic and energetic.

•APRIL•

On the 25th, Neptune becomes retrograde, accenting friends, groups and organizations. Direct your healing and counseling abilities. Avoid impractical visions. Romance may be encountered through friends or relatives with someone stable and devoted. Your finances are ambition-oriented. Use common sense. Don't confuse emotions with money. Avoid anger or impatience.

•MAY•

Uranus becomes retrograde on the 1st, highlighting friends, organizations and groups. Don't spread your time, talents and energies too thin. Research all original theories. Love appears flirtatious and hard to pin down. A romance may start right at home. You could be working creatively at home base, dealing with communications, arts and crafts, music, counseling or healing.

•JUNE•

Saturn moves retrograde on the 23rd, accenting new beginnings. Take your time and be constructive with plans. Try not to show your temper or insist upon confrontations with relatives or neighbors. Lovers and children are in the spotlight. You may feel nurtured by your love affairs and offspring. Mercury retrogrades on the 13th, so be cautious in communications and travel.

•JULY•

Jupiter turns direct on the 2nd, releasing tension around foreign trips, publishing, education, the law and the occult. Mercury becomes direct on the 7th, lessening irritations with children and lovers. Mutual understanding is evident. Trips may be planned with success. You may make a change in residence or purchase a second home, a boat or trailer. Romance appears stable.

•AUGUST•

On the 6th, Pluto turns retrograde, indicating that now is the time for action. Your employment sector offers recognition, approval and rewards for your talents. A position of authority or power is a potential. Love appears balanced, harmonious with mutual respect and goals. Avoid permissiveness toward lovers and/or children. Face necessary confrontations with empathy.

•SEPTEMBER•

A love union is indicated with someone who is supportive, practical and devoted. There is a possibility of an attractive legacy and a balanced outlook regarding mutual funds. Equality and worth are key words. Romance is exotic and intense with someone from another country or background. Friends and groups are important. Use persistence and common sense in achieving practical goals.

•OCTOBER•

Uranus and Neptune become direct on the 2nd, lessening restrictions on friends and groups. Healing and counseling and progressive concepts blend harmoniously. Public recognition and reward are suggested. Venus turns retrograde on the 13th and Mercury on the 19th, affecting foreign lands, the law, publishing and education. Separate your intellect and emotions. Avoid jealousy.

•NOVEMBER•

Saturn turns direct on the 9th, lessening frictions around new beginnings. Venus becomes direct on the 24th, taking the pressure off foreign travel, education, publishing, the law and occult studies. You may discover romance on a visit abroad or with someone ambitious and vital at study groups or social activities. Work is upbeat. Combine charisma with your leadership talents.

•DECEMBER•

Much emphasis is on your career and public image sector. New and expansive opportunities are available. Focus is on changes, travel and communications. Your love of the unexplored and untried accompanies potential learning opportunities. Working with the public is accented. Radio, TV, writing, teaching, lecturing, acting, public relations and travel agencies all come within this influence.

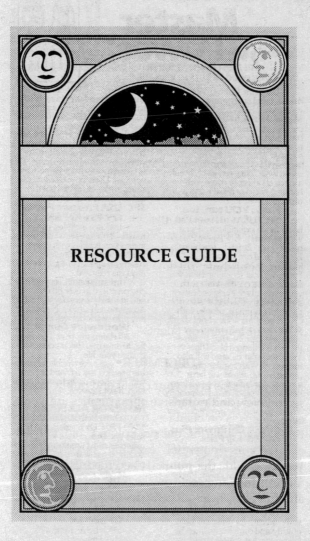

RESOURCE GUIDE

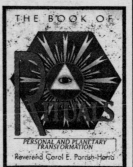
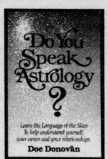

Charlotte's Mystical Web

P.O. Box 1177, West Memphis, AR 72301
(501) 735-1413 • 1-800-833-3056 • Contact Shari

♊ ♓ ♉

Astrological
Profile
Serbices

♌ ♎ ♏ ♒ ♑ ♍ ♋

We offer a complete line of mystical products and
supplies. We also offer astrological charts and reports.
Natal charts, plain talk explanation of the charts,
transit, life progressions, and friends and lovers
reports. All in easy-to-understand words.

Mystical supplies catalog and order form: $2.00
Astrological catalog and order form: $1.00

I am looking forward to doing business with you!
Blessed Be! Shari

Sensual Products

**How to order them without embarrassment.
How to use them without disappointment.**

Today, people are interested in improving the quality of their lives and exploring their own sensuality with options from the **Xandria Collection**.

What is The Xandria Collection?

It is a very special collection of sensual products. It includes the finest and most effective products available from around the world. Products that can open new doors to pleasure (perhaps many you never knew existed)!

Our products range from the simple to the delightfully complex. They are designed for the timid and the bold. For anyone who has ever wished there could be something more to their sensual pleasure.

The Xandria Collection has had the same unique three-way guarantee for nearly 20 years.

First, we guarantee your privacy. Everything we ship is plainly packaged and securely wrapped, with no clue to its contents from the outside. All transactions are strictly confidential and we <u>never</u> sell, rent or trade any customer's name.

Second, we guarantee your satisfaction. If a product seems unsatisfactory, simply return it for a replacement or refund.

Third, we guarantee the quality of our products for one year. If it malfunctions, simply return it to us for a replacement.

Send for the **Xandria Gold Edition Catalogue**. Its price of $4.00 is applied in full to your first order.

Write today. You have absolutely nothing to lose, and an entirely new world of enjoyment to gain.

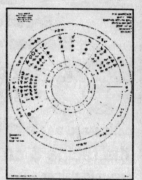

Spellbound
Metaphysical Shop

Crystal Empowered
Astrological Oils

**Based on Your Horoscope
Blended especially for You**

Only
$24⁹⁵

1oz of your crystal
empowered personal oil

a copy of your chart

the recipe & an explaination why

12 sticks of your personal Incense

$5 gift certificate off your next
purchase of 1 oz of your personal oil

When ordering please include:
Full Name, Birthday, Time & Place of Birth

Sorry, No COD's. Please add $3 shipping
Send Check or Money Order to:
Spellbound
480 Washington Ave. Belleville NJ 07109

AMAZING PSYCHIC PREDICTIONS

Now you too can experience the Astonishing Accuracy of the world's most gifted psychics!

Discover *YOUR* Destiny! Ask About
LOVE • SUCCESS • MONEY
LIVE ANSWERS TO ALL YOUR QUESTIONS!

1-900-370-3722

IS THIS REALLY THE "END TIME"?

The
Little
Book

From a woodcut by
Albrecht Dürer

As we approach the end of the millennium and the great changes due to result, you, being a responsible human, cannot afford to overlook the facts that say . . .

"YES, IT TRULY IS"!

Send $15 today for 3 Chapters from the "Little Book" of the "Mighty Angel" (Rev. 10:2):

1. "The Secret Purpose of Christianity"

2. "A Prophecy Fulfills; Christianity Must Change"

3. "The Quandary of Religion and the Quest for Truth"

Send $15, check or money order to Lester G. Murphy, 633 Cora Pl.#1a Rahway, NJ 07065-3726. Thank you.

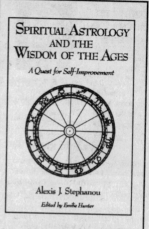

Classifieds

Products

NEW AGE SOFTWARE. Astrology, numerology, tarot and much more! Great prices. Catalog $1. Amazons' Realm, Box 60591, Reno NV 89506

Publications

CIRCLE NETWORK NEWS – Quarterly newspaper/journal of Paganism, Wiccan Spirituality, Goddess Studies, Shamanism, Magic and Nature Spirituality. FREE sample copy. Box 219, Mt. Horeb WI 53572

EXCITING NEW NATIONWIDE photo magazine for singles. Send name, address, age. Send no money. Exchange, Box 2425, Loveland CO 80539

Readings

EXTRAORDINARY PSYCHIC COUNSELOR, Randal Clayton Bradford, will tell you the best possible future in any situation, and how to make it happen. "Cuts straight to the truth…accurate, detailed and specific." Established worldwide clientele by telephone. AMEX/MC/VISA, 310-823-8893 or 213-REALITY

LIVE 24 HOURS! One on one! Psychics, astrologers, tarot. 1-900-773-7374. The Psychic Network_{sm}, Box 499-M, Deerfield FL 33443

CLAIRVOYANT, TAROT NUMEROLOGY or astrological readings. Taped: $35. Free information! The Psychic Network_{sm}, Box 499-M, Deerfield FL 33443

PSYCHIC PHONE READINGS, incredibly accurate. Need answers on love, health, finances? JoAnna 516-753-0191, NY, $35

GIFTED PSYCHIC TAROTIST shares insight and wisdom on love, health finances. Phone consultations, $30. Call Jerel-Lynn 516-271-8540.

Find New Meaning in Magical Myths

"Laura Simms is one of those rare and indispensible souls who keeps the oral tradition alive for us. She carries within her a tremendous range of material – from all over the world."
—*C.G. Jung Foundation*

Find new meaning in magical myths with the new **1994 Myth and Magic Calendar**. In this premiere calendar come twelve original full-color paintings from Llewellyn artists Hrana Janto and William Giese. Myth comes alive with exciting narrations by renowned storyteller Laura Simms.

Unleash your imagination and find new meaning from the gods and goddesses from around the world including Osiris, Isis and Horus; White Buffalo Woman; Sekhmet; and Pegasus. Order today!

- Behold the brilliance of 12 original full-color paintings
- Learn about symbolic myths that have meaning in our world today
- Keep track of your day-to-day appointments and personal notes
- Explore mythological legends from around the world
- Realize your everyday life is full of myth and magic!

Llewellyn's 1994 Myth & Magic Calendar
24 pp. ✦ full-color ✦ 12 x 12 ✦ Order # L-909 ✦ $10.00
Please use order form on last page.

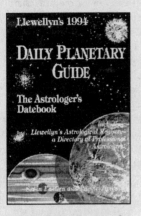

Llewellyn's Computerized Astrological Services

Llewellyn has been a leading authority in astrological chart readings for over thirty years. Our professional experience and continued dedication assures complete satisfaction in all areas of our astrological services.

Llewellyn features a wide variety of readings with the intent to satisfy the needs of any astrological enthusiast. Our goal is to give you the best possible service so that you can achieve your goals and live your life successfully.

When requesting a computerized service be sure to give accurate and complete birth data including: exact time (a.m. or p.m.), date, year, city, county and country of birth. (Check your birth certificate for this information.) *Accuracy of birth data is very important.* Llewellyn will not be responsible for mistakes made by you. An order form follows for your convenience.

Computerized Charts

Simple Natal Chart
Before you do anything else, order the Simple Natal Chart! This chart print-out is programmed and designed by Matrix. Learn the locations of your midpoints and aspects, elements, and more. Discover your planets and house cusps, retrogrades and other valuable data necessary to make a complete interpretation.
APS03-119 . . . . $5.00

Personality Profile
This is our most popular reading! It makes the perfect gift! This ten-part reading gives you a complete look at your "natal imprint" and how the planets mark your destiny. Examine your emotional needs and inner feelings. Explore your imagination and read about your general characteristics and life patterns. Very reasonable price!
APS03-503 . . . . $20.00

Life Progression

Discover what the future has in store for you! This incredible reading covers a year's time and is designed to complement the Personality Profile Reading. Progressions are a special system with which astrologers map how the "natal you" develops through specified periods of your present and future life. We are all born into an already existing world and an already existing fabric of personal interaction, and with this report you can discover the "now you!"

APS03-507 . . . . $20.00

Transit Report

Know the trends of your life—in advance! Keep abreast of positive trends and challenging periods for a specified period of time in your life. Transits are the relationships between the planets today and their positions at the moment of your birth. They are an invaluable aid for timing your actions and making decisions. This report devotes a paragraph to each of your transit aspects and gives effective dates for those transits. The report will begin with the first day of the month. Be sure to specify present residence for all people getting this report!

APS03-500 – 3-month report $12.00
APS03-501 – 6-month report $20.00
APS03-502 – 1-year report $30.00

Biorhythm Report

Ever have one of those days when you have unlimited energy and everything is going your way? Then the next day you are feeling sluggish and awkward? These cycles are called biorhythms. This individual report will accurately map your daily biorhythms. It can be your personal guide to the cycles of your daily life. Each important day is thoroughly discussed. With this valuable information, you can schedule important events with great success. This report is an invaluable source of information to help you plan your days to the fullest. Order today!

APS03-515 – 3-month report $12.00
APS03-516 – 6-month report $18.00
APS03-517 – 1-year report $25.00

Compatibility Profile

Find out if you really are compatible with your lover, spouse, friend or business partner! This is a great way of getting an in-depth look at your relationship with another person. Find out each person's approach to the relationship. Do you have the same goals? How well do you deal with arguments? Do you have the same values? This service includes planetary placements for both individuals, so send birth data for both. Succeed in all of your relationships! Order today!

APS03-504 . . . . $30.00

Personal Relationship Interpretation

If you've just called it quits on one relationship and know you need to understand more about yourself before you test the waters again, then this is the report for you! This reading will tell you how you approach relationships in general, what kind of people you look for and what kind of people might rub you the wrong way. Important for anyone!

APS03-506 . . . . $20.00

Tarot Reading

Find out what the cards have in store for you! This reading features the graphics of the traditional Rider-Waite card deck in a detailed 10-card spread, and as a bonus, there are three pages explaining what each Tarot card means for you. This report is also custom made to answer any question you might have. Order this exciting tarot reading today!

APS03-120 . . . . $10.00

Lucky Lotto Report

Do you play the lotteries? Bet on horses? Make trips to the casinos? This reading will determine the best numbers and dates based on specific planets, degrees and other indicators in your own chart. With this information you will know when planetary influences are in your favor, and when you are more likely to win. Learn what numbers are best for you, and begin your journey to financial success today!

APS03-512 – 3-month report $10.00
APS03-513 – 6-month report $15.00
APS03-514 – 1-year report $25.00

Numerology Report

Find out which numbers are right for you with this insightful report. This report uses an ancient form of numerology invented by Pythagoras to determine the significant numbers in your life. Using both your given birth name and date of birth, this report will accurately calculate those numbers which stand out as yours. With these numbers, the report can determine certain trends in your life and tell you when the important periods of your life will occur.

APS03-508 – 3-month report **$12.00**
APS03-509 – 6-month report **$18.00**
APS03-510 – 1-year report **$25.00**

Ultimate Astro-Profile

This report has it all! Receive over 40 pages of fascinating, insightful and uncanny descriptions of your innermost qualities and talents. Read about your burn rate (thirst for change). Explore your personal patterns (inside and outside). Examine the particular pattern of your Houses. The Astro-Profile doesn't repeat what you've already learned from other personality profiles, but considers often the neglected natal influence of the lunar nodes plus much more.

APS03-505 . . . . **$40.00**

SUPER DISCOUNTS ON
LLEWELLYN DATEBOOKS AND CALENDARS!

Llewellyn offers several ways to save money. With a four-year subscription you receive your books as soon as they are published. The price remains the same for four years even if there is a price increase! We pay postage and handling as well. *Buy any 2 subscriptions and take $2 off! Buy 3 and take $3 off! Buy 4 and take an additional $5 off!*

Subscriptions (4 years, 1995-1998)

- ☐ Astrological Calendar $40.00
- ☐ Sun Sign Book $19.80
- ☐ Moon Sign Book $19.80
- ☐ Daily Planetary Guide $27.80
- ☐ Organic Gardening Almanac $23.80

Order *by the dozen* and save 40%! Sell them to your friends or give them as gifts. Llewellyn pays all postage and handling on quantity orders.

Quantity Orders: 40% OFF
1994 1995

- ☐ ☐ Astrological Calendar .... 12/$72.00
- ☐ ☐ Sun Sign Book .... 12/$35.64
- ☐ ☐ Moon Sign Book .... 12/$35.64
- ☐ ☐ Daily Planetary Guide .... 12/$50.04
- ☐ ☐ Magical Almanac .... 12/$50.04
- ☐ ☐ Organic Gardening Almanac .... 12/$42.84

On single copy orders, include $3 p/h for orders under $10 and $4 for orders over $10. We pay postage for all orders over $50.

Single copies of Llewellyn's Almanacs and Calendars
1994 1995

- ☐ ☐ Astrological Calendar $10.00
- ☐ ☐ Sun Sign Book $4.95
- ☐ ☐ Moon Sign Book $4.95
- ☐ ☐ Daily Planetary Guide $6.95
- ☐ ☐ Magical Almanac $6.95
- ☐ ☐ Organic Gardening Almanac $5.95
- ☐ Myth and Magic Calendar $10.00

Please use order form on last page.

Astrological Services Order Form

Include all birth data plus your full name for all reports.

Service name and number _____

Full name (1st person) _____

Birthtime _____ ☐ a.m. ☐ p.m. Date _____ Year _____

Birthplace (city, county, state, country) _____

_____

Full name (2nd person) _____

Birthtime _____ ☐ a.m. ☐ p.m. Date _____ Year _____

Birthplace (city, county, state, country) _____

_____

Astrological knowledge: ☐ Novice ☐ Student ☐ Advanced

Include letter with questions on separate sheet of paper.

Name _____

Address _____

City _____ State _____ Zip _____

Make check or money order payable to Llewellyn Publications, or charge it!

☐ VISA   ☐ MasterCard   ☐ American Express

Account Number _____

Exp. Date _____ Daytime Phone _____

Signature of Cardholder _____

☐ **Yes!** Send me my **FREE** copy of **New Worlds!**

Mail this form and payment to:

Llewellyn's Personal Services, P.O. Box 64383-910,
St. Paul, MN 55164-0383. Allow 4-6 weeks for delivery.

LLEWELLYN ORDER FORM

Llewellyn Publications
P.O. Box 64383-910, St. Paul, MN 55164-0383

You may use this form to order any of the Llewellyn books listed in this publication.

Give Title, Author, Order Number and Price.

_____

_____

_____

_____

_____

Shipping and Handling: We ship UPS when possible. Include $3 for orders under $10 and $4 for orders over $10. Llewellyn pays postage for all orders over $50. Please give street address (UPS cannot deliver to P.O. Boxes). Minnesota residents please add 6.5% sales tax.

Credit Card Orders: In the U.S. and Canada call 1-800-THE-MOON. In Minnesota call 612-291-1970. Or, send credit card order by mail. Any questions can be directed to customer service 612-291-1970.

❐ Yes! Send me your free catalog!

❐ VISA   ❐ MasterCard   ❐ American Express

Account No. _____

Exp. Date _____ Phone _____

Signature _____

Name _____

Address _____

City _____ State _____ Zip _____

Thank you for your order!